SAFETY
Preparations for
CRUISING

SAFETY

Preparations for

CRUISING

Jeremy R. Hood

SHERIDAN *S* HOUSE, INC

DOBBS FERRY, NEW YORK

First published 1997 by
Sheridan House Inc.
145 Palisade Street
Dobbs Ferry, NY 10522

Library of Congress Cataloging-in-Publication Data

Hood, Jeremy R., 1952–
    Safety preparations for cruising / Jeremy R. Hood.
        p. cm.
    Includes biographical references (p. 000) and index.
    ISBN 1-57409-022-4 (alk. paper)
    1. Sailing—Safety measures.   2. Sailboats—Safety measures.
    3. Yachting—Safety measures.   4. Yachts—Safety measures.
    I. Title
    GV811.53.H66   1997
    797.1'246'0289—dc21   96–50072
                                                      CIP

Edited by Janine Simon
Design by Jeff Fitschen
Illustrations by William C. Grobe

Printed in the United States of America

ISBN   1-57409-022-4

Acknowledgements

Working at building up a business does not allow much time to write a book and inevitably there were times when I felt pulled in all directions. Without the constant support of my partner, my friend, and fellow single-handed sailor Janet Grobe this book would never have been finished, let alone published. Her contributions have been invaluable from reading and re-reading the early drafts, making suggestions of additions and changes and for her final proof reading.

The illustrations have been drawn immaculately by Janet's father Bill Grobe. A sailor, boat builder and sometime architect, he has been able to capture the essence of my limited text and the quality of his drawings is truly impressive.

After writing the first complete draft I was fortunate in being able to ask my friend Mike Firestone for his comments and suggestions. Not only is he the most meticulous marine surveyor I have met, he has sailed more miles than he can add up and, as if this were not sufficient, he is also a published author. The points he raised have all been incorporated into the final text.

Additionally I would like to thank my colleagues here at Blue Water Cruising for their support during this project and especially Joni Robertson for her assistance as the project progressed.

And finally, I would not have been in a position to write this book were it not for the many students who have attended my classes and who have asked astute questions and for the opportunities provided by many of them for me to sail many different boats here in the bay, across the Gulf of Mexico and occasionally beyond.

Yet despite all this assistance, I am the one who has made the final decision as to what to include or omit. And as skipper of this book, I am responsible for the inevitable errors that remain.

Jeremy R. Hood
Clear Lake, Texas
January 1997

Contents

Introduction

From the time that I began sailing I have heard skippers and crew curse their bad luck. "We were just unlucky to be caught out in a particularly strong storm" or, "We were unlucky to just catch the edge of the reef; another foot away and we wouldn't have even holed the boat!" All too often it is not luck at all but poor preparation; and given a well-found, well-equipped boat and an experienced crew, it would probably not have happened. Of course we can all make mistakes; I have certainly made my share and know there are others to come; and things can escalate from a minor emergency to a catastrophe extremely quickly. None of us are immune from disaster but we can significantly reduce the risks by being prepared.

No one in their right mind would dream of piloting an airplane without hours of instruction and practice. Yet all too many would-be cruising sailors potter around on lakes or bays, never venturing forth in inclement weather until they set out, inexperienced, for their offshore passage. And unfortunately many either return all too soon, disillusioned with cruising, or end up making a serious mistake that necessitates outside assistance, the loss of their vessel, or perhaps worse.

But it need not be like this. This book alerts the reader to those areas of preparation that may have been overlooked or not seriously considered. With a few exceptions, you will not find advice on specific actions or equipment, but rather increased awareness of potential problems and of some possible solutions. A skipper who will have to make hundreds of independent judgments while at sea can begin now, not by being told what to do, but by making informed decisions in advance. Every person will have differing priorities. While some may be prepared to venture across an ocean in a lightweight vessel, others may not be prepared to do so unless the hull is at least two inches thick. I've seen those.

Several years ago I attended a talk given by Steve Callahan, who in 1986 wrote *Adrift* about his time aboard a liferaft drifting across the Atlantic. And at the time he, too, was reluctant to advise those attending just what safety equipment they should have. There are risks involved in cruising, as there are in all pursuits. When you do leave, do so knowing what these risks are and be prepared to deal with them without needing to resort to outside help.

Chapter One deals specifically with preparing yourself while subsequent chapters deal with the vessel, its systems, and equipment. Each chapter begins with a short retelling of an incident that has happened to me, and ends with a checklist that summarizes the main points covered. If you already have your boat, you may wish to go through these checklists to identify those areas that you have yet to deal with. The checklists can also be used a week or so before departure to confirm that no major items have been left unattended.

Enjoy the planning of your voyage and the preparation of your boat, but don't neglect the need to prepare yourself. And then you can set off and begin to enjoy your cruising.

CHAPTER ONE

Preparing Yourself

It was Easter week and still cold on the water as I began one of my early English Channel crossings. I was just one of the crew taking advantage of an opportunity of a week's sailing to the Brittany coast of France. We set off from Falmouth, heading out past Black Rock into some largish swells, and as we cleared the Lizard the full southwesterly wind and seas made the motion uncomfortable. Despite the dodger, it was wet in the cockpit as we beat to windward, our friends on a sister ship behind us.

In anticipation of the passage the skipper had prepared a watch schedule, and we were soon taking advantage of our off-watch times to rest and warm up below. As night came it became evident our skipper was suffering from *mal de mer* despite the medication he had taken, and without really excusing himself he failed to appear for his watch. Next to go was our navigator who, after feeding the fishes profusely, went to his cabin and remained there all night, apart from a couple of brief and unpleasant trips on deck. So it was that with little experience I found myself having to do more than the others.

Sometime in the night I decided we needed to reef, and despite feeling not so great myself, I completed the task without incident. It seemed prudent to plot a position on the chart, which again I did. I then spoke on the radio with our friends somewhere off our starboard quarter and together we discussed our situation. With the wind from the southwest it was evident we would not be able to make our intended destination. We chose the alternative of L'abervrac'h, which we could lay more easily. The situation was discussed with the skipper, who rationally listed our options, "We can carry on beating to windward for the next 24 hours and make our intended destination, or we can head for L'abervrac'h and make landfall tonight, or we could heave-to and make our entrance to L'abervrac'h in the morning."

We chose to make a night approach and I set about plotting a course to steer. From my earlier plotted position I calculated the rhumb line course and then allowed for leeway in setting a compass heading. After I informed the skipper of this, we changed course and I called our friends on the radio to advise them of our decision. They concurred with our choice and they, too, altered course. A short while later they called us on the radio, "Hey, Jeremy, what course did you calculate?" I looked at the log and repeated our course. "We just plotted it and that's not what we got," came the reply. As it turned out, I had been wrong. All my calculations were correct but I had plotted our initial position one whole degree wrong. Fortunately they spotted the mistake. We corrected our course and eventually made our entrance to L'abervrac'h, surfing down some huge seas as the water shallowed. As the motion lessened once we were in sheltered waters, our seasick skipper re-emerged to take charge and, with some anxiety, we headed in and anchored. That night we all slept well.

Though we made our harbor safely, it was with a great deal of luck, for a number of mistakes were made. First, with both the skipper and navigator suffering from seasickness, we should have been hesitant at closing the coast at all—but that is one of the dangers of inexperience. Then, I made what could have been a disastrous mistake in the navigation. Again it was inexperience, as I was having to cope with too many new and different responsibilities all at once. And last, I now shiver at the thought of our entry into a strange harbor at night in rough conditions and with little experience. The saw-toothed rocks we saw the next morning only served to reinforce the real dangers into which we had put ourselves.

Most sailors planning to set off cruising spend months or years preparing their vessel. They spend thousands and often tens of thousands of dollars on safety equipment, making their ship ready for almost anything. Yet all too often they spend little or no time in getting offshore experience themselves. The folly soon becomes obvious to many. One couple who set off recently in a boat well-capable of ocean crossings are now planning a cruise along the Intracoastal Waterway, where I suspect their sails will remain permanently furled. Preparing for a safe passage not only requires a sound ship but a knowledgeable and experienced skipper and crew.

The Skills You Need

It is perhaps because of the eclectic range of knowledge and abilities that I find sailing so rewarding, the demands it makes upon me being returned in a sense of accomplishment and self-reliance. At times I have delved into the mathematics and astronomy of celestial navigation and in so doing stretched my intellectual self. Yet, at other times I have had to be a plumber, solving the lack of fresh water in the galley, or an electrician, a carpenter, a medic . . . the list is almost endless.

Clearly there are some skills that are essential if you are contemplating offshore passagemaking. Others are perhaps desirable, and some helpful, but you can manage without them.

Navigation

If you are to enjoy your sailing, be able to relax on a passage, and make a safe landfall, then you will need some navigational skills. I know many have set out on ocean voyages with little or no ability in this area and have survived to learn the necessary skills and subsequently write about them. Some have learned the hard way, losing their boat as a result of serious errors yet surviving themselves. And who knows of the many who don't make it, who are lost?

You can easily acquire the necessary basic knowledge by reading, self-study, or taking a formal class in the subject. But that in itself is not sufficient, for the theory is only part of what is required for sound navigation. You need practice and experience. Plotting a position on a chart is not hard, neither is calculating a course—allowing for magnetic variation, compass deviation, leeway, and set and drift—but if you have to

think about all of this while sitting at the chart table at the beginning of
a long passage, when you have many other concerns, it will not be that
simple and you will make mistakes. So it is important to have the theoreti-
cal knowledge and then some experience using it, preferably in a less
demanding situation than as skipper at the beginning of a major passage.

In my experience, you will do well to develop both your knowledge
and practical experience in the following areas of navigation:

Keeping a log

Learn which information is essential to record for safe and efficient
passagemaking. Practice keeping a log on a short coastal passage and
see how easy, or difficult, it can be.

Plotting on a chart

Using parallel rules and dividers to plot positions and courses on a
chart takes some skill, even in the classroom. Learn how difficult it can

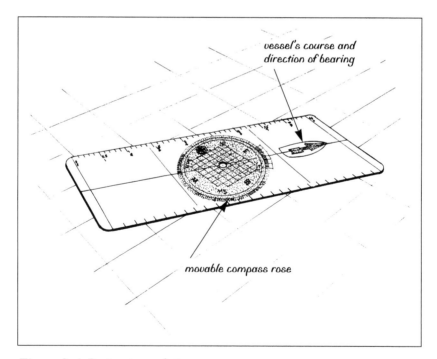

Figure 1. A Breton type plotter.

be sitting at a bucking chart table. Try using some of the different types of course plotters, which may make the job easier and more reliable. I prefer using the Breton plotter invented by a French navigator and named after his region of France. This plotter has a built-in compass rose that avoids having to step across a chart to calculate a course, and a large boat symbol you point in the direction of your travel, thus avoiding the possibility of calculating a reciprocal bearing in error. It is unlikely you will be taught to use such a plotter, yet after you begin using one you will realize how much easier and safer it makes your navigation.

Before departure you should be able to quickly and easily plot a position on a chart and work out a DR (dead reckoning) or an estimated position (EP).

Using the ship's compass
One of the hardest things to learn is to steer a vessel on a compass heading and unless you have had practice you will find it tiring and difficult. But more than this, you will frequently steer in the wrong direction risking an accidental jibe. Steering by the compass is just one of the many things that cannot be learned from a book but has to be acquired through experience.

Using your electronics
Electronics are great fun, a real asset to have, and normally reliable. But only if you know how to use them. Don't put yourself in the position of having to read the instruction manuals as you motor out at the beginning of your voyage. Just like other areas of navigation you need to learn just how much, and how little, you can rely on them. Practice using the display on your GPS, entering waypoints, and reading your position. Make sure it works and is as accurate as you anticipate it will be. And make sure you and your crew know how to activate the man overboard facility it will almost certainly have.

Just because your electronics give you a course to steer does not mean it is a safe course. Unless you plot the course on a chart and check that there are no rocks, wrecks, or other obstructions in the way, you will not know. But even if you do this and confirm the course is safe, you could still have made an error in entering your waypoints. There are so many opportunities for a mistake to occur: It could be in plotting the position from the chart, writing it down, reading your notes, or entering it into your electronics. Unless you plot your course when underway, you will have no way of knowing about the mistake until it is too late. And learning to plot your position on a chart as you go out the jetties is not the best time.

If you have radar, don't wait till you need it to learn how to adjust the display or read the screen. It will merely confuse you and perhaps cause you to make a mistake by a false interpretation of the display, or you will be below messing with it when you should more prudently be in the cockpit watching what is actually happening around you. Are you aware the navigation rules require that if you have an operational radar aboard you must know how to use it, and that you do so when the circumstances call for it?

Celestial navigation

Many would-be cruising people buy a sextant and then set out with a book, anticipating they will teach themselves how to use a sextant and tables in the spare time that they inevitably will have on a long passage. While some may achieve this, they will be in the minority. Learn the necessary skills before departing.

In these days of advanced electronics, when even a small sailboat may have aboard more navigation equipment than an ocean liner had a few years ago, celestial navigation may seem redundant and old-fashioned. For a while I, too, was beginning to think along these lines, until I reflected on what real backup I had to my main navigation. When crossing the Atlantic in 1988, which was before the GPS was available, I used the NavStar satellite navigation system, which gave me a regular fix every hour or so. But in order not to rely on this, I had a number of backup navigation systems. First was my RDF (radio direction finder), which could pick up a radio beacon 30 to 200 miles from a coast, depending on the beacon and signal, and allow me to home-in on the signal or, if more than one beacon was available, get a fix from them. Then, as I approached a strange shore, I could expect to make a landfall on a lighthouse visible perhaps 20 miles or more from shore. And as a final backup I had my sextant. But now it is difficult to find a RDF if you want one and many of the radio beacons are being discontinued. This also applies to many of the lighthouses around the U.S. coast as well as on foreign shores. And so when you depart on your voyage, what will you backup your GPS with besides celestial navigation?

The rules of the road

Learning the navigation rules is a chore that seems easy to put off. However it is really essential that you know the rules and have experience in relating them to actual situations at sea. For me, it seems I only really remember an unusual combination of navigation lights after I have seen a vessel at sea displaying them. If you know the rules, at least in theory, you are ahead and should have no problem answering the following questions. I'm not giving the answers here because this is not a manual on navigation, but you should have a copy of the rules on board.

- What do two all-round red lights set one above another on the same mast indicate? What does this mean in terms of your responsibilities?
- Under what situations should you use your whistle to communicate with another vessel? When may you communicate by VHF radio instead of using the whistle? And what is a whistle anyway?
- In what parts of the world should you leave red channel buoys to starboard when entering a channel from seaward? And in what areas should you leave them to port in order to stay in the channel when entering from seaward?
- What are cardinal marks and where may you see them?
- If you are sailing, under what circumstances do the navigation rules require you to give way to a power driven vessel? I can think of at least six.

Sail Handling

If you are planning an ocean, or even a coastal, passage, you should know how to handle your sails. If you trim your sails inefficiently, you will go more slowly than you need. Being race-trim ready is not so essential, but knowing how to reef is. Skills you have learned in protected waters will be much more difficult to accomplish offshore and some may not be appropriate at all. Before you leave you should have had real experience at sea, at least in accomplishing the following:

Reefing

Have you actually had practice in putting a reef in at sea? What about a second or third reef? Can you tension them and cleat them easily? If the lines are led back to the cockpit, does the system work under real conditions as opposed to the light breeze that was blowing when the rigger demonstrated your new system to you? Do you need to take any sail slides out in order to reef and if so can you easily open the track gate? If you lose this gate, do you have a spare for it? If you are planning a shorthanded voyage with just you and your partner, can you reef the vessel on your own or does it need both of you? Ironically, some single-line reefing systems need two people to use them effectively at sea.

Jibing

Jibing is one of those sailing techniques that often causes anxiety because of the potential damage that can occur when the maneuver goes wrong. Because of this, you may have avoided learning how to undertake this safely. Knowing how is not enough; practice is essential.

Have you ever used a preventer to help avoid a jibe? It is seldom needed in flat water but is essential offshore, particularly at times when heavy weather is abating and your vessel will be rolling around in some pretty big swells. How will you rig one aboard your boat? If you have run all other lines back to the cockpit, how can you do so with a preventer? How will you release it easily in an emergency?

Changing headsails

If your vessel has a roller-reefing system can you change the sail easily? Can you do this easily at sea? Many of the roller-furling systems I have seen use specially sized shackles to attach the head and tack. These can easily be lost overboard from a bucking foredeck. Do you have spares? Can you tie a bowline in a line at night? Can you untie one? Being able to accomplish these things at the dock is not sufficient though it clearly helps. Ideally, you will be able to practice before you depart.

Riding turns on a winch

Inevitably this problem will occur and you had better learn how to

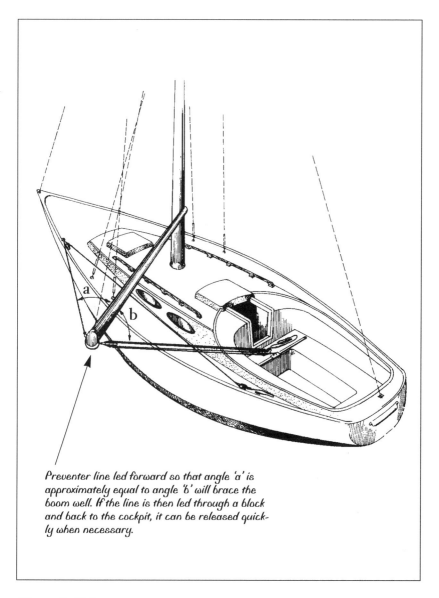

Preventer line led forward so that angle 'a' is approximately equal to angle 'b' will brace the boom well. If the line is then led through a block and back to the cockpit, it can be released quickly when necessary.

Figure 2. *Using a preventer.*

deal with it. When it happens to a genoa sheet and the wind is strong, you will be faced with a difficult task in removing the line. I was taught how to do it by using a rolling hitch on the line led to another winch.

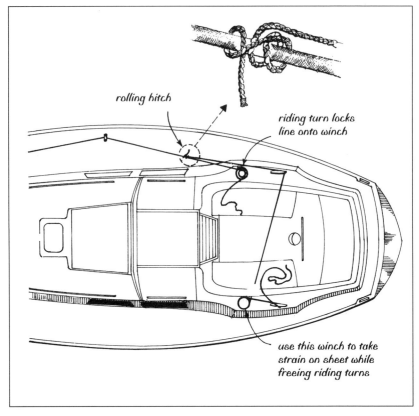

Figure 3. *Removing a riding turn from a winch.*

Knots

This is Boy Scouts for real. Unless you know how to tie a few knots, at a minimum the task will take an inordinate amount of time and will distract you perhaps from other tasks. Tying a knot incorrectly could threaten your safety or that of your crew. Can you tie a rolling hitch as mentioned above? What about the bowline? I use very few knots aboard and these include the following:

- Square (reef) knot
- Round turn and two half hitches
- Bowline
- Rolling hitch
- Cleat hitch

I use other knots but in my experience these five are really the minimum you should be able to tie quickly and easily.

Avoiding Fatigue

If you are planning a shorthanded trip or you are the only experienced person aboard, coping with and avoiding fatigue will be difficult. On the many passages I have made with owners new to offshore sailing I have to be available constantly to check our course, the proximity of shipping, the set of the sails, and the condition of the crew. Normally I will set a watch system, including myself in the schedule, but then I expect to be called whenever the on-watch crew are worried about anything, or whenever they see any shipping. The result is that initially I am often called when I am off watch, and so I have to manage my time effectively to not become overfatigued. These same duties and more will be required of the new offshore skippers, and since they lack experience, each situation will take longer to assess and longer to deal with. When going below they will find they are still worrying about details; they will probably find it hard to sleep and as a result become overtired very easily. It is in these situations that errors are mostly likely to be made, with the possibility of an escalating situation that may end in a real emergency. Fatigue is just as dangerous at sea as it can be on the freeway.

As a crewmember, fatigue can still be a problem, particularly if you find it hard to sleep when off watch. Often this will be because of tension and anxiety as you find yourself in an unusual environment. Becoming familiar with the motion of a vessel at sea, with being down below and accepting the experience of the on-watch crew cannot be accomplished overnight. It pays to gain this experience before you really have to be responsible for the vessel.

Being a Skipper

No matter how much experience you have sailing as a crewmember, when you become a skipper you suddenly realize how much there is to consider: how many things you have to pay attention to, allow for, make decisions about. If you enjoy a challenge and responsibility, then being skipper—captain of your ship—is rewarding and satisfying. You are the one in charge and the other crewmembers will look to you for guidance.

But reflect for a moment. Your crew accept you as the one in charge, the person who will make the decisions, not because you are a good leader or organizer, though you may be both, but because you have experience they lack. Sailing, even in protected waters, calls for considerable knowledge if you are to avoid damage to boat and crew; and it is your experience that makes a sail relaxing and enjoyable.

Before you become an offshore skipper you should gain some experience offshore as a crewmember, when you can learn how to cope with seasickness, catnap to avoid fatigue, and undertake the navigation under less than ideal circumstances. You will be able to get used to night sailing, recognizing lights offshore, making landfall at night, all at a time when you are not in charge. These experiences will then stand you in good stead when you do embark aboard your own boat.

When you do depart on your cruise as skipper there will still be new demands upon you even if you have undertaken considerable offshore sailing. Maybe this will be the first time that as skipper you have to trust others while you sleep, or try to. How should you arrange the watch schedule and should you be on it or not? Will you do all the navigation yourself or will you share it? What will happen when you encounter shipping or squalls, or your instruments quit working?

I enjoy the demands placed upon me as skipper. I like being able to make the decisions and I enjoy the relaxation and adventure of offshore sailing; but there are still times when I get fatigued, things becomes difficult, and I can't wait for the end of the passage. And like all experienced sailors, I still make mistakes. Knowing this, I try to develop methods of checking on myself. Expect that you will, too, and gain sufficient experience before your departure.

Other Desirable Skills

It is impossible for any crew to have all the knowledge and experience necessary to cope perfectly with all situations, and with a small crew this problem is exacerbated. Clearly there are some areas of knowledge essential to safe passagemaking, such as the sailing and navigation skills discussed above. Having expertise in other areas is desirable and the more areas of knowledge you feel comfortable with, the better. But within this broad category there are those skills that will be needed more often, or will be more critical should the circumstances occur, and it is these that are discussed here.

Knowledge of the boat

Being familiar with your boat is important. Knowing where the wires run to the navigation lights, where the water-tank shutoff valve is, or how to access the steering quadrant will be of immense help should you need to fix any of these things. Of course, much of this knowledge will come automatically as you prepare your vessel, so long as you either undertake the work yourself or follow closely the person you are paying to do it for you. Getting the steering cables replaced before you leave may be a prudent decision but the value will be doubled if you do it yourself, for then you will know how to adjust their tension and where the turning blocks are for later inspection. And more importantly, you will know that you have aboard the tools for undertaking this work should it become necessary.

Important areas of knowledge include all of the parts of the boat and the equipment that affect its safety and that of the crew. It is these areas that are covered in the remaining chapters of this book.

Going aloft

Let us hope you will never have to go up the mast at sea, but if you do have to it will be easier, safer, and quicker if you have done it before when tied to the dock. It's often not easy to persuade yourself to do this, so get this bit over before you depart. Make sure you know how to go aloft safely. This is especially necessary at sea when the boat will be rolling. Consider how you will rig a safety line in addition to the halyard you will be using.

Using tools

Having aboard the most expensive tool kit might be great, but knowing how to adjust a vise grip is probably more important. It is inevitable that repairs will be necessary—some will be imperative—and at least one of the crew should be familiar with using the tools. This is yet another reason for undertaking the fitting out yourself.

The ability to improvise

Though this is a much needed skill, it is hard to know how to go about gaining it. One method is to play *what if* when you are out sailing. *What if* the instruments suddenly go out? *What if* the engine stops? *What if* the stove goes out? The list is endless. But thinking along these lines and training yourself to consider how you will cope should something unexpected happen will be an extremely useful exercise, and the time for practice is before your actual departure. Using this technique you will be able to develop your own list of spares to take, independent of this or other books. It will lead you to consider what are the more serious things that could occur and how you could cope with them. For example, *what if* the engine fails will prompt you into thinking about how to repair it or the need for an alternative means of charging the batteries. *What if* is good seamanship.

CHECKLIST

	YES	NO
Do you have a ship's log book?	❑	❑
Have you decided which columns you will use?	❑	❑
Are there other columns you will need?	❑	❑
Have you practiced using it at sea?	❑	❑
Do you have a quality plotting instrument in addition to		
parallel rulers?	❑	❑
Can you easily use it at sea?	❑	❑
Can you:		
Plot a position on a chart at sea?	❑	❑
Plot a DR and an estimated position?	❑	❑
Can you steer a vessel using a compass?	❑	❑
Are you familiar with how to use and set your:		
Speed and depth instrumentation?	❑	❑

	YES	NO
GPS?	❏	❏
Chart plotter?	❏	❏
Radar?	❏	❏
All the other electronics?	❏	❏
Do you have on board:		
A sextant?	❏	❏
The necessary sight reduction tables?	❏	❏
A current nautical almanac?	❏	❏
Sight forms with which you are familiar?	❏	❏
Can you use these to obtain a position while at sea?	❏	❏
Do you know the most important navigation rules?	❏	❏
Do you have a book on board to refer to if necessary?	❏	❏
Can you:		
Put in a reef easily?	❏	❏
Jibe the vessel safely?	❏	❏
Easily set and release a boom preventer?	❏	❏
Change headsails on your roller-furling system?	❏	❏
Safely remove a riding turn from a winch?	❏	❏
Can you tie the following knots in the dark:		
Square (reef) knot?	❏	❏
Round turn and two half hitches?	❏	❏
Bowline?	❏	❏
Rolling hitch?	❏	❏
Have you learned how to avoid becoming overtired on a long passage?	❏	❏
If you will be skipper:		
Have you been a skipper before?	❏	❏
Had experience in coastal sailing?	❏	❏
Had offshore sailing experience?	❏	❏
Are you familiar with all the important systems aboard your boat?	❏	❏
Are you familiar with how to use the tools that you have aboard?	❏	❏
Are you able to improvise if necessary?	❏	❏

CHAPTER TWO

Hull and Deck Construction

I was anchored in the small fishing harbor of Lagos, Portugal, when someone buzzed across in a dinghy. "Ahoy, *Melos*," I heard from below. After coming on deck Mark introduced himself and proceeded to tell me how he knew my boat. "I had a look at her when she was for sale," he told me. "On the Hamble River, wasn't she," he continued. "Yes, I thought about it for a while but I decided I wanted something a little nicer." So much for never insulting a person's boat! Despite this introduction, I got to know Mark a little during the couple of weeks we spent in the harbor together. He was a computer consultant from England who had managed to get his company to give him a year off so that he could go sailing. His plan was to cross the Atlantic in the fall, spend the winter in the Caribbean, and then head on to Florida and up the East Coast before setting off back to England the next summer. It was a tight schedule but a realistic one if he didn't mind missing a lot of places on the way.

Mark had eventually bought his French built Gib'Sea 34 after seeing numerous boats and he was happy with it. The vessel was furnished with a large U-shaped galley, and a round dinette with plush cushions. It had an open, airy feel to the main cabin with plenty of hatches and opening ports. As I helped him on one occasion check out an electrical problem I found myself wondering whether I had made the right decision in choosing my very traditional and somewhat plain Rival 32 over his modern and airy Gib'Sea.

I left about the same time he did, Mark heading for Madeira, while I navigated toward the Canary Islands where I had arranged to meet a friend. It was a rough passage for me, with the storm jib set for three days as I ran toward the southwest with the gale force winds on the quarter, but I made good time and arrived safely.

Later I was to meet other friends in the south of Tenerife who had called at Madeira before heading to the Canary Islands. I asked if they had seen Mark. Yes they had, and I then learned how he and his boat had fared during those gale force winds as he made his passage across to Funchal, Madeira. Sometime during the passage he had become concerned as the main bulkheads of the boat came loose during the pounding it was taking. He reduced sail, headed off the wind some more, and eventually made his landfall in Funchal. But it was a tired, anxious, and chastened skipper who arrived. He had by then realized how poorly constructed his boat was and how vulnerable he had become in that one period of rough weather. By the time of his arrival he had already abandoned his plans of an Atlantic crossing and was considering how he could strengthen his boat sufficiently to get her back to England.

And when I learned this story I recalled my envy at his boat and was shamed by my thoughts of how dowdy my boat had seemed. Back aboard, I patted the bulkheads fondly and proceeded to give her a good clean-up. I was rightly proud of my yacht.

In planning to go cruising it is important to have a boat fit for the task. Mark's Gib'Sea was not a bad boat, but it was not the right choice for the ambitious, double Atlantic crossing that he had planned. Preparation demands a basic design of the hull and deck suited to the planned voyaging.

Choosing a Cruising Yacht

Uffa Fox, a great sailor and yacht designer of some years ago, once made the astute observation that you need a foot of boat length for every year of your age. There is some truth in the statement, for as we get older we want more room, more luxuries, more things around us. The 15-foot dinghy that was enjoyed in our youth is now too spartan, too small, and too wet.

A lot of considerations go into choosing the right boat for our needs. I want to emphasize requirements that affect safety.

Fiberglass Boats

A fiberglass boat is essentially one big patch made up of strands of glass soaked in a resin. And as such almost anything about it can be changed. But beyond a certain point it becomes more feasible to start from scratch than to improve an existing hull and deck. What are the essentials that a cruising yacht should really have?

Hull strength

Hull strength is critically important as it is basic to the integrity of the vessel. For cruising, when your boat will be your home and when you will sometimes be venturing far from shore, you need to have a boat sufficiently strong that it will not fail in rough seas or be easily holed if you hit an object at sea. But however strong your hull is, there will still be a risk, and only you can decide what level of strength will be satisfactory for you. Many people have set off cruising and crossed oceans in vessels that I would not consider seaworthy, yet at the same time many have thought me crazy for going in my boat.

The following are factors that affect hull strength and that you should consider in selecting a boat for cruising.

Fiberglass boats are manufactured using different types of fiberglass mat and using different techniques, though it is generally true that older boats were built with thicker—and hence stronger—hulls than more recent boats.

Normally on an assembly line a gun will be used that cuts the fiberglass, mixes it with resin, and sprays it onto the mold. Conversely, when hulls are made individually a hand-laid glass cloth will be used where the strands of fiberglass are kept longer and where the orientation of the strands can be controlled. A hand-laid hull will generally be stronger than a "blown" fiberglass hull of the same thickness.

In building the hull it is necessary to thoroughly wet all the fiberglass strands with the resin, but too much resin will weaken the final product, as it is the fiberglass and not the resin that affects the strength of the hull. Some modern techniques use vacuum bagging to suck out excess resin, which results in a stronger hull for a given thickness.

Cored hulls

In order to produce a lighter hull that will perform better under sail in light airs, some manufacturers make an inner and outer hull mold with a core material glued between them. This core is usually made of short lengths of balsa wood pressed together (end grain balsa) or a man-made material, the most common of which is known as Airex. The result is a lightweight yet rigid structure, with the additional benefit that it offers insulation to the hull and reduces condensation. But cored hulls are susceptible to two problems. Under certain conditions the two thin hull layers may delaminate from the core, resulting in a weak and flexible area that could fail. This can happen when a vessel has been pounding into heavy seas for a long time or as a result of a grounding or a failure consequent to poor construction. The other problem associated with balsa cored hulls is that once the balsa becomes wet it will begin rotting and the hull will lose its rigidity. Because a balsa core will wick water, once water gets into the core it can spread extensively. To help prevent this, balsa core material is now treated to seal the fibers and prevent wicking.

While some manufacturers use core material in the whole of the hull, others only use it above the waterline, preferring a solid fiberglass hull section below the water.

In choosing a cruising boat, find out whether it has a cored hull, what material the core is made from, and whether it extends below the waterline. Then decide if the benefits of this type of construction (weight, price, insulation) outweigh the disadvantages.

Cored decks

The use of core material in a deck is so common that it is rare to find one that does not use a core material to add strength to the fiberglass. As with the hull, both balsa and Airex are used with plywood being another favorite, especially for side decks. Cored decks are subject to many of the same problems as cored hulls and the same considerations apply.

The majority of problems with cored decks result from water ingress and subsequent rotting. This can occur where deck fittings have been secured through the deck, as strain on the fitting will compress the core and then, when the tension is eased, a gap remains where water can enter. But the most common problems occur when teak decks have been laid over a cored fiberglass deck. With each screw holding down the teak there is a potential source for a leak and inevitably some of these will.

Bulkheads

As essential to a vessel as the hull and deck, the bulkheads are structural features of most boats, preventing the hull from collapsing inward against the pull of the rigging and the force of the seas. While dockside, a thin plywood frame wedged in place may achieve this satisfactorily, but it will not be sufficient when the vessel is under full canvas pounding into steep seas. Then, as the whole hull flexes and works, the bulkheads need to be strong enough to take the high compression loads and rigid enough so that they do not flex or slip out of position. Looking at the design, thickness of the bulkheads, and how they are secured to the hull will tell you much about the boat as a whole.

For cruising the inland waterways or short coastal passagemaking you will not need the bulkheads to be as strong as if you are planning to double Cape Horn in the winter. Only you can decide what is good enough, but in doing so consider:
- The thickness of the bulkheads.
- Whether they are tabbed to the hull at strategic points or continuously bonded around their perimeter.
- Whether they are bonded to the deck molding or not.
- How they are secured where the vessel has a cored hull.
- How much material is left where doors and passageways are cut.

Hull to deck joints

Most fiberglass boats consist of two separate moldings, the hull and the deck. (There are sometimes three: The hull is made in two halves— port and starboard—that are then fiberglassed together to make the solid hull to which the deck is later added.) Usually the deck is not fitted to the boat until a late stage of production so that the engine, tanks, and furniture can all be installed more easily. Then the deck is lowered on to the hull and fixed in place. How this is done affects the strength of the boat. On some production boats a layer of sealant is placed around the joint and the two are then bolted together. On other boats the two moldings are both bolted and fiberglassed, while in some only a strong fiberglass bond is used.

Whatever method is used, it needs to be strong and watertight. Older boats with thin hulls and a sealed and bolted deck will often leak when the sealant becomes old and the vessel works when underway.

Wooden Boats

In 1969 Robin Knox-Johnston became the first winner of the single-handed round the world race in his wooden ketch *Suhaili*. He still sails the boat today. The Vikings used wooden boats. So did Columbus.

Wooden boats are fine for ocean cruising but are susceptible to failure just like any boat. Part of this depends on the original design and part on the present condition. Clearly both are important. If you are considering a wooden boat for cruising it is likely you will already be familiar with the design and construction. But if you are not, now is the time to find out how well the boat was made and in what condition it is. Cracked frames may have no effect as you quietly fit out the vessel at the dock but if they lead to a sprung plank at sea it could be goodbye to your boat. The same is true for corroded fasteners or keel bolts and rotten bulkheads. Find out about these potential problems and then make your decision as to whether your boat is suitable or not.

Steel Boats

As a construction material for a cruising boat, steel is about the best. That's why the majority of commercial vessels are made of steel. It is strong, malleable, easily joined and repaired. The design and manufacture of a steel boat is clearly of importance, what thickness steel was used, how well were the welds done, and how was the inside of the hull treated. Steel boats rust. You can see it on the outside of nearly all commercial boats, around the sharp corners of ports or rails. But rust on the outside of the boat is not so bad because you can see it and get to it for treatment or repair. But the inside of the boat is often permanently hidden once built. Hull sides are hidden on the insides of built-in fuel or water tanks and seams are hidden by foam insulation. Unless the inside of the hull was treated properly at the time of construction, rusting on the inside could lead to early and unexpected failure.

Aluminum Boats

Strong, light, malleable, easily joined and repaired, aluminum has a big advantage over steel in that it does not rust. It's used regularly to build commercial vessels and is a proven construction material for boats. But it does suffer from one potential problem: electrolysis. Because it is more chemically reactive than steel, aluminum is much more susceptible to electrolytic corrosion and without protection your vessel could dissolve away. So long as this is recognized and the boat has always been protected, an aluminum boat is likely to be fine. But of course it is still important to consider the design, specifications, and quality of manufacture. Just because it is aluminum does not make it automatically suitable for world cruising.

Keel Configuration

Prospective buyers are often told that they need a full keeled boat for ocean sailing by an advisor who has never been cruising and despite the fact that most cruising boats don't have full keels. As with every aspect of your boat, there is no absolute standard that is safe; you have to weigh the advantages and disadvantages depending on your needs and the level of risk you are prepared to take. On occasions the greater windward ability of a fin keel may mean that you can beat away from a lee shore and save your boat. Conversely, if you do go aground, less damage is likely to occur if you have a long keel. Whatever configuration you decide upon, however, you want to be sure that the keel is strongly and securely attached. My boat has a modified fin keel that is encapsulated within the hull of the boat.

Fin keels

A fin keeled boat will be faster and more responsive than a similar vessel with a different keel arrangement. It will point higher into the wind and have a greater resistance to leeway. In other words it will sail better. This is why nearly all ocean-racing monohulls have fin keels. But these advantages are gained at an expense. Fin keels have a greater depth than other types so that the vessel will need more draft and may not be able to get into some anchorages. And because all the weight of the keel is held from a relatively small section of the hull, the stresses are greater so that if a fin keeled boat goes aground, structural damage is more likely to occur.

Modified fin keels (long fins)

This type of keel is a compromise. It's longer than a standard fin keel with a consequent reduction in depth so that the vessel will draw less water and the stresses imposed by the keel will be spread over a greater area. But these benefits are gained at the expense of sailing performance.

Full keels

Full keels are a more traditional design where the keel runs the entire length of the hull. Because of this, a long keeled boat may draw less water and tolerate more added weight than fin keel boats of the same size. But even with a long keeled boat, the weight of the keel is rarely spread along the entire length of the keel. Most often the keel weight is contained in the forward half or two-thirds of the keel with a deadwood area making up the remainder and so stresses imposed by the weight of the keel will be similar to those on a modified fin keel.

Advantages of a long keel include the ability of the vessel to track very well, requiring less attention from the helm. A long keeled boat will often sail a straight course with the helm tied off so long as the sails are well balanced. And an additional benefit is that the vessel can be careened—laid over as the tide ebbs, enabling work to be undertaken on the underside of the vessel.

But as always there is a trade off. Long keeled boats have a greater wetted surface below the waterline that results in poor light-air performance. They will often be hard to tack (a disadvantage of their tracking) and make greater leeway.

Rudders

Along with differing keel designs, rudders have changed, too, from the traditional aft-hung barn door attached to the trailing edge of a long keel to a balanced spade rudder. Each design has advantages in different circumstances, and again you have to choose where to set your limits.

Keel hung rudders

A keel hung rudder offers a high degree of safety. It is attached by bearings—often pintles and gudgeons—at the top and bottom of the keel and is well protected from damage. But this type of rudder requires the vessel to have a long keel and because of the tracking feature of a long keel, the rudder often has to be large—hence the derisive *barn door*. Keel hung rudders are heavy and often require a long tiller or lots of turns on a wheel to make them sufficiently easy to use.

Skeg hung rudders

When a vessel has a fin keel that does not reach to the stern, a small additional structure (skeg) can be fitted to the hull like a small keel from which to hang the rudder. The skeg design is sometimes strong and deep so that a rudder can be supported top and bottom while other designs have only a partial skeg allowing the rudder to be a balanced type.

The skeg performs two functions. It supports the rudder and it protects it from damage. Not all skegs are designed to be sufficiently strong for ocean sailing. In my opinion, the rudder is such an important yet vulnerable part that a cruising boat needs to have a strong, full skeg if one is used. Make sure yours is. If the vessel runs over a line at sea or goes aground, a strong skeg will help protect a rudder from damage that could otherwise disable the boat.

Spade rudders

Spade type rudders fall into two categories: the balanced type where part of the rudder can be placed forward of the rudder post, making the rudder much lighter and more effective to use, and a more traditional type where all of the rudder is aft of the rudder post. On most racing boats a balanced rudder will be fitted while some cruising boats, such as those having a better sailing performance, will have either a balanced or a traditional spade rudder. These rudders are more vulnerable to damage as they are not protected by a skeg, and so the strength of the design bears careful scrutiny. Flimsy balanced rudders using a hollow and small-sized rudder post have no place aboard a cruising boat, but if the rudder is well built and strongly supported by two bearings, it can be stronger—and more resistant to damage—than the protective skegs found on some boats. If your boat has a spade rudder, make sure it is strong enough. You can compare the size of the rudder stock and the method of construction to that of other cruising boats of a similar size, and you should be able to see which ones are built more strongly.

Transom hung rudders

Some vessels, particularly smaller ones, will have the rudder attached to the boat's transom using pintles and gudgeons. An advantage is that the rudder is often relatively easy to remove for repair or replacement. But it must be protected by a skeg or long keel, it is too vulnerable otherwise and has no place, in my opinion, on a cruising boat.

Deck Design

While you can change many things aboard your boat, changing the layout and design of the deck is not realistic for most owners, especially if they want to begin cruising in the next ten years. And so it makes sense to choose a vessel that has the design features on deck that you really want.

Cockpits

The cockpit aboard a cruising yacht has to double for two widely differing functions: At sea it is the control center of the vessel and needs therefore to be safe and secure; but in port it will be your living room where you read, entertain, and eat. These two contrasting needs lead to the wide variety of cockpit designs seen aboard cruising vessels.

For safe passagemaking the cockpit should be small so that you can hold on easily and not get thrown around, deep so that you are held

securely when the vessel is heeled, and comfortable to sit in while lean-
ing against the coamings and bracing yourself against falling to leeward.

Center cockpits

Traditionally cockpits have always been at the rear of a boat though
many vessels are now built with a center cockpit, which can have a
number of significant advantages.

Center cockpits are often a safer location from which to pilot the
vessel and they will generally be drier. But when a center cockpit has
been designed to allow a passageway below decks to an aft cabin, it can
result in a conning tower cockpit with the cockpit sole high above the
waterline, and in these cases the crew will be more vulnerable when the
vessel heels.

On smaller cruising vessels a center cockpit becomes less desirable
as it breaks up the main areas both on deck and below. This tends to be
the case on vessels of less than 35 feet though you will find a number of
blue-water capable vessels considerably shorter than this, such as the
center cockpit version of the Northsea 27.

Bulwarks and Toerails

While modern racing sailboats often have an extruded aluminum
toerail along the outer edge of the deck, traditional deep-sea fishing boats
have a raised bulwark several feet high. At sea you need to be able to move
forward on deck with minimum risk of slipping off the wet and sloping
deck. In these conditions a raised bulwark of even a few inches is considerably better than a slippery aluminum toerail of perhaps one and one-half
inches in height. An aluminum toerail has some advantages when racing:
A low toerail, or even no toerail, lets a racing crew lean out over the sides,
keeping their weight as far to windward as possible and thus allowing the
vessel to carry more sail. Slotted aluminum toerails allow snatch blocks to
be placed along the entire length of the deck, which can facilitate sail trim.
Although this is also helpful aboard a cruising sailboat, it is not significant
compared to the increased safety of a raised bulwark. Generally it is a case
of the higher the better, though high bulwarks will need plenty of scuppers
along their length to allow water to drain off the deck.

Non-skid Decks

For the crew to be able to move forward on deck and work there, the deck needs to have a good non-slippery surface even when wet. All sailboats have some form of non-skid surface to the working areas of the deck, though the efficiency of these can vary enormously.

Teak decks

Teak decks are both traditional and highly efficient. Though most teak decks are liable to result in leaks below—from the screw holes used to secure them—teak is about the best non-skid surface around even when wet. But don't ever think of varnishing it. Any treatment at all, other than the application of salt water, is liable to reduce its natural non-skid properties. If you are considering a vessel with a teak deck, check to see whether any treatment has been applied to the teak surface and the thickness of the wood, which will give some indication of its future life expectancy.

Fiberglass non-skid

Many quality sailboats, my own included, have areas of the fiberglass deck designed with a raised non-skid pattern that works fairly well when the vessel is new. But after a number of years the raised edges get worn and the non-skid properties begin to deteriorate. When this happens you should either paint the deck with a non-skid paint additive or put down a commercial non-skid deck.

Stick-on non-skid

Some manufacturers, most notably Westerly Yachts in the U.K., use a patented non-skid material on deck that is more effective than teak. It is strong, lasts well, and is relatively easy to replace. The downside to this material is that its dark surface becomes extremely hot in the summer and its coarse pattern is uncomfortable to sit on, even for a few minutes.

Improving an Existing Hull and Deck

In *Sensible Cruising: The Thoreau Approach,* Don Casey and Lew Hackler suggest that the boat you have already is the best boat for cruising, but not necessarily without modification or improvement. This section is about changes relating to safety that should be considered for an existing boat.

Any boat, no matter how thick the hull, how strong the bulkheads, can be improved. But whether you consider this necessary is up to you. As with all aspects of safety, there is no absolute level that will guarantee a problem- and accident-free cruise. You have to decide what you will be happy with and accept the risks consequent to this.

Collision Bulkheads

The most likely cause for a vessel to sink is a collision, and the most likely area on the boat to be damaged is the bow. For this reason, many serious ocean-cruising yachts are built with a watertight bulkhead toward the bow. Often this is accessed only from the deck though there is no reason why a watertight door could not be used, as is seen on large ships. If it is possible to fit a watertight bulkhead or door on your vessel it is worth considering. Many owners do not use the forward cabin much at sea. Why not have a watertight door here and keep it closed when at sea? There is not much chance that your vessel could sail with the forward cabin full of water but it would probably stay afloat, giving you time to either repair the damaged area at the bow or await rescue.

Flotation Bags

If a vessel does begin to go down because a damaged hull cannot be repaired quickly enough, it would be nice to be able to keep the vessel afloat using air bags. A system is available commercially that will do just this. Bags are installed under berths or in lockers that can be inflated using integral air cylinders. If sufficient bags are used, a vessel can be kept afloat pending rescue. If you decide that the risk of sinking is sufficient to warrant fitting these bags, that's fine. But don't let it lead you into omitting a liferaft, believing this will be no longer necessary. *What if . . .* what if the boat catches fire?

Cockpit Drains

Recently I found my boat with several inches of water in the cockpit. This resulted from clogged cockpit drains, which were probably too small. I had always intended to fit larger ones, but . . .

Cockpit drains installed by a manufacturer are intended to drain the cockpit from rain or spray; they are not usually designed to quickly empty a cockpit that has been deluged by a sea breaking over the stern. The reasoning behind the need for large drains is that a cockpit full of water will slow a vessel so much that subsequent seas are more likely to break over the stern and fill the vessel until she founders. Though there is a need for adequately sized cockpit drains, the risk of a cockpit being deluged from the stern can be minimized by keeping up boat speed in heavy weather. But when you do need them they'd better be large. Just try blocking your existing drains, filling the cockpit, and then timing how long it takes to empty. In order to empty an average cockpit the drains need to be several inches in diameter. Two four-inch pipes leading directly to the stern would be ideal, on either side of the cockpit. But these will need to be plugged in normal conditions to avoid water swilling around the cockpit as it enters from the stern, particularly when the vessel is heeled. If PVC waste pipe is used, it can be glassed into the hull with bungs fitted to lanyards that are tied off. In the event of a breaking sea these can be quickly pulled without being lost.

Seacocks

The seacocks on your vessel are valves placed wherever there is a hole in the boat below the waterline so that, in an emergency, they can be closed to prevent flooding of the vessel. If they fail then you will have a problem on your hands. The least you can do is to inspect the existing seacocks thoroughly to make sure that they are not seized-up, corroded, or brittle. If any are doubtful you should seriously consider replacement.

Deck Fittings

A line coming adrift under tension can easily cause an injury. A deck fitting coming adrift is even more dangerous. Because of the loads imposed upon deck hardware when the conditions get tough, all fittings need to be sufficiently strong and well secured. But how strong is strong? Of course this depends mostly on the size of the vessel. It is likely that most boats appropriate for ocean sailing will by and large have strong deck hardware, but to be sure, why not compare the size of your sheet blocks, mainsheet traveler, and winches to other vessels of a similar type and size? Any fittings that are obviously small should be suspect. But mostly what you need to look for are those fittings that have been added later or replaced temporarily, only to be left aboard. This includes any shackles, padeyes, or other deck fittings that are bent or otherwise distorted or are too small. The time to replace them is now.

Check to see that all deck hardware is through-bolted, at least with backing washers and preferably with solid backing plates. In particular, check the following for secure fittings:

- Cleats (especially where these will be used to attach harness jacklines)
- Genoa sheet tracks
- Mainsheet traveler systems
- Sheet padeyes
- Vang fittings

Mast Pulpits and Handrails

At sea it is nice to have plenty of strong points to hold onto. That's why your vessel probably has handrails along at least part of the cabin top. What are really necessary are sufficient handholds to allow you to work your way forward, at least to the mast while holding on all the time. If this is not possible, consider fitting extra handholds along the cabin top and mast pulpits around the base of the mast. When you have all the handholds you need along the cabin top, don't tie your dinghy oars, windsurfer mast, boat hook, or whatever along them, for then they become next to useless as handholds.

Marine Surveys

Because it is almost impossible for most sailors to gain sufficient knowledge of boatbuilding methods, of construction problems, and of common problems or faults, it is important to employ an expert. This may be done at the time of purchase or prior to departure, but it is really essential that you get some professional and independent assessment of the structural integrity of your boat.

Choosing a Surveyor

Marine surveyors are not licensed, may have no professional qualification, and are responsible only to themselves. Because of this it is important to choose someone qualified to survey your boat. And the problem is that you have to make this assessment yourself. Here in the U.S. there are two professional organizations that a surveyor may belong to: SAMS (Society of Accredited Marine Surveyors) and NAMS (National Association of Marine Surveyors), and membership in either or both of these is an indication that the person is recognized by his colleagues as a marine surveyor.

The best method of selecting a surveyor is to ask others for a recommendation and then for you to interview the person involved. The following questions can be asked:
   • What are your qualifications?
   • Are you a member of either of the two marine surveyors organizations?
   • What is your experience? Are you a "buyer" or a "seller" surveyor?
   • Do you sail?
   • Are you familiar with this type of boat?
   • Have you ever made an ocean passage on a similar boat?
   • Can you give the references of satisfied customers?
   • What does the survey cover and what does it not cover?

What a marine survey usually covers

Because of the differing experiences and abilities of marine surveyors, items covered during a marine survey can vary considerably, and even when an item is covered it may or may not be something with which the surveyor has much experience.

You can expect all surveyors to cover the integrity of the hull. Whether the hull is sound and as good as new, or whether there are problems such as osmotic blistering or delamination between the layers of fiberglass or between the fiberglass and the core. You can expect that the rudder and rudder bearings will be checked, the propeller, propeller shaft, and stern bearings will be examined. The deck is to be checked for delamination, rotted core material, or structural damage. Inside the vessel the interior of the hull should be checked, the bulkheads examined, as well as the frames and stringers if used. All of these are structural items that impinge upon the safety of the boat and you will be relying on the expertise of the surveyor to tell you if there are any problems.

It is also normal to expect the survey to include the systems and equipment on the boat. You should expect the fuel and water tanks to be examined, the engine to be run, and obvious problems brought to your attention. Any electrical or electronic equipment that does not work should be noted. Because the survey is on a sailboat you should make sure that the rigging and sails will be checked and find out if the surveyor will attend a sea trial.

What is not always covered

A marine survey is primarily concerned with the structural integrity of hull and deck. Not all surveys cover the engine, though most surveyors will run the engine and report any obvious problems. If you want to be sure that the engine is O.K. you will probably need to arrange a separate engine survey. While you may expect that the rigging on a sailboat is covered during a survey, a surprising number of surveyors do not go up a mast to check for problems there. And because this is extremely important if you are planning to go cruising you should make sure in advance that this is done. The same applies to the sails if you need these to be checked.

Though most surveyors will check equipment, they will not all be knowledgeable enough to report adequately on all equipment, especially the very old or extremely new. Find out during the survey whether all items have been fully checked out.

Most marine surveyors, though not all, will be experienced sailors and will be able to offer useful advice on the appropriateness of the vessel for your planned sailing. But normally this won't even be mentioned in a survey unless you specifically request it.

One important consideration is absent equipment or items. You cannot expect a surveyor to report on missing equipment or advise on the need for certain items unless this was agreed in advance. Even when a survey has been completed by an extremely competent and experienced surveyor, I have often produced for a new owner a list five or six pages long detailing equipment, modifications, or additions that should be considered for cruising. Details on most of these items are the subject of the rest of this book.

During a survey

If you are planning to take time off from work to go cruising there is no excuse for not taking a day off to be present during the survey. Even if it means postponing the day or flying to where the vessel is lying. Being present during the survey will allow you to see how carefully the surveyor examines your boat and you will probably get a better job done. When problems are found you will have the opportunity to ask questions and to see for yourself exactly what is wrong and what needs doing. When you see something that you don't understand you will be able to ask questions about it and find out the answer from someone who has considerable experience with boats of this type. And most of all, you will learn more about your boat during a survey than at any other time.

CHECKLIST

	YES	NO
Does the hull thickness provide sufficient strength for your intended sailing?	❏	❏
Do you know if the hull has a core?	❏	❏
If so, does it extend below the waterline?	❏	❏
Are you certain that the core is in good condition?	❏	❏
If balsa cored, has the balsa been sealed?	❏	❏
Is the deck cored?	❏	❏
If so, is the core in good condition?	❏	❏
Are the bulkheads:		
Thick enough for your intended sailing?	❏	❏
Substantially bonded to the hull?	❏	❏
Strong enough after doors and passageways have been made?	❏	❏
Is the hull to deck joint strong enough for your intended sailing?	❏	❏
If sealant was used, is it still in good condition?	❏	❏
If your vessel is constructed of wood:		

	YES	NO
Is there evidence of rot?	❏	❏
Are the frames in good condition?	❏	❏
Are they strong enough?	❏	❏
Are they close enough together?	❏	❏
Is the planking thick enough?	❏	❏
Are the fasteners still sound?	❏	❏
If you have a steel vessel:		
Was it built by a reputable yard?	❏	❏
Was the inside well-protected against rust?	❏	❏
Is there evidence of serious rusting?	❏	❏
If you have an aluminum boat:		
Is it built strongly enough?	❏	❏
Is there evidence of electrolysis?	❏	❏
Is it correctly protected against this?	❏	❏
If your vessel has a fin keel:		
Is it strong enough?	❏	❏
Securely attached?	❏	❏
Is there evidence of grounding (that may have resulted in unseen hull damage)?	❏	❏
Is the rudder securely attached to the vessel at the top and bottom?	❏	❏
Is it in sound condition?	❏	❏
Is the cockpit:		
Deep enough with high coamings?	❏	❏
Small enough at sea?	❏	❏
Designed so that you can easily brace yourself when sitting to windward?	❏	❏
If the vessel has a center cockpit is this so high that it will be unsafe (and uncomfortable)?	❏	❏
Does the vessel have a substantial bulwark?	❏	❏
Have you considered fitting:		
A forward collision bulkhead?	❏	❏
Flotation bags?	❏	❏
Larger cockpit drains?	❏	❏
Are all the seacocks sound and easily closed?	❏	❏

	YES	NO
Are all the deck fittings securely fastened?	❏	❏
Have you considered installing mast pulpits?	❏	❏
When your vessel was surveyed:		
Was the surveyor a member of a recognized organization?	❏	❏
Experienced in surveying this type of boat?	❏	❏
Experienced in ocean sailing?	❏	❏
Did the survey report on the condition of:		
The engine?	❏	❏
The rigging (deck level and aloft)?	❏	❏
The sails?	❏	❏
The soundness of the vessel for your intended use?	❏	❏

CHAPTER THREE

Spars and Rigging

The beef Stroganoff that I had eaten our last night ashore must have been bad because I had been sick since we left Madeira heading across the Atlantic. At first I thought my upset stomach was due to sea-sickness, but the days passed and it got no better. I found myself growing tired easily and spending too long in the head.

The passage was, however, proceeding according to plan. Once we were far enough south to catch the trade winds we made good progress for most of the time, the wind vane doing the steering and few sail changes required. A couple of weeks into the voyage, the weather changed and overcast skies foretold a shift in the wind that faded almost to nothing one night so that we found ourselves rolling along in the big swells, the sails slatting and the boom jerking alternately at the main-sheet and preventer. This situation of light winds and leftover seas is one I detest but there was little we could do other than wait for the seas to calm down some.

Soon after first light I was up for my watch and once again sitting in the head when I noticed it. A wire stay lying on the deck, clearly visible from the open port. My energy returned in an instant as I rushed on deck to check what was wrong. Going forward I found the port forward lower shroud lying on deck. The swaged hook fitting at the end had fractured. With the boat on port tack the port shrouds were carrying the load, though sailing downwind the forward lower shrouds were perhaps the least necessary. But even so, a broken shroud is a great cause for concern and I wondered which of the other shrouds would be next to fail.

Initially I secured the spinnaker pole topping lift to a stanchion base and winched it tight to take some of the strain while I planned a more permanent repair. Though we had spare rigging wire aboard and cable clamps to join it, we did not have a spare T-ball fitting to go in the slot in the mast, and replacing the stay was not going to be easy. Eventually I tied a dockline around the mast just above the spreaders and I took the end down to the chainplate using the boom vang to tension it. The tension on the mast was approximately right and once the jury rig was in place I began to relax a little, though for the remainder of our crossing I remained somewhat anxious that another shroud might fail in a similar way.

I still have the wire stay with the broken T-ball fitting. I use it to show my students how an apparently solid stainless steel rod can crack and fail. It seems that this particular fitting broke because of a bad casting, yet it had already made two previous Atlantic passages. Before my passage I had inspected all of the rigging for visual signs of failure and found none. Perhaps if this particular shroud had been removed and the T-ball dye tested a hairline crack might have been detected.

Rigging failures aboard a sailboat are potentially disastrous, perhaps second only to hull damage. Safe preparation necessitates that all spars and rigging be checked carefully before departure; but even if this has been done, or even if all the rigging has been replaced, there is still the possibility of unforeseen failure and so part of preparation involves having sufficient items aboard to cope with the unexpected.

Mast and Booms

Failure of a spar at sea is an unusual occurrence unless precipitated by some other event, such as a failure in the rigging or, in the case of a boom, a broach or severe roll where the end of the boom is in the water. Prudent preparation demands that all spars be examined carefully prior to departure. If you are contemplating other work that requires removal of the mast, this will provide an ideal opportunity to check the spars thoroughly.

Mast and Boom Size

It is unlikely that you will be prepared to fit new spars to your vessel unless they are severely damaged, yet attention to the size of the spars may indicate potential problems when under sail. Generally the trend in sailboat manufacturing has been towards lighter, smaller diameter spars along with thinner, lighter hulls. Older vessels are thus likely to have larger and stronger spars than vessels of a similar length built more recently.

Smaller and lighter spars may be fine for the majority of sailors but for cruising you need to know that this could result in failure at sea. While most spars fail as a consequence of a rigging failure, a thin walled small diameter mast having multiple spreaders is much more likely to break when a shroud fails than is a larger and stronger mast.

If you are choosing a cruising boat give this as much attention as the hull strength. Compare spar sizes on vessels of similar length and displacement to the one you are thinking of buying to get an idea of where your spar fits along the range of sizes. Considerable variation will be found, and if you are looking to buy a production boat the sizing of the spars may give you an indication of strength in other less obvious areas of the vessel. Bear in mind that vessels built for racing will generally have thinner, taller masts to enhance sailing performance at the expense of ultimate seaworthiness.

If you already have the vessel pay particular attention to signs of damage and to the set of the rigging, which becomes progressively more important as spar size diminishes.

Keel or Deck Stepped Masts

Though traditional boat building required the mast to sit directly on the keel of the boat, many manufacturers now choose to step the mast at deck level, transferring the compression loading from the mast to the keel with a compression post fitted in the cabin immediately below the mast.

While traditionalists argue that a serious cruising boat must have a keel stepped mast, there is a trend among cruising boat manufacturers towards deck stepped masts. Either method is fine so long as it is done well. Both methods of seating the mast have advantages and disadvantages, as with all aspects of yacht design. Generally, keel stepped masts are preferred on racing sailboats because of the greater ability to induce mast bend and hence affect sail shape. However the downside of this aboard a cruising boat includes the existence of the spar in the middle of the cabin and an area for potential leaks. For cruising, perhaps the only advantage of a keel stepped mast is that if the mast breaks you are less likely to lose the whole thing over the side than with a deck stepped mast.

Aluminum Spars

A visual check of mast and boom will quickly reveal any cracks, dents, or severe electrolytic corrosion, any of which could easily lead to premature failure.

Cracks or dents in a mast or boom usually indicate previous damage, perhaps as a result of impact or rigging failure when the spar was under load. If cracks exist, a thorough inspection of the spar should be made to check for other hidden damage before a repair is undertaken.

Electrolytic corrosion on aluminum spars is potentially serious. Evidence will often be found where cleats or winches are bolted to the spar, the telltale signs being bubbling paint or a gray/white coating around the fittings. While some evidence of corrosion is often present, due to poor insulation between dissimilar metals, serious corrosion could result in a fitting parting from the spar or, worse still, a portion of the spar coming away with the fitting. Electrolytic damage is also frequently found at the mast step, particularly on keel stepped masts where the mast base is hidden in the bilge and perhaps often soaked in salt water. Corrosion here can easily lead to failure at sea where the mast is under a compression load.

Wooden Spars

Though it is extremely unlikely that you will find wooden spars aboard a new boat, you will see a surprising number of them when you are cruising. Wooden spars really are fine; they look great and are plenty strong enough. Problems that occur generally result from lack of maintenance. All of these can be fixed though some time and skill may be involved.

Check wooden spars for shakes—longitudinal splits in the grain caused by the wood drying out too much—cracks along glued joints, and areas of soft wood caused by rot. Problems are often found at the mast step where water is easily trapped, at the spreader base, on the tops of spreaders, and at the mast top.

Though they do require more maintenance, wooden spars will not suffer from electrolytic corrosion and will almost certainly be repairable anywhere in the world.

Unstayed Masts

Some vessels, most notably those built by Freedom Yachts, have large section masts that require no wire stays or shrouds to hold them up. Many of these masts are manufactured of carbon fiber, giving them a characteristic black finish.

This method of construction may not seem adequate for the rigors of ocean sailing, but many such vessels have proved that this is very definitely not the case. The large diameter spars are clearly strong enough— though they appear somewhat ugly—while the strength of the hull and deck required to support the mast results in an extremely sturdy and rugged vessel. If you are considering a vessel with an unstayed rig don't be put off by this aspect of the design; rather assess its other features.

Mast and Boom Fittings

The majority of problems with spars result from a failed cleat or some other fitting. On aluminum spars the bolts and rivets corrode, while on wooden spars screws pull out of soft wood. Prior to departure any suspect fittings should be removed and replaced in order to fully evaluate the situation. Soft wood at one fitting is a good indication of the problem in other areas. The same applies to electrolytic corrosion on aluminum spars: If one fitting is failing then you will probably need to check all the others.

Assuming that all fittings are sound, the size and strength of the fittings, particularly those that may have been added after the boat was built, should be checked. Mast cleats may be too small or turning blocks on the boom for jiffy reefing may be inadequate. If some fittings are smaller than others, ask yourself why. Is the load less on these fittings or is it similar to other loads that are provided with a larger fitting? When cruising, the loads imposed on mast and boom fittings are considerable, not just in heavy weather but often when the vessel is rolling or when big seas are abating.

Standing Rigging

A mast will usually break as the result of a failure in the standing rigging. Check the rigging carefully for indications of failure prior to departure.

Because of the concern over losing a mast at sea, some authors have suggested that all standing rigging should be replaced periodically, a realistic life expectancy of ten years being quoted for stainless steel wire rope. This is being over prudent rather than relying on hard fact or empirical evidence. I have not found this recommendation in other fields such as the aircraft industry where it could well be expected. Indeed, wire rope manufacturers I spoke with indicated that there is no specific life expectancy for their product and that it should be replaced only after signs of failure.

Chainplates

Chainplates are the fittings used to connect the standing rigging of the vessel to the hull and so are as important as the rigging itself. Chainplates have to be of sufficient size and be securely connected to the hull or bulkheads. In both cases bolts of sufficient size and number must be used, with backing washers. If there is any sign of elongation of the chainplate holes or looseness in the chainplates—as may be evidenced by leaks—the whole fitting should be removed for further examination. Look for hairline cracks directly above the chainplate holes.

If you believe the chainplates or bolts are too small, get some expert advice early in your preparations.

Stays and Shrouds

Whenever a fitting, stay, or shroud appears to be deteriorating it should be replaced. Doing so dockside prior to departure will be a small inconvenience compared with a similar procedure underway. As preparation for every long passage I make it a habit to check all of the standing rigging carefully both at deck level and aloft.

Stainless steel wire

Most vessels use a 1 x 19 construction wire rope for the standing rigging. So long as toggles or other devices are used to ensure a straight pull, and the wire is open to the air, stainless steel wire rope will last almost indefinitely, though problems with stainless steel wire often begin unnoticed with the inner strands that are not exposed to the air.

This type of wire is fairly rigid and works well so long as there are no sharp bends along its length. Toggles used at either end of the wire should ensure a straight pull but seized toggles can result in a forced bend at deck or mast top, and almost all cap shrouds are forced to bend at the spreaders. In all of these areas work hardening of the metal can occur that will eventually result in failure of the wire. Broken strands (meat hooks) are an early indication of this, and just one of these should be sufficient notice that the wire needs replacing.

Despite its name stainless steel does corrode. The majority of problems with standing rigging seem to occur as a result of oxidation (rusting) rather than electrolysis. When stainless steel is not exposed to air circulation, rusting begins and will often be seen around turnbuckles that have been taped over, thus trapping water against the wire, or where covers are used over the shrouds to protect sails against chafe. If either of these are used on your vessel regular examination of the wire is important, for problems could be occurring unnoticed. If you have to tape up turnbuckles, do so in a way that does not trap water. If you use chafe protection on the shrouds, try and ensure that it does not trap water and dirt inside. Whenever rust is evident on turnbuckles the fittings become suspect in strength, though in practice the problem may be only surface discoloration.

On metal hulled boats electrolysis could be a problem, though it is more likely to affect the hull than the rigging due to the relative inertness of stainless steel.

Stainless steel rod rigging

Because a rod of a smaller diameter can be used instead of a wire of the same strength, rod rigging is often seen on racing boats where weight and windage of the rigging are critical factors. Rod rigging has an advantage over wire in that there are no hidden inner strands that can be corroding unnoticed. However, with only one strand—the rod itself—failure will almost always occur with no warning signs. For this reason it is particularly important that rod rigging should not be subject to undue bending, which will induce work hardening. Toggles must be used and the rigging set up carefully.

Galvanized wire

Though rarely used these days, galvanized wire standing rigging has a significant advantage over stainless steel in that there is almost always advance warning of impending failure, as evidenced by rusting of the outer strands of the wire. Use this as an indication that replacement is required.

Turnbuckles and toggles

The turnbuckles can be the weakest part of the standing rigging. They need to be of adequate size for the wire and in good condition. After the introduction of stainless steel wire, stainless steel ones replaced the galvanized and bronze kind as the turnbuckles of choice. However, it has been recognized that where stainless steel threads run in a stainless turnbuckle, galling can occur between the threads, thus weakening the fitting. For this reason it is now recommended that bronze turnbuckles be used with stainless steel rigging. Of course this in turn leads to the possibility of electrolytic corrosion, which has to be monitored, though in practice it is rarely a problem aboard non-metal hulls.

Turnbuckles are manufactured in a number of designs, some totally enclosing fittings that screw into them while others are of an open body construction. This latter type allows easier inspection of the fitting and as a result I prefer this design, though all types are fine so long as they are inspected regularly.

Assuming the turnbuckles are of adequate size, they should be taken apart and cleaned prior to departure. The threads are then examined for wear and the body checked for cracks or distortion. Cotter pins should be replaced as a matter of course. Any problem at all should lead to replacement. When reassembling turnbuckles a little light grease can be used, though this will later serve to collect dirt, exclude air, and could exacerbate oxidation—particularly of the stainless threads. For a similar reason, if you decide to tape the fittings to protect sails and lines from the sharp edges of the cotter pins, do so in a way that does not permanently trap water and dirt.

Toggles are used to ensure that a non-linear strain is avoided between the wire and chainplate. Both toggles and turnbuckles are usually cast stainless or bronze, which is fine so long as the manufacturing process is satisfactory. I have seen a number of these fittings fail, an apparently solid piece of stainless one-half inch thick steel cracking into two pieces. This can happen when stress is induced during manufacturing as a result of uneven cooling. Avoid cheap toggles and turnbuckles. Most will be fine but even a small risk is not worth taking.

End fittings

A number of different devices are used to connect the standing rigging to the mast at one end and to the turnbuckle at the other. The most common are the rolled swage fitting and the mechanical Sta-Lok and Norseman type of fitting.

Rolled swage fittings will be seen on most production boats. These fittings are cheaper and quicker to install in a factory setting, and work well as long as the swaging machine is in good condition and the operator well-trained. Banana shaped swages are just one sign of poor equipment, operator, or both. When examining swage fittings look for signs of swelling or cracking around the swage body. This occurs when corrosion is taking place inside the fitting and it is a definite sign for replacement. Other signs are significant rust on the outside of the swage and at the wire where it enters the swage, broken wire strands, or indications that the wire has been pulling out of the swage. Swage fittings require that wire and fitting be matched for size. Use of metric-sized wire with American swages, or vice versa, will almost always lead to premature failure.

Sta-Lok and Norseman fittings—the two most common brands—are impressive in their strength and may be fitted without the need for special equipment, though they cost significantly more than swage fittings. While the fitting body has to be matched in size to that of the wire, the cone fitting used inside has to be matched to the type of construction of the wire (1 x 19, 7 x 7, etc.). Assuming that this is done correctly, the fittings may be installed at sea if necessary, so having one or two spares aboard is a great idea. The fitting body may also be taken off one wire and reused later so long as a new cone fitting is used inside. Another advantage of this type of fitting is that you can easily undo it to check for rusting, broken strands, etc.

When assembling Sta-Lok or Norseman end fittings, clear silicone sealant should be used to prevent salt water from entering the fitting. A thread locking compound such as Loctite should be used on the body of the fitting to prevent loosening; it seals the thread from salt-water intrusion.

If your vessel's rigging is currently fitted with swaged ends, and both these and the wire appear sound and in good condition, it is unnecessary to replace them as a matter of course. However, having spare wire and a couple of Sta-Lok or Norseman fittings aboard will enable you to make any necessary repairs at sea.

Running Rigging

Though perhaps easier to replace and less disastrous than the standing rigging if it fails, running rigging should be checked before departure on a long cruise and replaced if necessary. If a halyard led inside the mast breaks at sea it can be a considerable inconvenience, and quite serious if it results in the boom falling or the vessel getting out of control. It is instructive to inspect all running rigging carefully for signs of wear and find the cause. While some lines will wear from constant use, most will fail as a result of chafe. Sheaves at the masthead can cause halyards to fray, exposed cotter pins on the lifelines result in the genoa sheets catching every time you tack, and incorrectly mounted turning blocks cause lines to chafe and part.

Halyards

Wire halyards
While some vessels may be fitted with existing wire halyards, these are an inconvenience and a hazard when cruising. Wire halyards were used originally when racing to avoid a sagging luff due to halyard stretch. With cruising in mind and the resistance of modern pre-

stretched Dacron line, wire halyards only have disadvantages. At best the wire will have just a few meat hooks to catch your fingers as you raise the sail. But if you have a few now, more will be on their way as work hardening causes the strands to become brittle and crack. With wire halyards, chafe of the masthead sheaves is another problem. All in all it is a good idea to replace these before you depart.

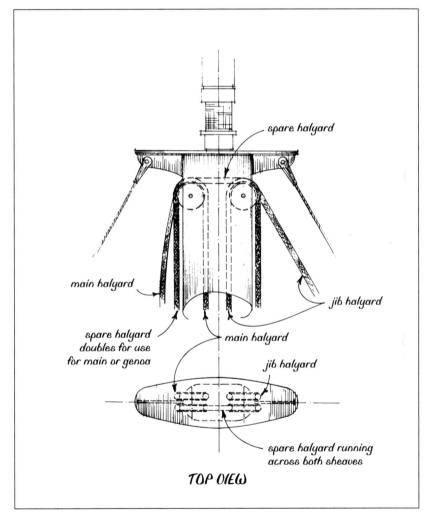

spare halyard

main halyard

jib halyard

spare halyard doubles for use for main or genoa

main halyard

jib halyard

spare halyard running across both sheaves

TOP VIEW

Figure 4. *Rigging spare halyards for main and genoa.*

Spare halyards

Assuming your existing halyards are in good condition or have been replaced, you now need to give some consideration to backup halyards. Should a halyard break at sea it is considerably easier and safer to use a spare to raise the sail than it is to replace the old one, which will almost always mean a trip aloft.

For the main halyard, the boom topping lift can be used; but this can only be done if the topping lift runs through a block at the masthead and back to a cleat at deck level.

Many topping lifts are secured at the mast top and adjustable from the boom. If a topping lift cannot be used consider fitting a spare halyard with an existing, unused masthead sheave, or provide a swivel block at the mast top for this purpose.

On one occasion I used a spinnaker halyard to replace a broken main halyard; this meant running the line over the upper shroud, which would not have lasted long as a result of chafe, but we only needed it for a short while.

The spinnaker halyard can be used as a spare for a genoa but having an additional genoa halyard is better still. At the masthead of most vessels are four sheaves with usually only two in use, one for the main halyard and one for the genoa. If these are run internally on one side of the mast, the two remaining sheaves may be used to run an external halyard that can double as a spare for both main or genoa.

Sheets

With sufficient spare line aboard, you could probably rig a spare sheet in an emergency. However when fitting out for cruising it may be prudent to replace the main and genoa sheets and keep the old ones for spares. If you have a separate storm jib you will need sheets for this in addition to your genoa sheets. Make sure that the storm jib sheets are of a similar size and length to your existing genoa sheets so that these can be used as replacements if necessary. When replacing any sheets, get them longer than the existing ones to allow for shortening because of future chafe.

Other Running Rigging

All other running rigging should be checked for wear, especially near splices or where the line passes through turning blocks or cam cleats. If wear exists it may be possible to completely replace the line but try and find the reason for the original chafe first. On a vessel I sailed, one of the steering lines from the wind vane would chafe through within a day or so because the turning block, though angled with a custom-made spacer, was not angled correctly. If this type of problem is noticed and diagnosed before departure it will save a great deal of frustration, stress, and difficulty later on.

Emergency Rigging

Mast, Boom, and Other Spars

While it is not realistic to take a spare mast with you, it may be possible to have the tools and equipment to repair essential fittings on the existing one. Cleats may pull off the mast, sheaves crack, aluminum rivets fail, and bolts disappear overboard. Take a look at what you have fitted to the mast, boom, and other spars, and mentally prepare a plan for what you would do if each failed. The result should be a list of tools and fittings to take with you.

Standing Rigging

Should a stay or shroud part at sea and you are lucky enough not to lose the mast, how will you replace it? Though I had spare rigging wire and cable clamps when I lost a shroud, these were of no use as the fitting that went into the mast had failed. In that instance I was able to effect a temporary repair by attaching a line around the spreaders, but if I had fitted a T-ball fitting on to one end of the wire before I departed I could have made a permanent repair at sea using a Sta-Lok or Norseman terminal at deck level. And even if the wire had not been long enough I could have made a strong temporary repair.

Have aboard wire of the correct diameters, together with a couple of end fittings and a bunch of cable clamps. These clamps are made to match the wire size and are available in both stainless and galvanized steel. I prefer the galvanized because of their greater friction coefficient and hence holding power.

Running Rigging

Make sure that you have sufficient line aboard to replace a sheet that parts at sea. In this case maybe a three-strand Dacron dockline will do, but other running rigging requires use of a specific size of line. If you have a wind vane steering system you should make sure that you have a few sets of replacement lines for this. Similarly, roller-furling lines need to be the correct diameter and length. If a furling line parts you cannot join it easily and using a larger diameter line will fill the drum before the sail is fully furled.

Reefing lines or others that go through turning blocks and end at sheet stoppers also need to be of a similar size when replaced, so having at least one spare of the longest length required is a good idea.

In addition you should have a bag of various spare lines for the 101 uses that will occur at sea but that even the most experienced ocean sailor could not anticipate.

CHECKLIST

	YES	NO
Is the mast of sufficient size?	❏	❏
Are there:		
Dents?	❏	❏
Cracks?	❏	❏
Severe areas of electrolytic corrosion (or rot)?	❏	❏
Is the mast step sound?	❏	❏
Are all the fittings strongly secured?	❏	❏
Are the boom, spinnaker pole, and other spars of		
sufficient size?	❏	❏
Do they suffer from:		
Dents?	❏	❏
Cracks?	❏	❏

	YES	NO
Severe areas of electrolytic corrosion (or rot)?	❏	❏
Is the standing rigging in good condition?	❏	❏
Is there any evidence of broken strands?	❏	❏
Are toggles used?	❏	❏
Are the turnbuckles in good condition?	❏	❏
Are they of sufficient size?	❏	❏
Is there evidence of:		
The threads galling?	❏	❏
Cracks or corrosion?	❏	❏
Does the wire have swaged ends?	❏	❏
If so, are they:		
In good condition (not swollen or rusty)?	❏	❏
Straight?	❏	❏
Secure?	❏	❏
Does the wire have Sta-Lok or Norseman terminals?	❏	❏
If so, have you checked them all by opening them?	❏	❏
Does the vessel have wire halyards?	❏	❏
Are they in good condition with no meat hooks?	❏	❏
Have you considered replacing them?	❏	❏
Are the mast sheaves in good condition?	❏	❏
Do you have:		
Spare halyards rigged for all sails?	❏	❏
Spare genoa sheets?	❏	❏
Line for a spare mainsheet?	❏	❏
If you have roller furling do you have a spare furling line?	❏	❏
If you have wind vane steering do you have spare steering lines?	❏	❏
Have you checked all other running rigging?	❏	❏
Do you have sufficient spare lines aboard?	❏	❏
Do you have tools and spares for rigging repair?	❏	❏

CHAPTER FOUR

Engines, Transmissions, and Propellers

From the east coast of Florida I chose to take the Okeechobee Waterway from its start at the St. Lucie River, at Stuart just north of Palm Beach, passing along the St. Lucie Canal to Port Mayaca. Then we went across Lake Okeechobee, via the Caloosahatchee Canal under the railroad lift bridge with its 49-foot clearance—that had me up the mast to be sure we had clearance. We continued on down the Caloosahatchee River to Fort Myers and finally anchored off Captiva Island. The trip was memorable for the winding rivers and canals, the flat Florida landscapes, and the opportunity to stop in several small towns that I would never otherwise have visited.

With its steady rumble, the old Volvo diesel ran and ran, starting each morning and continuing each day as we made about five knots along the winding, windless waterway. I checked the oil each morning and topped it off as necessary. At Port Mayaca we filled our jerrycans at the local gas station and transferred more diesel to the tank. We motored onwards secure in the knowledge that, if necessary, the engine could take us all the way to Clear Lake, Texas, which was our destination.

After a couple of peaceful nights anchored behind the barrier islands we set off one afternoon, heading out under engine into the Gulf of Mexico until we could shut off the noisy rumble and sail north-wards along the coast towards Tampa, which we made the next morning. After provisioning and picking up a friend who was to join us for our Gulf crossing we were ready to depart, but the emergence of a tropical depression over the Florida Keys led us up the Tarpon River where we anchored in anticipation of the coming storm. As often happens, we were ready but nothing really happened, and once the storm was north of us and dissipating as it headed inland we were ready to leave.

Back down the Tarpon River we headed out to sea again, first using the engine and then we began sailing in the light wind. By late afternoon the wind began to fade and by dusk we were again motoring. Later a breeze returned and we started sailing once more downwind at only a couple of knots. By midnight I decided to start the engine and motor again; perhaps farther from land we could pick up a steady ocean wind. I turned the key and the engine started, ran for a couple of seconds and died. I tried again but nothing. I removed the engine housing and operated the decompression levers, allowing it to run freely before closing just one of the two levers. It started on the forward cylinder but then stopped again. And that was it. It was dark, I couldn't figure out what had happened. I was both annoyed at the engine's untimely demise and anxious about our prospects without it. We sailed on that night and in the morning I tried to start it again but without success. Eventually I gave up and pondered whether to head back to Tampa or continue with our passage. I chose the latter, figuring that away from land we were probably fine, that both options meant a landfall under sail, and that we really wanted to be in Texas. And so we continued with our passage without an engine, arriving at Galveston some seven days later.

Until the old Volvo failed me I had really given it little thought. It had always started when I needed it and, though I didn't use it that often, it was there as my backup when a freighter appeared to be getting too close or to keep the boat moving while I doused the ripped mainsail. When the wind died as I closed the land after a passage I was always able to count on it to get me into the port safely.

I recall reading the accounts of cruising yachtsmen earlier this century making a passage across the English Channel to the Channel Islands in their small engineless boats. Within sight of land, they had to wait for several days to get into port as the wind was light and the adverse currents strong. In recent years, there have been a few cruisers who swear by their engineless sailboats, but the reality is that there are very few sailors who plan to go offshore without a reliable engine.

Engines are not just a convenience. They almost constantly affect the decisions that are made aboard the cruising sailboat. Just as I have chosen to enter a harbor in thick fog using a GPS, radar, and the skills of a good crew (a decision I would not have made in the absence of any one of these), engines affect decisions about what is safe to attempt and what is not. Departures and landfalls would be very different without them. Passages are made that otherwise may not be started. I know that I have made voyages in the Gulf of Mexico during hurricane season by staying closer to the coast than I would normally, planning to use the engine to put in should a tropical depression form during the passage. Engines are relied upon and when they fail the safety of the vessel is sometimes in jeopardy.

Marine Gasoline or Diesel Engines

The choice is not hard to make as evidenced by the fact that most sailboats will be fitted with an inboard diesel engine. But there is a lot to be said for the philosophy espoused in Don Casey and Lew Hackler's *Sensible Cruising: The Thoreau Approach*, which advocates going cruising with what you have rather than postpone the venture until you have all that you need. And if you already have a boat with a gasoline engine you may want to consider setting off with it.

Gasoline Engines

Marine gasoline engines are essentially the same type as car engines. They have spark plugs and coils, contact breakers, and carburetors. They are lightweight, start easily, are powerful, easy to control, and easy to stop. With suitable spare parts aboard they are simple enough to repair and you can be sure that wherever you venture, someone will be around to work on them if you don't.

But against these advantages there are some serious disadvantages to gasoline engines aboard a cruising sailboat. First, they rely on electricity. They need a battery to run and a charging system, a coil to create high voltages for the spark plugs, and a contact breaker to time and distribute this voltage. In a salty marine environment electrical systems tend to fail.

The risk of fire and explosion is their main disadvantage. Gasoline, because of its volatile nature, is liable to build up high concentrations of vapor until it will explode if ignited by a spark. In your car this risk is minimized by the constant circulation of air around the engine, but in the closed engine room of a boat there is little or no circulation unless you specifically arrange for it. It is for this reason that all vessels fitted with gasoline engines will also have a bilge blower that should be used for several minutes before you attempt to start the engine. The blower will suck out the air from around the engine and blow it overboard, and any gasoline fumes that have built up since you last used the engine will be expelled before you create a spark to start the engine. Ideally these fumes will not build up in the first place but the risk of them doing so is increased by the way a gasoline engine works. The engine's carburetor contains a reservoir of fuel so that a steady supply may be mixed with the air and the gas/air mixture sucked into the engine. When you stop the engine, the carburetor reservoir remains full and this small amount of gasoline can easily evaporate and remain around the engine or in the bilge.

With appropriate use of the engine blower, the risk of a build up of fumes while the engine is dormant can be minimized but the risk of fire and/or explosion remains. Any leakage of fuel while the engine is running will create a very serious risk of fire. Gasoline dripping onto a hot engine will easily ignite and the hot, oily engine room can very quickly become an inferno. In addition there is the very real risk that a fire in the engine room will track back to the fuel tank with the consequent high risk of explosion.

If you already have a gasoline engine aboard your boat and you choose to set off cruising with it attention to these risks is essential. Always:

- Install a gasoline vapor alarm system.
- Ensure the tank is grounded to the deck-fill plate to avoid the build up of static electricity and the chance of sparks.
- Use the bilge blower for several minutes before attempting to start the engine.
- Check the engine room regularly for a build up of gasoline fumes.
- Check the fuel lines regularly from the tank to the engine.
- If you work on the engine yourself, or employ a car mechanic to do so, make sure that the correct marine spares are installed.

Marine starter motors and alternators are similar to those used in cars, but the marine parts are fitted with spark guards that reduce the risk of a spark within the unit setting off an explosion. Carburetors are also fitted with a spark guard.

Diesel Engines

With a diesel engine, there is much less risk of fire and explosion. For this reason, it has become the primary choice aboard any boat, whether it is for fishing, cruising, or commercial use. Diesel engines are also pretty dependable and more economical on fuel. In his first book, *The Log of The Maken*, Ian Nicolson, the Scottish naval architect and designer who has written extensively about small boat sailing, describes how on his first real passage the one-cylinder diesel engine had to be started. First the kerosene stove was lit and then the blowtorch:

"Then, carrying the torch aloft, and without singeing more than the minimum amount of paintwork, the operator would go up on deck and climb down the slippery vertical ladder into our Black Hole of Calcutta, the engine room.

"The engine room was not a pleasant place. It lacked both light and ventilation. In the center stood the massive single cylinder, a tower of rusty steel coated with oil, grime and soot. Various pipes meandered about with disconcerting lack of straightness and some sharp bends which were rank bad engineering. At the fore end of the engine was the flywheel. If everything else on the *Maken* was over-size the flywheel outvied all the other gear. It lurked deep down in the bilge, a thick circle of steel so ponderous in appearance that at first glance one could be excused for wondering if any human hand could turn such a vast piece of ironware. In practice even Mike, for all his strength, couldn't turn it; at best he could rock it gently backwards and forwards.

"Down the engine room ladder our operator directs the blowlamp on to the top of the engine. The idea is to get the top of the cylinder thoroughly hot. Meanwhile a second victim has climbed into the pit of horrors and is oiling various points on the engine. There are, dotted about in the most remarkably inaccessible places, little brass bowls, like egg cups, which have to be filled with oil from a battered old can. Doing this in the dark, with the ship pitching in a seaway, it is not surprising that plenty of oil was spilled into the bilge. Naturally the risk of an engine seize-up was not to be considered, so we were liberal with the oil. This merely doubled the quantity which went into the bilge.

"With the top of the cylinder almost glowing hot, one victim would pump the fuel into the cylinder while the other rocked the gargantuan fly-wheel backwards and forwards. If all went according to plan and prayer there would be a thumpety-thumpety-thump and the engine would go at once and for ever till the fuel ran out. That was the chief virtue of this primitive old grinder. It was reliable to the point of embarrassment."

Fortunately for us such seasickness inducing tasks are rarely required though the description illustrates many essentials about diesel engines: the difficulty in getting them started, the need for pumping fuel, and for lubrication. And not least their reliability. Diesel engines will run and run, as Ian Nicolson says, to the point of embarrassment, but they can and do fail as mine did on that Gulf of Mexico passage. When my engine failed it was the cylinder head gasket that blew and though I did have spares aboard it would not have been possible to repair at sea. But a major failure like this is rare. Most problems with diesel engines are simple and straightforward. With good maintenance and the appropriate spares and tools, many problems can be eliminated or solved.

The fuel system

The supply of fuel to a diesel engine begins simply enough though it is here that many problems occur. From the diesel tank fuel is sucked up to the engine by the mechanical lift pump. Then under a slight pressure the lift pump delivers the fuel to the injection pump which in turns delivers the fuel to the injectors. Because the fuel is under suction from the tank to the lift pump, any poor or leaking joint will not be obvious as air is sucked into the system rather than fuel leaking out. Air sucked into the fuel line is one of the major reasons for an engine either failing to start or stopping after it has been running for a short while. Knowing how to bleed the air from your diesel engine is essential and having practiced this while at the dock will certainly pay big dividends if you undertake this procedure at sea.

Fuel leaks from the lift pump to the injector pump will be more obvious as, under slight pressure, fuel will leak out. Small leaks will probably not affect the running of the engine as the lift pump delivers far more fuel than is normally required, but even diesel fuel dripping on a hot engine creates a risk of fire. A fuel return line for the unused fuel will run from the injectors back to the fuel tank under very low pressure, and any leaks along this line will not only affect the running of the engine but will also create a risk of fire.

From the injection pump to the injectors the fuel is under extremely high pressure and even a small leak will affect the running of the engine. Generally leaks will be obvious by a mist of diesel at the point of leakage.

The need for clean fuel

In order for the fuel injection pump to create the high pressures needed to supply the injectors, and for the injectors to deliver a fine mist of fuel to the cylinder, very close tolerances are required in the injection pump and in the injector nozzle. Even minute quantities of dirt can damage the pump, block the injector, or both. To eliminate this problem, diesel engines are fitted with two or more fuel filters to remove dirt before it reaches the injection pump. For the engine to run efficiently these filters need to be changed regularly, for if they become blocked they will so restrict the flow of fuel that the engine will lose power or die.

Under normal circumstances the amount of dirt introduced into the fuel at a fuel dock is minimal, though away from the U.S. it is sensible to filter fuel as it enters the tank to remove any debris. But dirt and sludge can also accumulate in a fuel tank as a result of algae growth. This occurs more in warmer climates and always where there is water present in the fuel. Before setting out it is good practice to remove the fuel tank inspection covers and physically check for the presence of water and/or dirt. If you find any you will need to remove it yourself or engage the services of a company specializing in fuel polishing. Once you are sure that the fuel is clean and free of water, use a diesel additive to combat algae growth and keep the fuel tank full whenever possible, as this will minimize the accumulation of water from condensation.

Engine starting

Though gasoline engines require an electrical system to run and diesels do not, starting a diesel engine requires considerably more power from a battery, and a weak one will make a diesel hard to start. Because no sparks are used to ignite the fuel, very high compression is required in a diesel cylinder to create the high temperature needed to get the fuel to burn. When you try to start a diesel engine, if it turns over too slowly the combustible gases will have time to seep past the piston rings and the pressure will not be sufficient for the engine to fire.

Engine starting batteries

If you want your engine to start reliably you will need a good battery. Though most boats are fitted with dual batteries and a battery changeover switch allowing Battery 1, Battery 2, or both to be selected, this is not to my mind a prudent system. It is too easy to inadvertently leave the switch set to both and then each battery will drain to a point where there is not enough juice left for starting. Additionally, because the system allows either battery to be used for engine starting or boat supply, there will be many times when a battery is not used for its correct purpose. Batteries generally are designed to give a high output for a short period—starting batteries like those designed for a car—or a lower output over a longer period—deep cycle batteries. For the most efficiency, a starting battery should be used. This should be a battery dedicated only for this purpose, which will allow it to be relatively small. If in an emergency you wish to use this battery for something else, such as emergency communications or for a bilge pump, then a set of automobile jump cables will allow you to do this without the risk of a switch ever being left accidentally in the wrong position.

Hand cranking

Although many small marine diesels can also be hand started with a handle, this operation is not always possible. It is essential to check out the system before you depart. Make sure that the handle fits the engine, that it can rotate 360 degrees and still leave sufficient room for your knuckles, and that you can get into a position to turn the crank with some energy. As previously stated, a diesel engine requires a brisk cranking speed to create the high compression needed for ignition. When hand cranking an engine it is normal to open the decompression levers first so that the engine may be turned easily. When you have built up speed, either you or a crewmember can close one of the decompression levers and hopefully the engine will start. Once it is running on one cylinder, the other levers should be quickly closed and the engine will be running. As with all aspects of your boat, practicing this at the dock before you leave is much easier than trying it for the first time when you are between the jetties of some foreign port, with large freighters coming in and out, and the current taking you sideways down the channel.

When I was cruising aboard *Melos*, the knowledge that I could hand crank my engine made me confident that, whatever else failed, it would be available when needed. As I found out later, complacency has no position aboard ship.

Emergency starting techniques

The most important point about emergency starting is that when it becomes necessary you almost certainly have another problem. Unless the reason is that your battery is too flat for the engine to attain a high enough cranking speed, it will be essential to save whatever power you have left in a battery until you have solved the problem.

If your engine was previously running but then died, quietly, without serious sounding mechanical noises, you should suspect the fuel supply. You may be out of fuel, low enough in fuel for the pickup to suck in air—especially when the boat is heeled as will happen when sailing or in steep seas—or a fitting may have broken or loosened, allowing air into the fuel system. Check to see if you have fuel at the injectors and if you do, bleed the fuel lines anyway to be sure that air in the injection pump is not the problem. Other things to look for are a blocked air intake, a blocked exhaust, or a clogged fuel filter.

If you are trying to start a cold engine, check that a cold starting device such as glow plugs or the air intake heater are working, or that a cold-start fuel enriching device is engaged. A very low battery will not have sufficient power to run glow plugs and start an engine simultaneously. Assuming these have been checked and are all operational you can try the following ideas:

- Try hand cranking or battery cranking with the decompression levers open (if fitted) while the engine builds up speed and warmth.
- Put a few drops of oil or WD-40 in the air intake. This will help to

seal a cylinder and increase the compression, hopefully enough to get it to start. Don't use starting fluid designed for a gasoline engine. It is too volatile and will explode too early, almost always damaging the engine.

• Warm the cylinder head using a propane torch, or even hot water boiled on the stove.

• Heat the air entering the air intake.

Lubrication systems

Making sure your diesel or marine gasoline engine has sufficient oil is an important maintenance procedure for the reliability of the motor, though checking the oil level and replacing the oil are often not easy to do. Rarely will there be a need to undertake this at sea, unless you plan to motor across an ocean. It will be a chore to be taken care of in port.

While checking, topping off, or replacing the engine oil is not easy, attending to the transmission (gearbox) oil is more difficult and often forgotten. Though it is not necessary to replace the oil regularly, this maintenance task should not be neglected. From a practical standpoint, buying several oil filters and fitting one of them before you leave is a sensible precaution. On one boat that I helped the owner prepare for an ocean passage, the replacement oil filters sold to us by an auto parts store would not physically fit in the space available, despite having the correct thread and seal.

Cooling systems

Next to fuel problems, engine overheating is the most common problem to be encountered. Sea water is used to cool the engine. In some engines, referred to as raw water cooled, the sea water is pumped through the engine, cooling the cylinders before being ejected via the exhaust system. In the majority of modern diesel engines, referred to as fresh water cooled, raw water is used to cool a separate supply of fresh water by means of a heat exchange which then circulates around the engine just as the coolant does in a car's engine.

Both engines will have a raw water pump that will suck up the sea water and force it under pressure through the engine. These pumps generally have a rubber impeller that does the pumping and that can and will fail from time to time. Preventative maintenance suggests replacing this impeller once a season and having a spare aboard. It is essential to know how to undertake this task. I recall motoring back up the Houston Ship Channel one afternoon, after a weekend teaching aboard an owner's boat, when I noticed the sound of the engine changing. A quick check revealed that cooling water was no longer being emitted from the exhaust. We pulled out of the channel (not always possible) and anchored to find out what was wrong. The pump impeller was the most likely cause and my first task was to find the raw water pump, which was more difficult than usual. Because of its location, simply removing the cover was not possible. Even with a good supply of tools aboard the task was not easy. First the alternator had to be loosened and the drive belt removed before the entire pump could be unbolted from the engine. Only then could the cover be taken off and the failed impeller—it was the impeller—replaced with the spare that was aboard. If the owner had undertaken this task previously at the dock, he would have known the location of the pump, that it was necessary to loosen the alternator, and been sure to have all the necessary tools aboard. And most importantly he would have known that the impeller in his box of spares was the correct one.

Engine alarms

Your marine engine will almost certainly fail with serious damage if it is run too hot for any length of time or with an oil pressure too low for even a short period. Knowing this, most engine manufacturers fit warning lights to indicate too high cooling water temperatures or too low oil pressure. Although these lights are usually reliable, actually seeing them is another thing. Either the engine controls will be below and thus not constantly in view or, if mounted in the cockpit, the lights will be difficult or impossible to see in bright sunlight. A warning buzzer or alarm is an essential piece of safety equipment for your engine. It should activate when you first turn the ignition on and stop when the engine is running. If you don't have an alarm consider fitting one before you leave. Just recently I was sailing a relatively new boat that was fitted with an alarm, and also with a switch on the engine control panel in the cockpit that silenced the alarm. This is an extremely poor system as it would be too easy to leave the switch off. Surely you need to be aware of the alarm at all times.

Transmissions

An engine transmission transfers the power from the rotating engine crankshaft to the propeller via a gearbox and propeller shaft. There are two main categories of gearboxes, mechanically driven ones and hydraulic ones. Both require oil: the mechanical ones to lubricate the gears and bearings, the hydraulic ones use oil to actually transfer the power.

Mechanical Gearboxes

As preparation for cruising, little needs to be done to a mechanical gearbox other than to check and/or replace the oil and to ensure that it is operational. Normal maintenance would indicate that the shift mechanism be checked and greased as necessary. An advantage to a mechanical gearbox is that when the engine is not running the gear shift may be engaged to stop the prop shaft from revolving when the vessel is under sail.

Hydraulic Gearboxes

Since hydraulic gearboxes are normally extremely reliable and long lasting, there is little that can be done to prepare for cruising other than to check for oil leaks, change the oil, and ensure that a sufficient supply of oil is aboard should a hose break when at sea.

Most hydraulic gearboxes use the engine raw water cooling circuit to also cool the oil, and thus if problems develop in this system it will also affect the gearbox.

V-Drives

Both mechanical and hydraulic gearboxes can be fitted as a V-drive; the engine is installed with the output shaft facing forward and the gearbox having its output shaft facing aft. Such an installation is often necessary to obtain the correct angle or position for the prop shaft and it is usually determined by the design requirements of the vessel. Having a

V-drive gearbox makes little difference in terms of performance though it does have practical considerations. While checking and changing the gearbox oil is usually extremely easy, getting to the shaft and stern gland can be almost impossible.

Prop Shafts

At one time revolving prop shafts were used to generate power while the boat was under sail, using a specially wound alternator fitted to the shaft. These units are expensive, have a relatively low output, and are now seen less frequently. In fact most cruisers wish to stop the shaft revolving to reduce noise and wear of the cutlass bearing. If the vessel has a hydraulic gearbox this will have to be accomplished using a shaft brake. Some hydraulic gearboxes can actually be damaged by allowing the shaft to rotate when the engine is not running, as the bearings will not be sufficiently lubricated. While this may not have been a consideration when daysailing, it could be an important consideration if you are planning an ocean crossing.

Ideally before setting off, the prop shaft should be removed from the boat and examined for wear at the sight of the cutlass bearing and for pitting caused by electrolysis, or a lack of straightness. Any of these problems will probably indicate the need for a new shaft.

While the shaft is removed it will allow inspection and replacement of the cutlass bearing if necessary, and even if not it will allow you to obtain the correct replacement as a spare. Similarly the packing gland can be checked and the packing replaced if a standard fitting. Spare packing material of the correct size can be put aside for later use. Some stern glands are now dripless and maintenance-free. They work fine until they fail, and then you are left with a difficult situation. For this reason I prefer the simpler, traditional type of gland even though it can be a pain to get to and needs adjusting occasionally.

With the shaft out of the boat, this is also an opportunity to replace the hose connecting the stern gland to the stern tube, as it is only possible to undertake this with the shaft removed.

Once these checks have been carried out and any necessary repairs or replacements fitted, a final procedure will be to align the engine correctly with the shaft. This will ensure a smoothly running engine, reduced noise, and, most importantly, will minimize damage that can occur when the engine is seriously misaligned.

Propellers

Checking and Replacing

If the boat you are taking cruising has been fitted with its prop for some time and all has been well, then the best approach is to leave it alone. If you do remove it from the shaft it should be checked and balanced as a preventative measure before being replaced. When fitting it back, ensure that the key-way or splines are a tight fit, that the shaft and prop tapers fit together correctly, and that the prop is tightly fitted to the shaft and the nut wired or pinned. I have known a number of people who have lost the prop from the end of the shaft.

Sizing

If you decide on a new prop make sure it is correctly sized for your engine and boat. Propeller sizing is partly a science but also partly trial and error. A prop with too small a diameter or too small a pitch will produce too little power and the boat will barely reach hull speed in flat water; too large a prop or pitch can overload an engine so much that it fails.

Two- or Three-Bladed, Fixed, or Folding

If you change the prop you will have a large choice. The boat may have been fitted with a two-bladed or folding prop for a little improvement in performance under sail, and you may choose to fit a fixed, three-bladed one for more power or maneuverability when using the engine. The opposite may also apply and you may decide that the fixed, three-bladed prop that you have now will produce too much drag when sailing long distances. The decision, like many, is individual and will be determined by your own plans or experience. My advice is that if you are not sure what to do leave the prop as it is and move on to some other area of the boat that needs attention.

CHECKLIST

	YES	NO
If your engine is gasoline powered, are you aware of the risks involved?	❏	❏
Are you familiar with the fuel system on your engine?	❏	❏
Are there any fuel or air leaks?	❏	❏
Do you have a separate engine battery for engine starting?	❏	❏
Is it a high-output starting battery?	❏	❏
Can you switch this for use in an emergency or do you have jump cables for this purpose?	❏	❏
If your engine has a hand cranking facility can you start it this way?	❏	❏
Is your fuel tank free of dirt and water?	❏	❏
Have you changed the fuel filters?	❏	❏
Do you have spare filters aboard?	❏	❏
Have you changed the lubricating oil?	❏	❏
Do you have extra oil aboard?	❏	❏
Have you replaced the raw-water pump impeller?	❏	❏
Do you have a spare aboard?	❏	❏
Does your engine have audible alarms for temperature and oil pressure?	❏	❏
If not, are you happy with this?	❏	❏
Have you changed the transmission oil?	❏	❏
Have you checked the cutlass bearing?	❏	❏
Can you stop the shaft revolving when under sail?	❏	❏
Have you replaced the packing in the stern gland?	❏	❏
Do you have spare packing aboard?	❏	❏
Is the prop correctly sized for the engine?	❏	❏

CHAPTER FIVE

Steering

I had prepared a long list of modifications and additions for the owner of the Morgan 41 and the majority of these had been completed when I arrived early Saturday morning at the boat. I was to be the skipper and teacher. The owner, a friend, and his two nephews were on the boat for a 600-mile passage across the Gulf of Mexico from Clear Lake, Texas to Destin, Florida. We surveyed the items yet to be completed and selected those essential for the trip, such as pulling out the anchor rode, checking that the bitter end was connected, and then faking it for easy use if needed.

By lunch time we were ready to depart. After a hurried take-out from McDonald's we set out, first to the fuel dock and then on towards Galveston, a short passage of around 20 miles in the protected waters of Galveston Bay. We had intended to carry on that evening, but the winds were picking up and it would have meant leaving for open water at dusk with a fairly inexperienced crew, so instead we opted to anchor for the night and set out early the next morning.

By first light we had our anchor aboard and by around 8:00 A.M. we were out of the jetties and in some fairly large swells and stiff winds. With a reefed main and only a portion of the genoa unfurled we set off, to windward inevitably, beating south southeast as close as we could. The conditions remained the same all day as we plowed on, first on port tack then on starboard, trying to get upwind. By dusk one of the crew was incapacitated with seasickness and another was suffering but still standing watch. It was pretty rough in the night and we had the storm jib set for some of the time. We all were wet and tired. Needless to say our progress to windward at night was not great, and overall we had not made too much progress by the next morning.

Dawn revived the earlier enthusiasm of the crew. With moderating conditions we carried on. After breakfast we experimented with the new and expensive autopilot. With an interface to the masthead wind instruments it steered us on a course relative to the apparent wind and our progress improved considerably, until it failed. By midday we were back to manning the wheel and I was getting some needed rest below when I was called on deck to witness the wheel spinning freely around and the boat broadside onto the wind and seas. One of the advantages of a below decks, quadrant-drive autopilot is the ability to use it for emergency steering in the event of cable failure. We did try again but found it still broken.

After reducing sail, we looked for the problem in the steering and found that the bolts securing one of the cables to the quadrant had come undone. We found them in the bilge and it was a relatively easy task to get the bolts back in the hole and the first nut on. We tightened it all up and I prepared to go back to bed for the remainder of my much needed sleep, but our crew in the cockpit reported that the problem remained.

It was time for the cumbersome and inelegant emergency tiller, which we got up on deck and proceeded to fit. But then we realized that the new quadrant arm for the autopilot had been mounted in such a way as to prevent use of the emergency tiller. With it not working, it was a simple enough decision to remove the arm from the top of the rudder stock so that we could mount the tiller. That done we were back in business, though using the tiller was extremely difficult. The short tiller required considerable force to move it, which was difficult to do sitting on the cabin top aft of the cockpit with no footholds to lever against. As we altered course and headed for land we took turns manning the helm for short periods at a time.

During the afternoon I rechecked the steering system and concluded that there was a problem in the steering pedestal. It could be that the short chain had jumped off the sprocket, which would have been simple to fix had we been able to disassemble the pedestal, but the stainless bolts in the aluminum housing would not budge. Our screwdriver was too small.

It was dark by the time we had passed the jetties at Calcasieu, Louisiana. That night, while we had some difficulty using the tiller, we maneuvered alongside an oil supply depot at Cameron. The next morning, with help from the depot staff, we were able to take apart the pedestal top and, sure enough, all that was needed was to replace the chain on the sprocket that had come off while the cable was loose. We had our wheel steering again but still no autopilot.

Steering Systems

A ship without the ability to steer is essentially a ship without a rudder and it is difficult if not impossible to go anywhere. You must pay careful attention to the steering system and carry an effective backup if possible.

Tiller Steering

If your vessel has a tiller then so far, so good. A tiller is a simple mechanical device and a joy to steer with, though if you are accustomed to wheel steering it may take a little getting used to. With a tiller you have a direct connection to the rudder stock and many potential problems in a steering system are eliminated. However under some conditions it is possible that the tiller could break, so having a spare aboard is sensible even if it is made of galvanized water pipe or rough sawn lumber. Try your spare before you depart, then put it aside somewhere deep inside the boat, for chances are you will never need it.

If you have a tiller but are contemplating exchanging it for a wheel, stop and ask yourself why. Is it because you feel more comfortable with a wheel? Plan first to make a few days' passage giving yourself time to get used to the tiller. Then decide whether to replace it or not.

Wheel Steering

The majority of cruising boats will be fitted with wheel steering in the cockpit and some perhaps will have an additional steering position either below decks or in the pilothouse. Wheel steering is easy to use and necessary aboard a larger boat. Vessels with a single steering position in the cockpit will most often have a cable drive from the wheel to the steering quadrant. On boats with more than one steering position, the drive is usually hydraulic, or it may be shaft driven.

Cable drive

Cable-drive steering systems are operated by running flexible wires from the steering pedestal back to the rudder stock where a steering quadrant is mounted. The cables may be of stainless wire, which runs back to the rudder via turning blocks, or they may be of a type similar to that used for the engine throttle, though much larger, with an inner control cable running inside a rigid outer cable.

Stainless wire cables should be inspected as carefully as the standing rigging for meat hooks, an early sign of impending failure. Where the cable reaches the wheel a short length of chain is usually connected with swaged eyes in the cable, and these swages must be inspected for signs of slippage or failure. If spare steering cable is to be carried, it may be sensible to have at least one swaged eye of the correct size already fitted. At the quadrant end of the cables, eyes are usually formed with stainless steel thimbles and galvanized cable clamps. Inspect the clamps for corrosion, replace if necessary, and get spares. Though subject to rusting, galvanized cable clamps are preferable to stainless steel because they have a much greater friction coefficient and will consequently hold more securely.

From the pedestal to the quadrant the cable will change direction at several points via turning blocks attached to a bulkhead or fiberglassed to the hull. The stress on these blocks is immense, especially in heavy weather, and consequently they need to be strong. They should be inspected carefully for signs of pulling out and also for their alignment. If possible this should be done with the boat under sail, though this will inevitably entail crawling into some difficult and confined space when at sea. If a long voyage is planned it may be prudent to have a couple of sheaves or blocks aboard as spares.

Steering quadrant

When cables are used for steering, a quadrant is mounted on the rudder stock around which the cables pass. Tension on the cable pulls on the quadrant, which turns the rudder, and so all forces in the cable are transferred to the rudder by the quadrant. Again, because of the loads imposed, careful examination of the quadrant is sensible. One area to pay particular attention to is where the quadrant is secured to the rudder stock. In order to transfer these high loads the connection must be strong and secure. Any sign of slip between these parts will need attention. Bolts should be tight and secured with locking nuts.

Hydraulic steering

This method of steering uses hydraulic oil and tubing to connect the wheel to the rudder. It is most often used aboard pilothouse boats or those with a wheel below decks because of the ease of setting up more than one steering position. A well-installed system will be virtually maintenance free, though all connections should be periodically inspected for leaks.

When hydraulic steering fails it is usually due to a blown oil seal resulting in the loss of hydraulic fluid. If you have hydraulic steering you will need spare seals, the ability to replace them when necessary, and sufficient oil to refill the system after repair.

Geared steering

This is a direct drive system in which the wheel is rigidly connected to the rudder with gears and shafts. Within this category are variations that include rack and pinion steering, worm drive units, and gearbox systems. If all shafts and gears are in good condition and well lubricated before departure there is every chance that the system will operate flawlessly for many years. Check to make sure that all bolts are tight, that there is no obvious wear or slackness in any of the connections, and that all gears are free from wear. When bearings or gears begin to wear, damage will spread quickly and so regular inspection is recommended.

Emergency tillers

Every vessel fitted with wheel steering should have an emergency tiller in the event of failure of the steering system. An emergency tiller usually consists of two parts: the vertical shaft that connects to the top of the rudder stock and the horizontal bar used for steering. These tiller systems are usually manufactured cheaply out of steel pipe and at best will fit loosely on the rudder stock.

Aboard center cockpit/aft cabin boats the rudder post will normally be below the berth so that cushions will have to be removed for access. Most boats have a removable deck plate above the rudder to allow access for the emergency tiller. On some boats the emergency tiller has to be used from below in the aft cabin.

In preparing for cruising you should anticipate that at some time, for some reason, the steering will fail. And while it may be repairable at sea, it will probably be necessary then to use the emergency tiller. It is thus sensible to spend a little time and money on it. Install the tiller to make sure all the parts are there and the deck plate can be easily removed. Often an emergency tiller will have to be unduly high to pass over the wheel or to clear other deck fittings, so now is the time to examine its design and to see if improvements need to be made. Perhaps the wheel can be easily removed and the tiller post made shorter, or perhaps recently added equipment—such as a liferaft fitted on the aft cabin top—makes it impossible to use without an additional extension.

Check the rudder stock for a good fit with the tiller shaft, as any play will only result in wear of one or both parts when using the tiller. A snug fit and the use of a round securing pin, rather than a threaded bolt, are good signs. There is often an extremely loose fit where the tiller post emerges through the deck, such as a two-inch pipe passing through a five-inch hole. Consider having a bushing made to improve the ease with which the tiller may be used and to prevent a lot of water from ending up below. The connection between tiller and tiller post may also be loose. Here it should be possible to have a welded fitting to accomplish the 90 degree turn and provide rigidity, and if this has not been done it may be sensible to make the improvement. The tiller itself may be uncomfortable to use without some covering such as wood or rope.

In some cases it may be necessary to remove a recently fitted autopilot or to disengage the quadrant to fit the tiller but with some redesign it should be possible to ensure they can remain in place when the tiller is installed.

To test your systems, the emergency tiller should be fitted and tried out in relatively calm conditions once the modifications have been made. Any difficulties may lead you to make further modifications or at least to a more zealous inspection of the existing steering system.

Electronic and
Wind Vane Steering Systems

If you are planning to sail with a small crew you will most likely be dependent on some form of automatic steering, whether it is an electronic autopilot or a mechanical wind vane system. On a short passage with two persons aboard, and on a longer passage even with a crew of three, long periods at the helm will be necessary. And should you plan on doing any singlehanding you will of course have to rely on your automatic systems.

Autopilots

An autopilot is electrically operated and electronically controlled. Most autopilots have an electronic compass that enables them to steer a chosen course. Many autopilots can interface with other electronics to steer relative to the wind or to a chosen position.

When an autopilot is installed as a necessary piece of equipment rather than a pleasant extra it will need to be as rugged and reliable as possible. Many are neither. Because an autopilot relies on electrical power it will be dependent upon the main engine or generator to operate, and if these fail the autopilot will follow quickly when the batteries have drained. If you intend to rely on an autopilot you will need a back-up charging system capable of providing sufficient power.

Cockpit mounted autopilots

Many boats have wheel mounted autopilots because they are considerably cheaper and easier to install than those fitted below decks. While satisfactory in light conditions in protected waters, they often fail under more arduous conditions, though I have seen such autopilots perform perfectly for many days.

Cockpit mounted autopilots are exposed to the damp sea air all the time and may on occasions be deluged by a breaking wave. Racking strains and movement in the steering pedestal will impose additional loads on the pilot and its gearing. There is also a chance of physical damage caused by a caught genoa sheet or a clumsy foot.

Below decks autopilots

An installation that drives a steering quadrant or the rudder stock directly is more rugged and reliable than a wheel mounted autopilot. These units are mounted in a warm and hopefully dry environment, away from the risk of physical damage while at the same time providing a back-up steering system should the wheel driven steering fail. For these reasons a below decks autopilot is essential if its use is anticipated in lieu of crew.

But even below decks autopilots are prone to failure. Because of the loads imposed on the drive unit, the mechanical installation will need to be extremely strong and often special mounts will need to be made and glassed to the hull or aft bulkhead. Any flexing in the mount will result in early failure.

The location of the autopilot electronics is extremely important. I have had a number of new and expensively installed autopilots fail because the electronics had not been installed well. In many cases the control box (computer) is sensitive to interference from motors, generators, radio transmitters, etc.; it therefore needs to be in a location away from all of these. Any electric motor is liable to cause interference, and aboard a modern sailboat finding a position away from all motors is not easy, though it will be necessary. Besides the control box, it is necessary to position the electronic compass where it will work satisfactorily and not suffer from magnetic interference. Most manufacturers recommend a position low down on the centerline and near the middle of the boat where motion will be minimized, and this often leads to an installation below the cabin sole. While motion is important, perhaps a more serious consideration is magnetic interference. If the compass is positioned close to any magnets or magnetic material it will be subject to considerable deviation. Any permanent compass deviation may be compensated or allowed for, but often the amount will vary if caused by moveable equipment stowed in a close by locker or wires carrying a substantial current, such as those from an engine alternator to the batteries.

The wear on an autopilot, and wind vane, will depend largely on the crew's ability to balance the sails on the boat, as with a light helm the wear will be negligible while with extreme weather helm there is a very real possibility of gear failure. The use of an autopilot does not free the crew from the need to set sails efficiently.

Wind Vane Steering

Wind vane steering systems are generally rugged and reliable and will easily steer a boat for weeks or months without failure. That is, so long as care has been taken in the installation, routine maintenance is carried out, and sails are balanced to avoid excessive loads.

Wind vane systems use wind power to steer the boat with a number of different techniques. The vane may steer the rudder directly (not common), it may steer a small trim tab attached to the rudder, or it may have its own rudder that steers the boat. But the most frequently encountered type uses a servo blade to increase the mechanical advantage of the steering system.

Installation

The effectiveness of a wind vane system depends on its installation. If a servo blade or auxiliary rudder is used, the unit must be mounted sufficiently low so that the blade or rudder remains in the water when the boat is pitching.

When a wind vane system fails it is usually because of mechanical failure from an overload. To reduce the risk of damage the wind vane must be of a sufficient size for the vessel. Some units are just not strong enough when fitted to larger boats.

When mounting the gear, attention should be paid to the strength of the hull at the mounting positions. Backing blocks should always be used and, if necessary, additional strengthening fitted.

Rigging

After a wind vane system has been fitted to the transom, one of the most difficult tasks will be to run the lines back to the wheel or tiller in a way both simple and effective. For the unit to operate effectively in light winds there must be as little friction as possible and the number of turning blocks should be kept to a minimum. But it is also necessary to run the lines in a way that will minimize interference with the crew and allow access to all cockpit lockers and other equipment. Because it is difficult to know how a system will operate until you begin using it, I recommend temporarily mounting the turning blocks and then using the gear before final positioning.

To avoid chafe the lines must run freely from each block and arrive at the wheel or tiller from the correct angle. On one installation I know, the lines leaving the vane pass through turning blocks on the taffrail mounted with specially made wooden spacers to ensure the lead is fair. But one of the blocks is not angled exactly enough because it causes the line to chafe on the block cheeks. When in use, this steering line has to be moved or replaced daily.

Even the most competent boat yard will have limited experience installing and rigging wind vane systems and probably little or no experience in their use. If you decide to have a yard complete the installation, this is one job where your experience will be important and you will want to check the installation carefully.

Because it is extremely difficult to completely replace steering lines when at sea, it is worthwhile to check out the system for problems, and any time spent doing so will be repaid later by the trouble-free operation of the wind vane. Because chafe will be greatest when the gear is under a heavy load, the problems of fraying or parting lines will almost always occur in strong winds—and for some reason at night. But even with a perfect installation you should carry one or more sets of spare lines of the correct diameter ready for installation.

Disengaging the gear
When a wind vane system is connected, it is impossible, except in very light conditions, to steer against it. The system has to be disengaged and on occasion there will be a need to do this quickly. Make sure that it is possible to disconnect the gear quickly and easily when under load, and that all of the crew know how.

Emergency Steering

Losing the ability to steer puts you in a vulnerable position and having the means to rig some form of steering is essential. Even having a plan for what to do in an emergency is better than nothing.

Balancing the sails is an important skill and if you are able to do this well it will assist greatly when you have a problem with the steering; but it is not that easy to steer a boat by sails alone.

Most wheel-steered vessels will have an emergency tiller to drive the rudder directly, as discussed earlier. But what about the rudder itself? What if the stock gets bent or it falls off? How can you rig some emergency steering? If a main or mizzen boom tied to the transom is to be used for steering, what spare parts could you take with you to make this temporary rig work? Is there a need for padeyes mounted at the transom?

Having some ideas now will help you in planning what spares to take with you. An emergency rudder could perhaps be fashioned from locker doors attached to the boom or to a spinnaker pole, but how will you actually attach them securely? And how will you control the emergency rudder? Make sure that you have aboard sufficient fasteners, fittings, rope, wire, wood, etc., for this.

CHECKLIST

	YES	NO
If your vessel is tiller steered, do you have a spare tiller?	❑	❑
If you have cable-drive wheel steering have you:		
Checked the existing cable for rust, wear, and corrosion?	❑	❑
Obtained spare cable?	❑	❑
Obtained spare cable clamps?	❑	❑
Inspected the turning blocks for secure mounting and alignment?	❑	❑
Obtained spare turning blocks?	❑	❑
Is the steering quadrant attached securely to the rudder stock?	❑	❑
If you have hydraulic steering do you have:		
Spare seals?	❑	❑
Spare hose?	❑	❑
Spare hydraulic oil?	❑	❑
If you have geared steering:		
Is it in good condition?	❑	❑
Are all the bolts tight?	❑	❑
Has it been lubricated recently?	❑	❑
Do you have an emergency tiller?	❑	❑
Will it still fit after installation of new equipment?	❑	❑
If you have a below decks autopilot is it securely mounted?	❑	❑

	YES	NO
If you will be relying on it, do you have a separate charging system for the batteries should the main engine fail?	❏	❏
Is the control box installed correctly?	❏	❏
Is the electronic compass mounted away from other magnetic influences?	❏	❏
If you have a wind vane steering system:		
Is it fitted so the blade will be immersed in the water at all times?	❏	❏
Do the lines run easily and without chafing?	❏	❏
Is it possible to disengage the steering system easily?	❏	❏
Do you have a plan for an emergency steering system?	❏	❏
Does it require additional hardware?	❏	❏

CHAPTER SIX

Safety Below Decks

We had stopped at Puerto del Rey Marina on the east coast of Puerto Rico to spend Christmas with friends and to pick up two more crew for an anticipated pleasant sail across the Caribbean Sea to the Yucatán Peninsula of Mexico. A more rugged winter crossing of the Gulf of Mexico would follow.

The worst of a winter storm had passed and, in about 20 knots of wind, we emerged from behind the harbor wall. Setting a reefed mainsail to reduce our motion, we began motoring straight into the swells with the boat's somewhat underpowered engine. Progress was slow and wet as we took turns at the wheel, clothed in sea boots and our full foul-weather gear, heading back toward the island of Culebra and the more distant St. Thomas. Our intention was to head east until we could clear the rocky shoals to the south and the restricted area around the naval base, then bear away, set some headsail and reach down to the southern coast where we would be running pleasantly downwind.

Despite setting off fairly early in the morning just after our breakfast of eggs Benedict, we were still motoring directly into the seas at around midday when I relieved Dave, one of our new crewmembers, at the wheel so he could warm up below and prepare lunch. He was to begin our galley duty roster and prepare our meals this first day, and then have a full night's rest as reward. Sandwiches it was to be, and Dave had just about managed to find our cold meats and salad items when I ordered a change of course and about two-thirds of our roller-furling genoa to be set. Immediately our speed increased and we were sailing at last, though now broadside, onto the swells. It was only minutes later that a sea caught us squarely and Dave,

95

in the middle of preparing our sandwiches, was sent crashing across the boat, landing in the navigation area with a crack to his head. Too late I realized that he was not using the galley strap—probably because I had not instructed our new crew on its necessity. Fortunately, he was only winded, bruised, and shocked, and was later able to join us back on deck. The error had been mine and we very nearly had a serious injury to cope with. Needless to say, we all used the galley strap from then on.

Though much attention is drawn to on-deck safety equipment or survival items, and marine catalogs contain many pages of such equipment, often little thought is given to below decks safety. Yet the cruiser will spend much time below decks and could get seriously injured. Clearly you will need to be careful in the galley, when using knives in preparing food, using both hands much of the time, and preparing hot food. Other areas of concern include safe sleeping arrangements, safe passage through the boat, and safe stowage of heavy equipment.

The Galley

The Stove

Fuel

All stoves need fuel and all fuels have their advantages and disadvantages. Perhaps the safest type of fuel is *alcohol* (methylated spirits) as a fire can be easily extinguished with water. However, alcohol is not readily available in many cruising locations; also it has such a low flame temperature that even an unwatched pot never seems to boil.

Fuel Type	Availability	Ease of Use and Control	Efficiency	Safety
Alcohol		•		•
Kerosene	•		•	
Propane	•	•	•	
Natural Gas		•	•	•
Electricity	•	•	•	

Table 1. Advantages of Different Stove Fuels

Kerosene (paraffin) or diesel can both be used for cooking, though most times the fuel needs to be pressurized to be efficient. The result is a fuel not easy to light—it requires a starter fluid of alcohol—and once started it is hard to control. It is all too common when you attempt to light the stove that a flame will burn two-feet high, with the risk of setting the whole boat alight. A kerosene burner can hardly be turned low enough to simmer without the risk of it going out. Once this happens a fine spray of atomized kerosene will coat the stove top, adding an unwholesome flavor to your dish, while at the same time causing sensitive stomachs to scramble for the lee rail. Though some cruising folks love their kerosene stoves they are definitely in the minority.

Most common of all is pressurized gas, with *propane* by far the most readily available. Propane cooking is similar to gas cooking at home; the stove is easy to light, easy to control, and hot enough to get the job done quickly. Propane cylinders can be filled almost anywhere in the world as the fuel is often used locally for cooking, with the result that it is usually relatively inexpensive. But the big disadvantage of propane is the possibility of explosion. Care must be taken in how the gas is stowed and in ensuring it does not leak into the boat because, being heavier than air, it will sink into the bilge and accumulate there until, in a high enough concentration, it will explode. To avoid the risk of propane leakage when the stove is not being used, the propane cylinders should be stowed in a locker sealed off from the remainder of the vessel, and with a drain near the bottom to vent any gas overboard. To facilitate easy use from the galley, a solenoid valve should be fitted, controlled from below but installed after the regulator in the propane locker, to turn off the gas when not in use.

An additional safety device well worth installing, though surprisingly rarely found, is a gas alarm. Various types are available, and different sensors can be used to detect specific gases so the installation may be used to detect gasoline (petrol) fumes as well as propane. In the best installations the alarm performs a self-test that will allow the solenoid to open only when it has checked for fumes. In the event fumes accumulate when the stove is being used, the alarm will sound and the solenoid will shut off the supply. With such a system to help protect against the danger of explosion, and with good practice and a seamanlike awareness of the dangers, propane in my opinion is the fuel of choice.

Because it is lighter than air, *natural gas* is an even better alternative, having all the benefits of propane without the danger of its accumulation in the bilge. For cruising in coastal waters of the U.S. it is a sensible though expensive choice, but because it is virtually impossible to obtain elsewhere it has to be ruled out as a serious cooking fuel for offshore cruising.

On larger vessels fitted with a generator, you can use *electricity* for the stove. Electricity is safe since there is no risk of fumes or naked flames. Nevertheless you could get an electric shock should the stove be dowsed with a hefty dose of sea water or a pan overturn on a swinging stove. Using electricity also makes you dependent on the generator, and if it fails you also lose the ability to heat or cook food. Larger, power driven vessels often have such an installation and so marine applications are not uncommon, though in the majority of these boats a normal domestic cooker is used. If you are considering such an installation, make certain the grounding is adequate and have the wiring checked by a qualified electrician.

Gimballing

A stove is gimballed when it is hung from pivots so that, as the boat rolls, the stove may remain level. Gimballing is not necessary on a multihull or on a large yacht of over 100 feet where the stove is set on the centerline of the vessel. But for most smaller boats a gimballed stove provides the only safe way to cook when underway in anything but the mildest conditions. Because on a monohull the greatest motion is from rolling as opposed to pitching, a gimballed stove will always be placed with the pivots fore and aft.

Merely providing for the stove to gimbal is not sufficient. On about 90 percent of the cruising boats I see, the gimballed stove actually becomes more dangerous because of the poor arrangement. A gimballed stove that cannot swing freely both to port and starboard, one where the connecting fuel line catches as it swings, or one with the angle of swing restricted in one or both directions, becomes extremely dangerous at sea. As the boat rolls the stove swings, gathering momentum. If brought to a sudden stop, pans on the stove top can fly off with considerable force. Just consider what a pan of boiling water could do if this happened at sea. For the gimballing to be safe, the stove must swing freely through a greater arc than may be anticipated. If the maximum expected heel of your boat is around 30 degrees, then the stove will need to swing to at least 45 degrees in each direction to allow for overswing of the stove, or the occasional extra heel caused by the vessel rising on the side of a beam sea. The fuel line must be arranged so that it cannot catch the stove as it swings, and no drawers or other items must get in the way of its arc of travel. Even factory fitted stoves are prone to these deficiencies, so before going offshore take a good look at your stove.

With a gimballed stove you also need a lock installed so the stove can be fixed in position. Many locks are unfortunately too flimsy or difficult to operate. Though it may at first seem you only need to lock the stove in position when in port, this is not so. In extreme weather it will also be wise to restrict its motion as the boat is flung around by big seas. In this instance, it will be clear that the lock needs to be positive and substantial as, if it should break, a considerable weight could be set in motion.

You should lock the stove when removing items from the oven. If the oven is being used at sea, the stove will most likely be allowed to gimbal to keep the food in its pan. However, if the oven door is opened, the stove becomes unbalanced and will no longer sit level. Merely opening the door on a gimballed stove is sufficient to deposit the oven contents onto your lap—it's happened to me. On one offshore passage I took advantage of a downwind leg to make an apple pie. Everything went well and several times I took the pie out, turned it around, and put it back for a little longer. When it was time for dessert I locked the stove to stop it from gimballing and opened the door. But as I did so the boat rolled a little more than I anticipated, I was caught unbalanced and the pie took a somersault, landing upside down on the cabin sole. We ate apple turnover that day! Though not an ideal solution, I nearly always lock the stove before taking items from the oven. Because it is locked, the pans will inevitably slide around and some food may spill, but it does allow me to open the door carefully and retrieve the pan. Once this has been done and the door closed, the stove may again be allowed to gimbal. It is advisable not to use the oven in rough conditions or for liquid foods that will spill easily.

Crash bars, fiddle rails, and pot holders

For any stove aboard ship, gimballed or not, a protective bar is required in front of the stove to stop the crew from falling onto the stove. Such a crash bar may also help to protect the stove controls from being operated accidentally and may be used as a stronghold by the crew in rough waters. Because of this, a crash bar must be well secured and be placed sufficiently in front of the stove so that when the stove is gimballed it cannot trap fingers. Often the crash bar will be used along with a galley strap to restrict the motion of the cook and allow free use of both hands in food preparation. Though usually strong enough, crash bars can sometimes be extremely uncomfortable. On one boat I sailed, all the crew had bruises on their hips from the round, stainless-steel crash bar. As the boat rolled we were constantly nudged against the bar in a part of our anatomy where we had little natural protection.

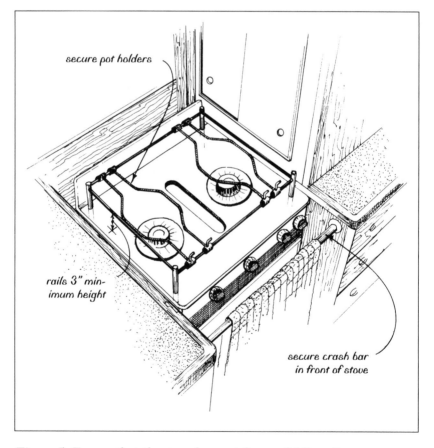

Figure 5. *Ensure that the stove has satisfactory fiddle rails, strong crash bar, and secure pot holders.*

Fiddle rails on the stove top prevent pans from sliding off the stove. Pot holders are often used in addition. For a fiddle rail to be effective it must be strong enough to take the weight of a sliding pressure cooker full of stew. In addition, it must be high enough so that it does not merely trip up the pot, turning it over as it slides from the stove. If used without pot holders, fiddle rails need to be at least three-inches high, and even higher on larger boats where bigger pans are used. Allowance will also have to be made for a stove's gimballing, as it is obviously important that the fiddle rail does not catch either on the hull or on the crash bar.

Pan holders are most often used to secure pans on a stove top. They can be extremely effective, but are also useless if they are too weak to secure properly and difficult to adjust when hot. The best type I have seen are sliding bars fixed to a stout fiddle rail, the worst type are pairs of pan holders pivoting from a corner of the stove. Like fiddle rails, pan holders must be strong enough to hold a heavy pan, high enough to be effective, and easily adjustable when the stove is hot.

Fire blankets

Though preparations for fire fighting are dealt with elsewhere, this is a good time to advocate the addition of a fire blanket for the galley. Fire blankets are manufactured by both Simpson Lawrence (U.K.) and Plastimo (France) and should be available at stores that carry items from these companies. Fire blankets are woven fiberglass cloths, taped at the edges, and stored in a container ready for use. In the event of a galley fire the cloth is pulled out and draped over the stove, smothering the fire by excluding air. These cloths are non-combustible, easy to use, effective, and can be reused. There is little danger of exacerbating the fire, as may occur with the force of a jet from a conventional fire extinguisher. Though they should not replace an extinguisher, their small cost makes fire blankets an extremely prudent addition to the galley of a cruising yacht.

Galley straps

It is almost impossible to obey the adage "one hand for yourself, one hand for the ship" when preparing food. Salad items and vegetables need to be held when being cut; you need two hands when lifting a pan off the stove, holding a pan while stirring it, and making hot drinks. It is necessary to be able to secure yourself in the galley so that a lurch of the vessel does not send you hurtling across the boat. On many of the more modern boats with a U-shaped galley the installation becomes relatively simple. Padeyes can be fitted across the galley and a strap made to fit between them so the cook is secured between the galley strap and the crash bar. Most items are within reach, but you must always remember to fit the strap. In other galley arrangements it is often necessary to use some imagination. Sometimes straps will be attached at either end of the crash bar, thus severely restricting movement, and if they are too low, they may trip the cook.

Like seat belts in a car, galley straps have to be comfortable to use and easy to fit. They should be easily adjustable yet not slip when under tension. Though they are sold in marine stores, the size is often inappropriate for a safe installation. The best straps will be custom-made and tailored to a specific boat, which makes me wonder why a substantial number of new offshore yachts are sold without them.

When you use a galley strap, you won't be thrown across the boat, but it will be difficult to quickly get out of the way of a hot pan. You should also use a protective apron.

Sinks

While a kitchen sink at home may be used to wash the dishes, the sink aboard an offshore yacht will have many more uses. Hot pans taken off the stove may be placed in a sink until needed, in rough conditions hot drinks will be poured into mugs already in the sink, and tall items used in the galley may be stowed so they cannot fall over. Ideally, a vessel will have double sinks with at least one of them deep enough to be used as a container. If dishes are to be washed below when underway, then having double sinks allows the washed items to be placed in the spare sink until they can be stowed.

While in many boats the sinks are served by a pressurized water system and a hot/cold mixer tap, it makes sense to have a manual pump fitted at least to the cold water supply for use at sea. Such a pump will provide a backup to the pressure system should it fail, while also allowing the use of hand- or foot-pumped water at sea to conserve supplies. A manual sea-water pump is sometimes added to allow easy access to salt water for cleaning fruit and vegetables in the galley or for washing dishes. The cost of such a pump is often an extra through-hull fitting, and the need for the pump will have to be offset against this. Unless you are planning a substantial number of ocean passages where the sea water will be clean enough to use and fresh water limited enough to warrant it, a sea-water pump may be unnecessary. For the occasional offshore passage, a small bucket on a lanyard may be all that is needed.

Refrigerators and Freezers

Because the subject of marine refrigeration is large enough to warrant a separate chapter, if not a whole book, it is not my intention to try and cover the subject here. However, a number of important considerations are often omitted in the all-too-frequent technical discussions of coldplates and eutectic solutions.

On a safety level, one important factor to consider is how to manage the locker lid of a refrigerator or freezer compartment. Often large and heavy, the lid may be hinged or not. If not, and the lid is removed at sea, you have to know where to put it. Maybe it will fit in the sink temporarily or atop the stove, but often both spots may be in use. When beating to windward the lid may be wedged in a corner on the downhill side, but what if you are sailing downwind and the rolling vessel has no permanent downhill angle? Sliding lids can cause chaos in the galley, shoot across the boat to hit the navigator, or perhaps smash the display on the all-important GPS.

Hinged lids are better, but, like cockpit locker lids, at sea they need to be secured while open. Though in port they may hinge far enough back to remain open, the motion of the boat may cause them to fall shut unless secured. Simple catches are not difficult to arrange but are rarely found.

From a practical point of view, as well as to help ensure that food stays fresh, it is necessary to store food in separate containers in a refrigerator compartment. On most boats, the opening will be at the top and easy access to items at the bottom will be necessary. When I worked with a charter company in the Caribbean, one of the least pleasant jobs was to empty the refrigerator after a boat was returned from a week's charter. Often the refrigerator was inefficient and had not drained

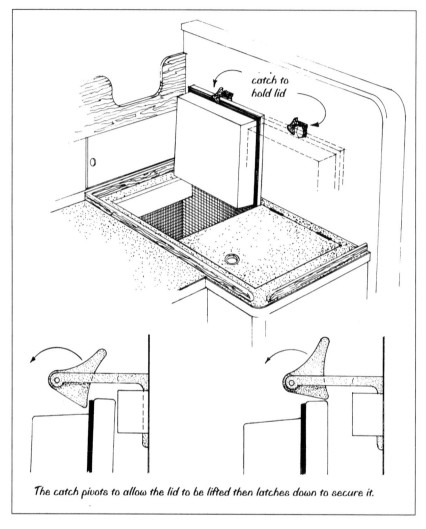

The catch pivots to allow the lid to be lifted then latches down to secure it.

Figure 6. *Safety catches to hold a refrigerator lid open.*

enough, and so I would find a putrid and decaying mass of food at the bottom. The smell of water drained from the refrigerator compartment is often worse than anything encountered elsewhere on a boat. Perhaps the simplest is to have plastic containers with lids, though the best arrangement I have seen consisted of stainless steel boxes, custom-made to fit the size of the compartment.

Microwave Ovens

With a microwave oven you will get hot food easily when under-way, yet you will encounter similar motion problems as with a conventional oven. On two occasions I have seen a microwave oven hung on gimbals, but in both instances the original stove had been removed to facilitate this. To date I have yet to see a factory-fitted microwave oven that is gimballed.

Assuming it is not possible to fit a microwave where it can be gim-balled, or that you choose not to remove the conventional oven, you will need to find a safe location. Since motion is minimized low down along the centerline of the vessel, this should be a starting point in considering where to place a microwave oven. But ease of use is also important. A microwave fitted at the level of the cabin sole will require the cook to lie belly down when using it. Like with everything else aboard a vessel, a compromise is required. Try keeping to the centerline as much as possible, with an athwartships installation being preferable, as you will be able to open the door more easily on either tack without spilling the contents. Mounting the oven at eye level may utilize unused space in the galley, but this is not sensible because of the risk of spilling hot food on yourself. A better height is around chest level. Unless the oven is securely installed within the surrounding cabinetry, straps will be necessary to hold it in place.

If the microwave is not gimballed, don't use it for heating liquids when underway as the containers cannot be sealed and may spill. However, for reheating stews, casseroles, or for defrosting frozen meals, a microwave can be wonderful, especially in rough conditions or when the cook prefers to not spend too long below.

Handholds

Making the passage from the companionway to the forward head can be a difficult process, particularly on larger boats with open plan saloons. Though handholds are often installed by the manufacturer, they are not always sufficient nor appropriately positioned for use at sea. Handholds need to be placed within easy reach of one another, low enough to be reached by children or small adults, and strong enough to take the weight of a lurching body. If handrails are not fitted and fitting hand-holds is not possible, an alternative is to run a line between padeyes through-bolted to the bulkheads. This was the method that I chose on my Rival 32 *Melos*. I managed to tension the line sufficiently, and it has remained satisfactory for years.

Strategically placed handholds are also extremely helpful in other sit-uations. For instance, a handhold close to the navigation area will allow you to hold on while perusing the chart, and a handhold in the head can help you brace yourself when your pants are around your ankles. Consider where you will need to spend time below when at sea and see where handholds can be fitted, such as by the main companionway, near the galley, and to assist in getting into or out of upper level bunks.

Handholds must be strong enough for the job. I recall seeing one charter boat after the crew had brought her from Europe to the Caribbean. It had not been a particularly rough passage but the down-wind rolling had clearly caught some of the crew off guard. Thrown across the wide main cabin they had obviously landed with some force, as the main settee had broken loose from its mount and the panels of two cabin doors had caved in. If there had been handholds I suspect these, too, may have broken loose as the standard of joinery work was just not satisfactory for an ocean going vessel. Handholds must be strongly made and securely fitted. If you are using wooden ones, check how the grain runs and how much wood is left to secure them after allowing for the countersink. With straight grain along the hold and deep countersinks they can easily fracture with a sideways pull. Rarely will wood screws be sufficient to secure a handhold. Pretend they are deck fittings and, if at all possible, through-bolt them with a backing plate to spread the load.

Sleeping Arrangements

When you are planning to go cruising you are essentially planning to use your vessel in two very separate ways. At sea you want performance, comfort, and safety, while at anchor you require a floating home. Nowhere will a compromise be more necessary than in the sleeping arrangements. For berths to be comfortable at sea they need to be nar-row so that you cannot be thrown around, and they should have sides so

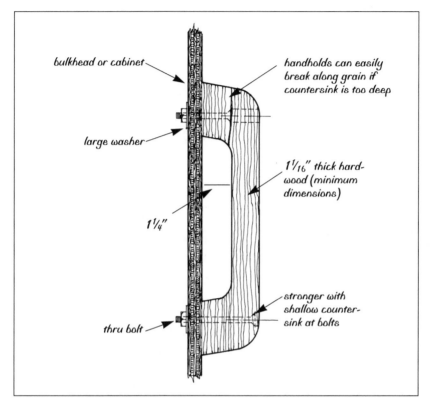

Figure 7. *Make sure handholds are securely attached.*

that you cannot fall out. At anchor you need room to move around, stretch and, if you are like me, turn around a dozen times a night. With some planning, most berths can be made to work in both situations, though not always.

Forward Berths

Though the forward cabin in many boats offers a spacious double berth, at sea the motion of the boat often precludes its use. However, the double berth can be converted into two separate sea berths if leecloths can be fitted. Often the bulkheads at either end of the berth are sufficiently strong to attach padeyes and the bottom edge of the cloth can be fastened with a thin strip of aluminum under the cushion.

Settee Berths

Settee berths in the main cabin are often fairly narrow when used as seats but pull out for sleeping. The narrow seating arrangement is often fine as a sea berth, provided either a leecloth or leeboard is fitted to stop the occupant from falling out. The choice of leeboard or leecloth often depends on the ease of fitting padeyes for the leecloth or cleats for the board. Only an inspection of the cabin will reveal which is to be preferred.

Aft Cabin Berths

Center cockpit/aft cabin boats are often the choice for cruising because the aft cabin provides a good berth both at sea and at anchor. However, this is not always so. Aft cabins with a center fore-and-aft double "island" bed from which one can step out on either side may be fine in port, but will be an extremely poor berth in most conditions at sea. Even running downwind a boat tends to roll sufficiently so that you have to continually brace yourself and such a bed will provide little rest. Others are better, particularly where the berth extends to the cabin sides and you can wedge yourself against the hull side. Athwartships berths in the aft cabin are often comfortable at sea, especially when the boat is on a definite tack, but when the boat tacks, it means either sleeping with your head lower or shifting around during the tack. A similar problem occurs with these berths when running downwind—you spend 50 percent of your time with your blood rushing to your head and the other 50 percent to your feet. The effect is not that pleasant.

Quarter Berths

Quarter berths are often ideal sea berths; they offer support on both sides and are located where the motion of the boat is at a minimum. Single quarter berths work equally well on either tack and there is rarely a need for additional support from a leecloth. Perhaps the only real disadvantage I have come across is the difficulty of climbing in and out, along with their proximity to the companionway where spray and water from foul-weather gear can interrupt a peaceful sleep. Double quarter-berth cabins may be fine in port, but offer only a single sea berth with the disadvantage of being too wide in rough conditions to make them comfortable, despite their location near the rear of the vessel.

Pilot Berths

Though they look narrow, uncomfortable, and have little head-room, pilot berths are often the best at sea. Usually located outboard of the settee berths in the main cabin or in the walk-through to an aft cabin, they are in the part of the boat where pitching motion is minimized. Because of their narrowness, you will tend to be held securely on a rolling boat, and the limited height that can seem a little claustrophobic in port will further help in rough seas to keep you safe. If given the choice of my own bunk at the beginning of a long passage I will always choose a pilot berth.

Leecloths

I have rarely seen a U.S. built boat fitted with leecloths, yet they are quite common aboard European cruising yachts. Usually made from canvas, they are frequently secured to the outer edge of the bunk below the cushion, and have grommets in the upper corners from which lanyards are used to attach them to padeyes mounted securely on the bulkheads. The leecloth will keep you from falling out when the boat is heeled in that direction. When sailing downwind you may find yourself rolling against it with each roll of the boat, and in heavy weather the leecloth will prevent you from being thrown out of the bunk.

For leecloths to work effectively they need to be strongly made and securely fitted. The bottom edge is often secured by a wooden cleat to the outer edge of a bunk using screws at about six-inch intervals. If you are undertaking the installation, avoid attaching it at the outer edge, because when using the leecloth the raised edge of the bunk that holds the cushions in place will often dig into your hips in an extremely uncomfortable way. If the bottom edge is secured some inches in from the outer edge of the cushion, this will not only be avoided, but when the leecloth is set it will force the cushion to pucker up and give some support at the side. Leecloths should be 12 to 18 inches high and stretch virtually the full length of the berth to offer support from the neck to the ankles. The corners need to be reinforced where the grommets are fitted. Though ready-

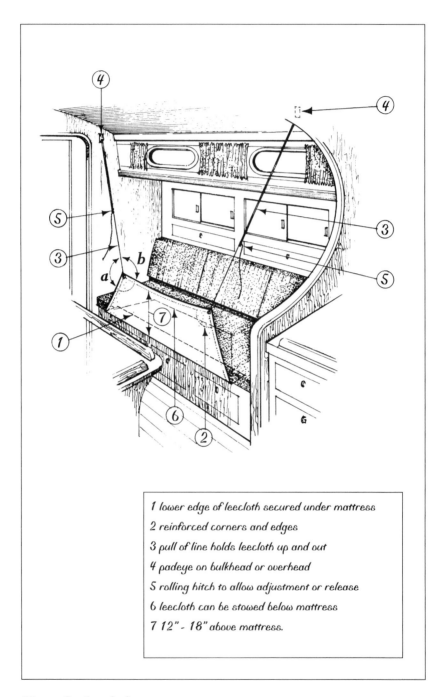

1 lower edge of leecloth secured under mattress

2 reinforced corners and edges

3 pull of line holds leecloth up and out

4 padeye on bulkhead or overhead

5 rolling hitch to allow adjustment or release

6 leecloth can be stowed below mattress

7 12" - 18" above mattress.

Figure 8a. Leecloths

made leecloths are available, they should be avoided as they are unlikely to fit well. Traditionally, lanyards attached to the corners of the leecloth are run through the appropriate padeyes and tied with a rolling hitch, allowing for easy adjustment. The knot may be tied and the line slackened to allow you to climb into the bunk, from where it can be tightened easily by sliding the hitch along the line.

Leeboards

Leeboards were traditionally used on sea berths and are still seen on some production boats (such as the British Westerly, which has removable leeboards for the main-cabin settee berths). Leeboards are often made to slot or hinge in place when needed and can be stowed out of the way. They are usually around six-inches high, and as a result often provide insufficient protection in severe conditions when a leecloth may

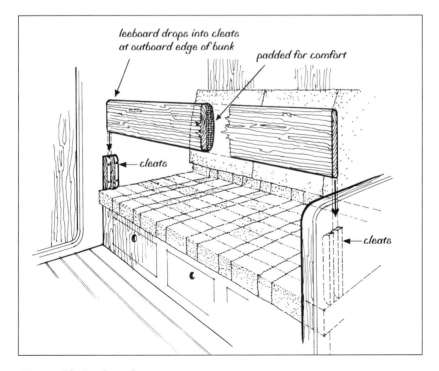

Figure 8b. Leeboards

be necessary in addition to the leeboard. In practice, leeboards work like the raised side on an upper bunk bed, offering just sufficient height to stop you from rolling out. But at sea on a rolling boat they need to be strong enough to take the weight of a heavy body. Leeboards are often less versatile than leecloths and certainly take up more room when stowed away, yet on occasion they may be the ideal method of turning a settee berth into a sea berth, for example, when there are no strong fixing points for the lanyards of a leecloth.

Cabin Soles

A perfectly varnished finish on a teak and holly cabin sole is often the pride of the owner. It will be protected in port by rugs, giving a homey feel to the boat. But at sea, when the rugs become crumpled against the lee side and the dripping water from the crew's foul-weather gear wets the cabin sole, the beautiful finish turns into an ice rink even for those wearing deck shoes or sea boots. A slippery cabin sole can be the cause of many injuries, and you must make sure this does not happen. Ideally, the cabin sole must have a functional non-skid surface, like those used on the side decks with a natural teak finish, or a quality non-skid coating like Treadmaster. The reality is that manufacturers don't sell boats prepared in this way and few owners are prepared to sacrifice the existing cabin sole in the interest of safety at sea. What are the alternatives? Perhaps the easiest solution is a piece of fitted carpet laid over the sole. Choose cheap indoor/outdoor carpeting and reserve it for sea use only. Alternatively, a non-skid additive can be used with a coat of varnish on the cabin sole. A partial solution, though not ideal, is to just ensure that the area of the cabin sole immediately below the companionway has a non-skid surface and then hope that you can contain water brought below in this one area.

Cabin Furniture

Settees and Berths

Most settees and berths will be fitted into the boat and secured to the hull or bulkheads or both. In most cases they will be strong enough to take a good deal of punishment from use by the crew and as a result of flexing of the hull, though occasionally the combined effects can result in the framing coming apart. If everything appears solid and secure, all that may be necessary is to round off any sharp corners. Pay attention to galley furniture fitted at head level as head banging will inevitably occur in a rolling boat. Even though the furniture itself may have rounded corners, the locker doors almost always have sharp edges. Work surfaces in the galley have to be used both in port and at sea, for different needs in each case. In port, large flat areas will be ideal with easy to clean edges; at sea, smaller areas bound by high fiddle rails will be more appropriate, so that items in use may be wedged easily and the vegetables you have just chopped up will remain in one place as the next big sea throws the boat to leeward. Fiddle rails need to be a minimum of one and one-half inches high to be effective and should have their sides perpendicular to the work surface.

Dining Tables

Most sailboats are fitted with a dining table in the main cabin. Some are hinged to the bulkhead and fold down for use while others are permanently secured to the cabin sole. Nearly all will be fitted with fiddle rails around their perimeter. These rails look nautical but are usually more of a nuisance than an asset. When you have dinner, they are uncomfortable and rarely useful. In practice I have found that, if there is a need for fiddle rails because the vessel is heeling, it is simpler and often safer to brace oneself and hold the bowl or plate. Non-slip mats are a good solution when the boat doesn't heel too much.

Dining tables permanently fitted to the cabin sole will inevitably be used by the crew as a handhold and they need to be strong enough to take the weight of a person thrown against them as the boat lurches. For the same reason rounded corners are an extremely desirable feature.

Companionway Ladders

For safe, easy use, companionway steps need to be secure and have wide, non-skid treads with closed, ladder-style sides. Wide steps are easy to feel with your foot when you go below in a heeling boat and the closed sides will give a secure footing. Open sided steps may be simple to install but are hazardous. Ideally each step will have an equal rise, making it easier and safer to use.

Safety Lights

Some vessels are equipped with small safety lights at foot level, which will help when you walk around the boat at night. Though often seen on power boats, they are less common on sailboats where they could potentially be of greater benefit. While saving electricity is always a concern for sailors, and many owners feel that they are familiar enough with their boat to make such additions unnecessary, I have always found having a little light does help. Where better could these lights be than at foot level rather than at head height where they will be less effective and more likely to affect night vision? Location will inevitably depend on individual circumstances, though at the base of the companionway ladder and on other steps seems sensible.

Securing Heavy Equipment

In preparing for cruising you must give some thought to securing equipment so that it remains put when at sea, and then give further thought to what would happen if the boat should receive a knockdown or, in the worst case, be rolled 360 degrees. It will be sufficient to stow most items in lockers with positive catches, but for heavy items—such as the stove or microwave in the galley, batteries, water or fuel tanks—it is extremely important to secure them tightly. The danger of any of these items coming adrift is considerable.

Any heavy item that starts moving will gain momentum and will be very hard to stop. Imagine swinging a heavy engine-starting battery through the air and the force required to bring it to an almost immediate stop. This is what happens when a boat falls off a wave or when it surfs down a sea and is brought to a sudden stop as it hits solid water. The forces are immense and only the firmest securing of heavy items will be sufficient.

It is often possible to secure tanks with webbing like that used for car seat belts, which is definitely strong enough, but might present two problems. First, will it chafe on the tank edges over time so that it could fail when needed? And second, how can it be secured and tensioned? Because of these difficulties it may be preferable to use rigging wire and turnbuckles (rigging screws) or wooden braces wedged and through-bolted. Given the weights of these items, finding sufficiently strong securing points may be difficult and, in some cases, it may be prudent to fiberglass some tabs to the hull as fixing points.

Batteries, because they are more accessible, may be conveniently held down with webbing. One simple yet ingenious securing device used by a local boatyard consists of a thick length of stainless steel all-thread (studding) above the batteries, held in place by insertion into holes in the bulkhead and securing with nuts. This relatively cheap installation is certainly strong enough and has a seamanlike utility to it.

Items such as tool boxes should not be ignored, and because easy access will be required, the problem of securing them becomes more

Batteries and other heavy objects (such as fuel or water tanks) may be secured strongly by using stainless steel all-thread inserted into the locker sides and secured in place using nuts.

Figure 9. *A simple and effective method of securing batteries.*

complex. In some instances, it may be possible to use the idea mentioned above for securing batteries. Another method would be to fit a removable locker shelf above the boxes to keep them securely in place.

Locker Catches

Recognizing that many boats are meant for the sea, lockers are often, though not always, fitted with positive latches. The most popular

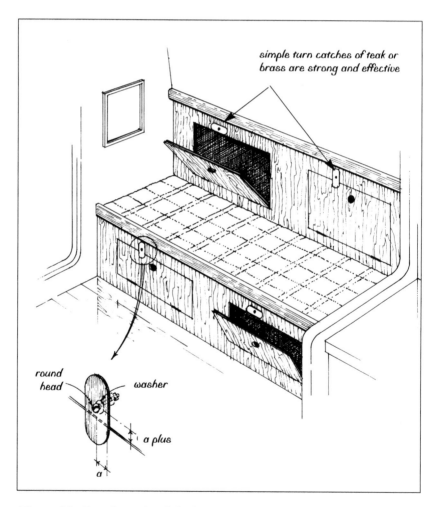

Figure 10. *Simple and safe locker catches.*

of these is the type where a finger is inserted through the locker door to release the spring-loaded catch from the inside. Catches similar to these are fitted on my boat *Melos* and they have generally served well, except in the wet locker where the salt water has caused the steel pivot pin to rust and seize on more than one catch. However, this type of catch is criticized often because of the risk of breaking a finger. Imagine the situation: You go below in rough waters, and with the roll of the boat you reach across to open a locker when a rogue wave causes the rhythm to change and the boat lurches back with your body weight held by your finger. To date, I have not suffered any serious injury from this type of catch, though I have bruised a joint on more than one occasion. If you decide to use these catches be aware of the danger.

Like with many efficient systems, simplicity often is the answer. A plain twist catch on the outside of a locker is easy to fit and efficient. For those wanting a little more elegance, the type of latch that requires you to push the door in a little to release the catch is satisfactory, though I have not seen marine-quality fittings of this type. Many catches, latches, and locks found in regular hardware stores will not work in a sea water environment. Springs will rust and break, and many brass hinges have pins of steel that will rust and seize.

CHECKLIST

	YES	NO
In the galley have you ensured that:		
The fuel used for the stove is safe?	❑	❑
The stove is able to gimball freely on both tacks?	❑	❑
When the stove gimballs, pots will not hit the surrounding cabinetry?	❑	❑
The stove can be locked securely in the non-gimballed position?	❑	❑
There is a crash bar preventing crew from being thrown against the stove?	❑	❑
The fiddle rails and pot holders are adequate?	❑	❑

	YES	NO
Have you also:		
Installed a fire blanket?	❑	❑
Installed a galley strap?	❑	❑
Ensured that the galley sinks are deep enough?	❑	❑
Fitted a manual fresh-water pump as a backup to a pressurized system?	❑	❑
Have you ensured that refrigerator and freezer lids are hinged or otherwise secured?	❑	❑
That they can be locked in the open position?	❑	❑
If a microwave oven is fitted, have you ensured it is:		
Securely mounted?	❑	❑
Can be safely used at sea?	❑	❑
Elsewhere below decks have you:		
Fitted handholds to ensure a safe passage through the vessel:		
By the main companionway?	❑	❑
Near the chart table?	❑	❑
Near the galley?	❑	❑
In the head?	❑	❑
To assist in getting in and out of upper bunks?	❑	❑
Have you considered the need for leecloths/leeboards:		
In the forward cabin?	❑	❑
On settee berths?	❑	❑
On pilot berths?	❑	❑
On island beds in the aft cabin?	❑	❑
Do you have a non-slippery cabin sole?	❑	❑
Does it remain so when wet?	❑	❑
Where there are fiddle rails on the cabin furniture:		
Do they have vertical sides?	❑	❑
Are they high enough to be useful?	❑	❑
Is the dining table securely fastened?	❑	❑
Are the companionway steps:		
Wide enough?	❑	❑
Fitted with non-skid?	❑	❑
Closed at the sides to ensure safe footing?	❑	❑
Have you considered the need for safety lights at foot level?	❑	❑

	YES	NO
Are all fuel tanks solidly secured in place?	❏	❏
Are all water tanks solidly secured in place?	❏	❏
Are all the batteries strongly secured?	❏	❏
Are all tool boxes strongly held in place?	❏	❏
Are all locker catches:		
Strong enough to resist opening unintentionally?	❏	❏
Easy to use?	❏	❏
Safe to use?	❏	❏
Non-rusting?	❏	❏

CHAPTER SEVEN

Navigation

I first met George in La Coruña where he arrived a few days after me. He had used a mixture of diesel and kerosene (paraffin) in his engine to get himself to windward and out of the notorious Bay of Biscay. We had both singlehanded from England and were at the start of our cruising. George had read a lot of books, bought his boat and spent a long time fitting her out, but had little sailing experience. He was of the school of sailors who learn as they go along, hoping to stay one step ahead of any difficulties.

From La Coruña we both set out for Bayona on the same day, though not really sailing together. It was a blustery afternoon and evening as I was beating to windward to weather Cape Finisterre. During the night an accidental jibe resulted in the mainsheet coming adrift, a shackle holding it to the track having sheared across the top. I, too, was learning and in the morning I chose to put into Finisterre, where I anchored and slept before continuing my journey.

Early the next morning, I was away in much calmer conditions and could sail free down along the coast. My only concern was to sail sufficiently far out to sea to avoid a reef some miles out that was shown on the chart. With the Aries wind vane doing the steering, I plotted a course and calculated a vertical sextant angle from the Cape Finisterre lighthouse. So long as my measured angle remained less than this figure I could be sure I would be to seaward of the danger area.

Everything proceeded smoothly that day as I sailed south, the weather noticeably warmer than farther north. By early afternoon the wind had died completely and in the glassy swells I began to motor, reaching the anchorage off the Yacht Club by late afternoon. That evening I met George and, together with the crew from another boat, we sat outside a café watching Spanish families parade past: parents, children, teenagers all dressed up and smiling, talking, laughing together.

It was some days later that George and I were talking about our respective passages from La Coruña. I told him of my problems that night and was chagrined to hear that he had coped easily and with no apparent problems. "It was not easy avoiding that offshore reef south of the Cape," I continued, expecting him to make light of this, too. But instead his reply was enlightening. "What reef?" he inquired. It became clear that he was navigating using a chart that covered the south coast of England down to somewhere in Africa, an offshore chart showing no detail close to land. On further prying, for I was now feeling a little more righteous, I learned that he did have aboard the correct volume of *Sailing Directions* but that he had not looked at it. I guess he was lucky that time but he must have learned to be a little more prudent in his navigation for I last heard from George when he reached Australia.

Navigation is at the very heart of a cruising lifestyle, essential to planning voyages to tropical hideaways and executing the passage safely and sensibly. With sound navigation you will be able to relax and enjoy the sailing, secure that you know where you are and where you are heading on the featureless ocean. But without the right equipment or the skill to use it you will be asking for trouble. Planning your voyage properly should be the first step.

Charts and Publications

Preparing for a cruise is fun and a great way to start is with the world-wide chart catalogs. Here in the U.S., two organizations produce official charts and publications. Information on the coastal waters is published by the National Oceanic and Atmospheric Administration (NOAA), though these are also sometimes referred to as National Ocean Service (NOS) publications, NOS being a branch of NOAA. For all waters away from the U.S., charts and publications are issued by the Department of

Defense, Defense Mapping Agency (DMA), but recently NOAA/NOS has begun to distribute DMA products.

Similar charts and publications are published by the British Hydrographic Office and are available worldwide.

Charts

If money and space are no problem, check the catalog and order all the charts listed for the areas you intend to sail. Most cruisers will not be in this position and both space and dollars will be at a premium. You will want to take a sufficient amount of charts but not all of them.

As a planning chart you will need one having a relatively small scale—it will cover a large area on one chart—and this can then be used for any offshore passages. Such charts will cover either all, or a substantial part, of an ocean, and will generally have a scale of greater than 1:1 million. For coastal sailing you will need more detailed charts of the areas and these are likely to have scales of less than 1:500,000. For landfalls and entrances even more detailed charts will be needed, with scales of less than 1:100,000. On occasion charts of even larger scale may be required, but in general you will probably not need charts having scales less than 1:40,000, particularly if you have information in other publications.

In general it is best to have more charts rather than less, but like everything about this process only you can decide what you will be comfortable with.

Choosing between U.S. or British charts may be a consideration, particularly for areas away from the U.S. Unlike the U.S. charts, virtually all British charts are the same size and folded once. This means that a chart table can be made to accept a half folded chart and that charts may be stored in a similar space. These charts are printed on thick paper that will withstand more rough treatment than the American ones. And a final significant advantage is that they are generally more up-to-date and accurate. However they cost significantly more than U.S. charts.

Chart Correction

If you have bought new charts, they will need to be corrected if you want them to remain as current and accurate as possible. U.S. charts are current to the date shown in the bottom left-hand corner and, even if just purchased will need to be corrected from this date. British charts should have been corrected for you by the chart agent up to the day of purchase.

Chart corrections are contained in *Notices to Mariners*. These are issued weekly by the DMA (Defense Mapping Agency) and recent copies should be available from chart agents. Local Notices to Mariners are issued for U.S. waters by the Coast Guard regions around the country and these cover more local information than is normally required for ocean-going commercial vessels. The British Hydrographic Office also publishes a weekly Notice to Mariners for their charts and publications.

Many people set off cruising with old charts obtained secondhand from stores, returning adventurers, or from commercial ships which update all their charts regularly. These charts will not be up-to-date and may have significant errors as a result. Recent wrecks or dangers may not be shown, channels may have changed, and lights may no longer be in operation, though generally land areas remain pretty much the same. To improve the accuracy of these old charts they are sometimes used with current Light Lists and Sailing Directions (Pilots) in a compromise between cost and the need for accurate up-to-date information.

Lists of Lights, Radio Signals, and Other Official Publications

Here in the U.S., both NOAA and the DMA publish books for commercial shipping relevant for any long passages or visits to new and unfamiliar ports. Like charts, these publications can be obtained secondhand, though the value of any information thus obtained is, unlike charts, practically useless. If you plan to take any of the following they will need to be current editions.

Publication	Publisher	Notes
Chart #1	NOAA	Symbols and abbreviations used on nautical charts (includes NOAA, DMA, and IHO symbols).
Tide Tables	NOAA	Times and heights of high and low water both nationally and worldwide.

Publication	Publisher	Notes
Navigation Rules	USCG	The International Navigation Rules (Colregs) and the Inland Rules, which cover bays and the Intracoastal Waterway.
Coastal Pilots	NOAA	Information on ports, entrances, and federal regulations concerning the area covered. Lots of useful information though it's not well organized.
Sailing Directions	DMA	The equivalent of Coastal Pilots for foreign waters. There are Sailing Directions covering all areas of the world. These should be carried if possible.
Light Lists	USCG	Latitude/Longitude, description and light characteristics of navigational marks in the area covered.
Light Lists	DMA	Similar information to the Coast Guard Light Lists, but for foreign waters and including radio aids and fog signals.
PUB 117	DMA	A worldwide list of Radio Navigational Aids giving information on: direction finder and radar stations, time signals, navigational warnings, distress, emergency and safety traffic, medical advice, and more that is really relevant to commercial shipping.
Pilot Charts	DMA	Chart atlases for each ocean showing winds, currents, and temperatures for each month of the year. Essential for ocean passage planning.
Bowditch, Vol. I	DMA	American Practical Navigator. A less than practical tome on navigation.
Bowditch, Vol. II	DMA	Companion to Volume I containing tables.
Time Zone Chart	DMA	Of some, though limited, use when cruising.
Sight Reduction Tables	DMA	Tables for obtaining position from sextant sights. Two types are available, the most commonly used by cruising sailors being PUB 249 (3 volumes).
Nautical Almanac	U.S. Navy	Celestial navigation data for the sun, moon, stars, and planets. Identical information is available in a commercial edition at a lower price.
VPOS Plotting Sheets	DMA	Used for celestial navigation plots.

In the U.K., the majority of the official publications are published by the British Hydrographic Office which also produces all the charts, though some are published by HMSO. These are the main publications:

Publication	Number	Notes
Chart Symbols	5011	Symbols and abbreviations used on Admiralty Charts.
Tide Tables	NP201-3	Times and heights of high and low waters for European waters (201), Atlantic and Indian Oceans (202), and Pacific Ocean and adjacent waters (203).
Sailing Directions	NP1-72	Information on navigation and regulations. Countries, ports and natural conditions in the area covered. Lots of useful information; essential if no cruising guides for the area are available.
Ocean Passages for the World	NP136	Useful information on routing, passage planning, world meteorological conditions, etc.
List of Lights	NP74-84	Eleven volumes covering the world giving Lat/Long, description and light characteristics of navigational marks and for signals in the area covered.
Radio Signals	NP281-6	Lists of marine radio stations and frequencies covering coast radio stations, radio navigational aids (NP282—the most relevant for cruising), vessel traffic services, weather broadcasts, etc.
Pilot Charts		Charts for each ocean showing winds, currents, temperatures for each month of the year. Essential for ocean passage planning.
Mariners Handbook	NP100	Information on Admiralty charts and navigational publications.
Plotting Sheets	5331-6	Used for celestial navigation plotting. 6 charts each covering a range of latitudes.
Sight Reduction Tables	AP3270	Published by HMSO (identical to U.S. publications 249). 3 volumes.

Cruising Guides

Most cruising guides will include information about port facilities; the location of official buildings (customs, immigration, etc.); shopping and tourist information on land; and diagrams or charts showing entrances, anchorages, and other navigational information. All such charts will be marked prominently with statements such as, "Not to be used for navigation," which indicate to the reader that the information contained may be inaccurate or out-of-date. While this may be so, and I have seen a number of serious errors in such guides, if the information is used along with all other information available and with a good amount of seamanship, they will be extremely useful.

Position Fixing

Once at sea, and with the relevant charts aboard, perhaps the most critical information is the ship's position. With this knowledge you can avoid physical dangers such as land, rocks, and reefs; stay clear of strong currents, eddies, and overfalls; and avoid areas prone to bad weather. Thought should be given to backup position-fixing systems should the main one fail.

Global Positioning System (GPS)

GPS is now the preferred navigational system by commercial and recreational vessels alike. Offering worldwide, continuous coverage, GPS gives a vessel's position more accurately than it can usually be plotted on a chart.

At the most basic level, a GPS receiver can be turned on hourly, or even daily, and the vessel's position noted and recorded on a chart. But many users will value other software included in the receiver, such as the ability to enter waypoints and steer to them using the displayed course and bearing or cross-track error. A GPS can be interfaced with other equipment such as autopilots, radars, chart plotters, and full computer navigation systems. Such is the value of GPS navigation that I am now reluctant to set to sea unless I have one aboard, despite the fact that I have sailed many thousands of miles without one.

But, as with all equipment and especially electronic equipment, a GPS can fail. Maybe an internal chip will fail, or a lightning strike burn out an essential component. Perhaps the unit will be damaged by a missile from the galley, or maybe it will be dropped. What will happen when the batteries fail? All of these are potential problems that could easily occur, and many sailors choose to take a second GPS unit as a backup. But this still leaves the user dependent upon the munificence of the U.S. Government which owns the system and could easily choose to turn it off at any time. This is unlikely to happen but be aware of this dependency and plan on having at least one independent backup to GPS.

Other Electronic Navigation Systems

With the advent of GPS, earlier electronic navigation systems, such as Loran C, NavStar, Decca, and Omega, are considered virtually redundant, and though all are still available at present, this will not be so for much longer. None of these systems offers the combination of accurate, continuous worldwide coverage available from GPS, yet any of these systems could still be considered for a backup navigation system.

Marine radio beacons were once used extensively for navigation and all major ports had marine beacons on the coast. But these are being discontinued. Despite the fact that many beacons still remain and that most small islands have usable beacons at their airports, finding a radio direction finder (RDF) is now almost impossible. As a result use of these beacons cannot be recommended, though I will continue to carry my own hand-held RDF.

Celestial Navigation

As a method of navigation perfected over hundreds of years and one that can make you independent of anything else, celestial navigation is perhaps now even more relevant than it was a decade ago for it will probably be your only backup to the GPS system. With a sextant, tables, and the skill to use them, it is possible to fix the ship's position within a radius of five miles or less, which should be sufficient for offshore use and even for making landfall if necessary. Celestial navigation should be seriously considered as a backup navigational system and you should know how to use it. While expertise is not essential, at a minimum you should have the skill to take and reduce sun sights to obtain a position.

Coastal Position Fixing

While GPS will probably be the main navigational system aboard (with perhaps celestial as a backup), having the knowledge, skill, and a handbearing compass will facilitate coastal navigation techniques. It may be used for obtaining a three bearing fix or to obtain the information for a running fix. It can help you determine set or leeway by taking a back bearing, or find out whether your vessel is on a collision course with another. Such a compass will also be a backup to the main ship's compass.

A sextant will help to obtain useful information, such as distance offshore, by use of a vertical sextant angle; and such an angle combined with a bearing will provide a position.

Depth sounders may be used in many areas to locate a contour, bank, or trench for use in navigation; and a depth reading combined with a bearing can fix a position.

Collision Avoidance

The International Regulations for the Prevention of Collisions at Sea (Colregs) and the Inland Rules (in the U.S.) are designed to help ensure that vessels stay clear of one another. Besides telling you which vessel in any given situation should give way, the rules include specifications for your navigation lights and how these should be used, use of sound signals in normal and restricted visibility, rules pertaining to the use of radar, and much more. Though you could put to sea without knowing the rules, and without even having a copy on board, it is not sensible. Knowing the rules in practice as well as in theory is all part of preparing yourself, as discussed in Chapter 1. Here the emphasis is on equipment to aid in complying with the rules.

Handbearing Compass

One of my most prized pieces of navigation equipment is a small, hockey-puck style, handbearing compass. Whenever I pack to go off-shore I take it along, as surprisingly few otherwise well-equipped boats have such a compass aboard. Besides being available as a back-up to the main steering compass, a handbearing compass is almost essential in determining whether two vessels are on a collision course. If the bearing remains constant they almost certainly are. But as with all equipment, it is essential to know how to use it. Almost without fail, every new crewmember using my handbearing compass will report a reading ending in a five or a zero degree—such as 135 degrees or 210 degrees—despite the fact that the compass is graduated in one degree intervals.

Navigation Lights

Next to keeping a good watch, appropriate navigation lights are essential to avoid a collision. Those cruising sailors who spurn the use of navigation lights at sea to conserve battery power—while often using more in a couple of hours for their refrigeration than the lights will use all night—are taking a bigger risk than they realize. When sailing off-shore, most other vessels have to give way to you and most large ships will do so if on a collision course. But if you cannot be seen easily, or your lights are wrong, you will at best be creating a confusing situation that could exacerbate the chances of a collision.

Tricolor navigation lights

When offshore, a tricolor light at the top of a mast is almost essential. Being high up and above the sails, such a light will be visible from a considerable distance and will not be obscured by sails or seas. An additional advantage for the energy-conscious sailor is that only one lamp is required, which combines the functions of port and starboard running lights and the stern light. Tricolor lights may be used by all sailing vessels up to 20 meters (65.6 feet) in length, but only when under sail. The rules require that such lights should be visible from a distance of two miles (one mile for the red and green sectors on a vessel less than 12 meters or 39.4 feet) though one bright bulb is likely to be visible for a considerably greater distance.

Some manufacturers of tricolor lights make a combined light including an all-round white light for use as an anchor light, and some models also include a high-intensity strobe light. While strobe lights have been favored by some sailors for giving high visibility with a minimum usage of energy, such lights are not recognized in the Navigation Rules except as a distress signal in the Inland Rules. I've seen them at sea, but prefer a tricolor light so that I can determine the direction of the vessel from the color of the light.

Side lights and stern lights (running lights)

While the use of a tricolor light offshore increases visibility, I have found that when navigating on inland or coastal waters where distances between vessels will generally be less, many lookouts may miss a tricolor merely because they are looking ahead rather than up. For this reason it is sensible to consider using bow-mounted side lights and a stern light when close to other vessels. But if you do so, remember that these lights have to be visible for the same distances as the tricolor light. Many side lights fitted to older vessels are so dim that they are hardly visible from a few hundred yards on a clear, moonless night. Because you will need to use these lights when under power, in conjunction with a masthead (steaming) light, and as a backup to a tricolor should the lamp fail at sea, these lights should be bright and clearly visible over the correct sectors.

Other navigation lights

All vessels will require a masthead (steaming) light for use when under power. The use of the word masthead here is confusing for sailboat owners, for the light should not be at the top of the mast but at a height somewhat above the side lights. Details are specified in the rules. All vessels will require an anchor light. If you are planning to do night diving from your vessel you will need additional lights to indicate this. In other situations additional lights will be required.

Navigation light switches

On many boats, switches on the electrical panel are connected in such a way that it becomes impossible to use the correct navigational lights in all situations. I recently saw a boat where the masthead light, side lights, and stern light all came on together. This is fine for motoring but clearly incorrect when under sail alone. To ensure that the correct lights are always available, and to give you backup lights to a tricolor light, you may want to wire your navigation lights as follows:

Breaker 1   Port and starboard side lights and stern light
Breaker 2   Masthead (steaming) light
Breaker 3   Tricolor light
Breaker 4   Anchor light

Under sail you can use either Breaker 1 or Breaker 3; under power Breakers 1 and 2 together.

Radar

In recent years, radar equipment has come down in size and price. It is possible now for many boat owners to consider its installation. Radar can be a wonderful asset to navigation, showing you a distance offshore, the range and bearing to another vessel, or the entrance to a harbor hidden in fog. The benefits can be considerable, but only if you are able to use the equipment correctly and you understand its limitations. A radar may not show you the land when the seas are rough and the coast is low lying; a bearing on an approaching vessel is often hard to read because of the yawing motion of your own boat in a seaway; and the visibility on the screen of a harbor entrance shielded in fog may entice you to enter a port when it is not safe to do so.

If you have radar or are planning to install it, learn how to use it before you depart. Be aware of the problems and limitations and of your requirement to use the radar, if fitted and functional, as determined by the navigation rules.

VHF Radio

Marine VHF radio was primarily designed to promote safety between vessels, though most recreational boat owners use the radio to communicate with friends aboard other vessels. However the VHF radio can be of use for navigation. When all other equipment has failed, it is often possible to obtain a position line from a Coast Guard or coast radio station. In other circumstances you may wish to call a freighter that is bearing down upon you or to obtain a position from them. In all cases you have to be sure that the vessel or coast station that you are speaking with is the one you think it is. VHF radio can increase a risk of collision as well as assist in its avoidance.

CHECKLIST

	YES	NO
Do you have the necessary planning charts?	❑	❑
Do you have sufficient coastal charts?	❑	❑
Do you have the necessary entrance charts?	❑	❑
Have you brought your charts up to date using *Notices to Mariners*?	❑	❑
Do you have current:		
Light lists?	❑	❑
Sailing directions?	❑	❑
Cruising guides?	❑	❑
Do you have a GPS receiver?	❑	❑
Can you use it independently of the ship's power supply?	❑	❑
Do you have a backup method of navigation?	❑	❑
If you are planning to use celestial navigation do you have:		
A current nautical almanac?	❑	❑
Sight reduction tables?	❑	❑
Sight forms?	❑	❑
Plotting sheets?	❑	❑
Do you have a handbearing compass?	❑	❑
Do you have a copy of the navigation rules aboard?	❑	❑
Are you familiar with them?	❑	❑
Does your vessel have a tricolor navigation light at the masthead?	❑	❑
Do the following navigation lights work:		
Side lights (red and green running lights)?	❑	❑
Stern light?	❑	❑
Masthead light?	❑	❑

	YES	NO
Anchor light?	❏	❏
Compass light?	❏	❏
Can you switch them independently?	❏	❏
Do you have spares for all your navigation lights?	❏	❏
If your vessel has radar:		
Does it work?	❏	❏
Can you use it?	❏	❏
Does your VHF radio transmit?	❏	❏
Have you checked it on the air?	❏	❏

CHAPTER EIGHT

Communications

Each year a local yacht club in the Houston area organizes a regatta along the Texas coast on the weekend closest to the full moon in October. The race starts around midday Friday, off the Galveston beach front, and ends at Port Aransas, a small town at the Gulf entrance to Corpus Christi. It covers a distance of about 150 miles along the flat and featureless Texas coast. The event has grown in recent years; about 200 sailboats now enter, ranging from the out-and-out racing crowd to the cruising couple making their first trip away from the protected waters of the bay.

In 1994 I was aboard two boats for the race, physically aboard a Hunter Passage 42 with a group of coastal navigation students as crew, and emotionally aboard my own boat that was being crewed by friends. For the first time since I have owned her, she was making a passage without me.

It was a typical fall day when we started, with blue skies and a light breeze from the east. The colorful picture of 200 boats was reminiscent of those grander and more adventurous races that most sailors only dream of. For many of the entrants, it was their first regatta and as such an impressive occasion. The vessels started in fleets at five minute intervals and after 20 minutes or so we could look around at all the vessels surrounding us as we ran spinnakerless behind the true racing yachts.

After a few hours the wind began slowly to veer and freshen. By dusk we were heading approximately on our course for the No. 6 channel marker at Port Aransas. As darkness grew, so did the wind. By 10:00 P.M. we had a steady 25 knots off the quarter and, as always happens in the shallow waters of the Gulf of Mexico, the sea began to build quickly. For those of us used to these winds it was great sailing. Aboard our Hunter we had begun surfing down the swells. I chose to reef the mainsail to ease the weather helm for the relatively inexperienced crew. My friends did the same aboard my own boat.

But the story was different for many of the boats that night. We heard cries of *Mayday, Mayday, Mayday* on the radio. Skippers were sick and unable to cope in these boisterous conditions. In all, six boats went aground during the night along the beaches of the Texas coast, some to be left there permanently. Had it not been for the radios aboard, their crews may not all have survived.

When fitting out for cruising, communications are high on most people's agenda. Too high perhaps, for they see their radio equipment as a means to get help whenever necessary, often ignoring the need for sound seamanship and preparation. But, assuming all other prudent preparations have been made, correctly installed and properly functioning communications equipment could save your life.

VHF Radio

It doesn't seem many years ago that friends were talking about fitting a VHF radio to their boat for the first time. Until then they had set out on a passage with only a receiver to obtain the weather. Now it is almost unheard of for a vessel not to have at least one VHF radio and many have two.

Permanent Installation

A fixed VHF radio is a skipper's primary means of communication with other vessels and shore side facilities, as well as a means of obtaining assistance in an emergency. At times it will be convenient to use it in the navigation area, where you remain dry, and can write down essential information or give your position. At other times you may wish to use the radio in the cockpit where you can keep an eye on what's going on around you. The physical location of the radio is important.

You may wish to consider installing two VHF radios, one at each location. This would also give you a good backup for this essential piece of equipment. An alternative is to install one radio in the navigation area and connect a cockpit-mounted external speaker to it. A simple method is to utilize an existing cockpit-mounted stereo speaker that can be switched between stereo and the VHF. You will be able to hear the radio while at the helm, though you will have to go below to transmit.

Electrical Installation

Because your VHF radio may be needed in an emergency, it is a good idea to mount it as high as possible. A further consideration is how it will be connected to your batteries. If it is wired via your switch panel and battery switches, any problems with these could result in the radio not working. You should consider connecting it directly to a battery via an in-line fuse. In the past it was recommended that a separate battery be installed as high as possible so that, in the event of the vessel beginning to sink, this battery would remain usable for the longest time possible. But with sealed gelcell batteries it is now not necessary to mount the battery high up, so long as you insulate the terminals completely. The battery can then be kept low down in a secure compartment and still function under water.

VHF Antennas

Permanently installed radios use permanently installed antennas, and aboard a vessel this is the weak link in your communications. The antenna and its cable will inevitably be exposed to salt and rain, lots of sunlight, and possibly chafe. In time, any joins or connections in the cable are likely to suffer from corrosion, and when this happens your ability to transmit at full power may be affected. Any problem whatsoever in the cable will cause some power loss before the signal reaches the antenna. While reception may remain fine, it's possible that nobody further away than a mile or so will be able to hear you. Unless you have two radios and two antennas, consider installing a backup antenna, having a spare on board, or learning how to make a dipole antenna from a length of coaxial cable.

Handheld VHF Radios

Handheld VHF radios are great. Having a handheld radio that you can keep in the cockpit and a permanently installed VHF at the navigation area is the way to go. In port or when close to shipping, the handheld radio will probably have sufficient power. Offshore, it can be kept with the grab bag for your liferaft in an emergency.

If your handheld is not waterproof consider getting a waterproof bag for it. A spare battery and a 12-volt charger are other useful items to have.

High Frequency (HF) Transmissions

Choosing between a Ham Rig and a Marine SSB (Single Sideband)

Offshore a VHF radio will allow you to communicate only with other vessels in the vicinity. If there are none, or you need assistance from land—such as medical advice—you will need to consider installing an HF transmitter. These come in two types: a ham radio designed for worldwide use on frequencies designated for amateurs, or an SSB transmitter designed for communicating on the marine high frequencies. Though these two types are apparently designed for differing purposes, the electronics inside them are remarkably similar, and I suspect identical in some cases. The difference is that when you purchase a ham radio it will only transmit on ham frequencies and it is not approved for any other use by the FCC. However most, if not all, ham radios can be modified extremely easily to transmit on all frequencies, and you can use such a radio for amateur band transmissions and for emergency communications on marine frequencies.

While modified ham radios can transmit on all marine frequencies, not all marine SSB transmitters can utilize all ham bands. But marine SSB radios are simpler to use as they have fewer user-adjustable dials.

Some vessels are equipped with both a ham radio and an SSB radio, yet most owners will choose one or the other because of space or money. Whichever you choose, you will have the ability to communicate over long distances—around the world given the right frequencies and conditions. If you are not sure which route to take, make contact with your local ham radio club and talk to a few of its members before making your decision. If you think cruising folk are friendly, just wait till you get to meet a few ham enthusiasts.

Licenses

For recreational boaters, getting a license for a marine SSB radio is simple. You just pay your fee and it will be mailed to you. A license to operate a ham radio requires that you pass a test, and if you wish to use the longer range frequencies you will also need to pass a Morse code test. None of these tests are that difficult and you will probably get lots of help from the local ham radio club if you ask.

Radio Installation

You will want to install your HF radio where it is easy to use. Often this will be in the navigation area though on occasions I have seen them installed very satisfactorily alongside the main cabin seating, and even in an aft cabin where you can lie down while on the air. Wherever you choose, bear in mind that the radio may be needed in an emergency. It should be accessible, convenient, and mounted as high up in the vessel as practical. Because HF radios draw a lot of power from your batteries when transmitting, the power cables need to be kept short to minimize voltage loss.

As with VHF radios, consider connecting your HF radio directly to a battery via an in-line fuse to eliminate potential sources of trouble in an emergency. If practical, install a separate battery—isolated from all others yet charged from the alternator, etc.—to run your radio and essential navigation equipment.

Grounding

For electrical reasons too complicated to analyze here, a VHF radio does not require much of a ground connection but an HF radio does. Indeed, the efficiency of your HF transmitter will largely depend on how satisfactorily you can provide a good ground. This can be accomplished in several ways: using a ground plane installed within the vessel or making a good electrical connection to the surrounding salt water, using either the keel (not very satisfactory) or a grounding plate.

Grounding plates work fine when first installed but tend to become clogged and fouled quickly, which reduces their efficiency. For these reasons a good ground plane is often chosen despite the difficulty of installation aboard most sailboats.

Antennas

In the past many amateur radio enthusiasts built their own radios; today this is extremely rare. However the pioneering spirit has not been entirely lost from the design of antennas and you will find much discussion on this subject from enthusiasts. If you get hooked on radio communications you will probably want to experiment with different types of antennas. For a regular antenna you need something simple and reliable. Most often this means using a portion of the vessel's rigging for the antenna. Insulators placed near the top and bottom of a backstay can isolate a section of the rigging without compromising the safety of your mast. If you need to fit insulators to a stay, bear in mind the following points:

Generally, the longer the section of wire that can be isolated the better, but:

- If the bottom insulator is too low, there will be a risk of injury to a crewmember close to the stay or touching the stay during transmission. An RF (radio frequency) shock is like a burn; it's not usually life threatening but is always unpleasant.
- If the top insulator is too close to the mast, it will detract from the antenna's efficiency.
- If the isolated length is too short, the antenna's efficiency will be compromised, particularly on the lower frequency bands.

Antenna Tuners

For an antenna to transmit the full power put out by your radio it must be tuned to the frequency you are using. This can either be done by physically altering the length of the antenna or by an electronic antenna tuner.

Antenna tuners vary from simple boxes containing few electrical components to sophisticated programmable units that tune to the frequency you are using automatically and save these settings in a memory for instant recall. Given that the radio you will be using is already high-tech, most owners will choose an automatic tuner unit also. It makes sense to choose an antenna tuner designed, and probably manufactured by, the maker of your radio so that the two pieces of equipment can communicate easily.

Installing the antenna tuner

Since the output of the antenna tuner unit is where your antenna starts transmitting from, the physical location of the tuner unit is important. If you are using an insulated stay as the antenna, the tuner unit should be mounted as close to the base as possible. But while most antenna units are designed to be waterproof, it is unlikely they would survive a dowsing of green water. Thus the tuner unit should be mounted inside the vessel if possible, yet still close to the base of the antenna.

Connecting the radio and tuner

While this is a relatively simple task, well within the abilities of anyone considering a cruising lifestyle, the efficiency of your radio depends on good electrical connections. The plugs used between radio and tuner for the antenna lead (PL 259's) are not that easy to connect and if you are at all unsure about installing these, get help. Remember that your radio may be needed in an emergency.

Connecting the control cable between radio and tuner is usually straightforward and is unlikely to present problems.

Connecting the antenna

The output wire from an antenna tuner is a single wire that connects to the antenna stay just above the bottom insulator. This connection is often made by using a small hose clamp, but this is not really a satisfactory method as the salty air in a marine environment is likely to corrode the antenna wire and result in electrolysis between the differing metals of antenna wire and stay. To ensure a reliable corrosion free connection, I have always followed advice I read years ago and have had no problems. First, about two inches of stay are wrapped tightly with Monel seizing wire. Then a two-inch length of the antenna wire is bared and laid over the Monel seizing wire while another layer of Monel wire is wrapped over the top to hold it in place. This provides a good electrical connection while separating the differing metals by the Monel barrier. The whole section is insulated with rigging tape to give a fully waterproof connection.

Radio Procedures

You have to know how to operate your radio, and for emergency use this must be simple and routine. As with all the systems aboard your ves-

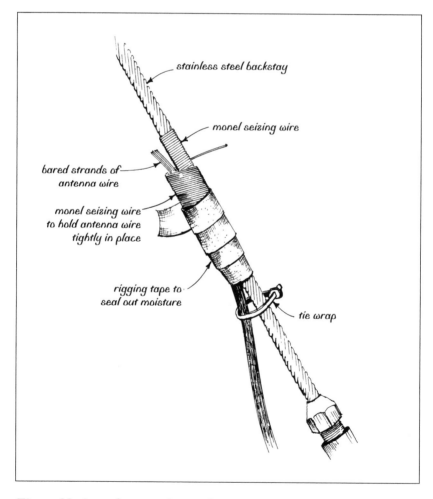

Figure 11. A good connection to the antenna is important.

sel, you will need practice in using the equipment before you depart. Make sure that you can transmit and receive on all frequencies. Check that the antenna tuner is working and that your radio is able to transmit at full power on most if not all bands.

There are frequencies set aside for emergency communications. On a VHF radio this is Channel 16. On an HF radio, a frequency of 2182 KHz is the distress and calling channel, though as with VHF radio any frequency can be used in an emergency.

Make sure that you are familiar with the three internationally recognized emergency signals (*Mayday*, *Pan-Pan*, and *Security*) and that you know how to transmit a radio distress signal. Have a reminder card close to your radio for an emergency.

Satellite Communication Systems

As communications technology advances, the options available to those setting out on a cruise become greater. Satellite communication systems are now available for all sizes of cruising boats and they offer new, more reliable methods of keeping in touch or getting help in an emergency.

Two systems are currently available for use aboard recreational vessels: Inmarsat-M and Inmarsat-C. The Inmarsat-M system offers a regular phone service with fax and data capabilities. However the antenna dome required is 65 to 80 pounds in weight and 24 inches in diameter; this option is only possible aboard larger vessels.

The Inmarsat-C system is a more realistic proposal, requiring an antenna only slightly larger than most GPS antennas. The system does not offer online voice communications but allows messages and faxes to be sent and received via a laptop computer. The system can be programmed to download important weather bulletins and to automatically transmit your GPS-derived position to a relative back home.

Both of these systems provide a method of asking for help in an emergency, and because they are satellite based, the communication is more certain than trying to make a phone call using an HF transmitter. But there are some drawbacks to these systems. Like cellular phones, they only allow you to call one number. They cannot be used for broadcasting a general request for assistance. If you are in the middle of the

Pacific and need help, your best chance of getting it is from another vessel close by, not from the Coast Guard back home. Radio communications still have a lot to offer.

CHECKLIST

	YES	NO
Do you have a permanently installed VHF radio?	❏	❏
Can you monitor it from the cockpit?	❏	❏
Is it connected directly to a battery?	❏	❏
Is the antenna in good condition?	❏	❏
Do you have a spare antenna?	❏	❏
Does the radio transmit at full power?	❏	❏
If you have a handheld VHF radio:		
Is it waterproof or in a waterproof bag?	❏	❏
Do you have a spare battery?	❏	❏
Can you charge the batteries from 12 volts?	❏	❏
If you have an HF transceiver:		
Do you have the necessary license?	❏	❏
Can it transmit on all frequencies?	❏	❏
Is the power cord connected directly to a battery?	❏	❏
Are the radio and tuner grounded satisfactorily?	❏	❏
Is the antenna:		
Insulated from the rigging?	❏	❏
Insulated against electrical shock at the lower end?	❏	❏
Satisfactorily connected to the tuner unit?	❏	❏
Are you familiar with normal radio-operating procedures?	❏	❏
Do you know how to transmit an emergency signal:		
On VHF radio?	❏	❏
On HF frequencies?	❏	❏

CHAPTER NINE

Safety Harnesses and Personal Flotation Devices

Before I left Madeira, I took a picture of the young Swede's boat, but my camera was later stolen with the film still in it. I had flown to this Portuguese island off the West African coast, in order to sail back a boat the owner had left there. The island is one of the prettiest I have seen with its mountainous landscape and winding roads. With the neat and orderly homes clinging to the hillsides on the south of the island, the impressively terraced hills with banana plantations, vines, and many tropical and subtropical fruits growing along the sides of the road, it seems too good to be true—an idyllic island.

It wasn't until I reached the high plateau of the mountains that here, above the clouds, I found sheep, cows, and goats roaming freely in the more temperate climate. Then, descending to the north shore I found the landscape became more rugged, more North European. The stark cliffs created overhangs and sheer drops around which the narrow road curved tenaciously, passing at times through man-made tunnels in the rocks over which water cascaded, running down from the high mountain. I parked the car I had rented and looked out to the north, toward Portugal, Spain, England. Some years before I had sailed there singlehanded on my way from Portugal to the Canary Islands. Somewhere out there was where they found the boat, sails set, yet more drifting than sailing—a boat without a captain, empty.

The Portuguese Navy had found her about 30 miles offshore and had towed her into port just a few days before I arrived. I passed her several times each day on my way from our slip to the town. More than once I went just to stand and look at her, about the same length as my own boat *Melos*. I reflected on my passages alone, on how this could perhaps have happened to me. It was a somber experience.

Apparently the owner of the boat was a young Swede known to the crew of another boat here in the marina. They had been in contact with him by radio as both boats headed south toward the island. They were talking with him one afternoon when he ended their discussion saying the weather had deteriorated and he had to reef the mainsail. He would call them back later . . . but he never did.

The boat was well-built, solid, and safe, and though not expensively equipped, it was clearly adequate for the task. It seems the young owner must have gone forward to reef without wearing his harness. Perhaps the vessel jibed accidentally, knocking him overboard, or perhaps he stumbled or was knocked off balance by a wave breaking the pattern of the swells. We will never know. A long search failed to find the body. I took one last look at the boat before I left.

Safety Harnesses

Of all the safety devices aboard a boat this is the one item that will be used most often. In my briefings before a passage I always tell the crew to make sure all harnesses are adjusted correctly. We look around the boat, discussing which are the safe attachment points and which ones are not. And I tell the crew when I expect them to wear their harnesses: always at night, always when I ask them to, but also whenever they would feel more secure in doing so. Wearing a harness is a sensible precaution, like a seat belt in a car. It is inevitable that before long you will slip or lose balance, trying perhaps to use both hands at once to accomplish a difficult task. And without a harness to keep you aboard or at least attached to the boat, a minor accident with perhaps a little bruising can become a major emergency and result in loss of life.

A harness should be comfortable and should not interfere any more than necessary with your freedom of movement. It should be adjustable so that it can fit your body satisfactorily, both over a thin T-shirt and over your foul-weather gear. It needs to be strong enough for the job and have solid, easily usable clips. The lanyard used to attach the harness to the boat needs to be of an appropriate length, strong enough for the job, and the clips or shackles adequate for the task.

Adjustment

If a harness is too tight it will be uncomfortable, if loose or too low on the body it can pull off over the head easily. A safety harness should be adjusted to be as tight as comfortably acceptable, with the lanyard attachment point about one third of the way above the sternum. With a good harness this should be easy to accomplish for men, though it is more difficult for women to attain a comfortable yet securely fitting harness. There seems to be a need for a different design for harnesses for women, yet I am not aware of any being made.

Though most harnesses are not fitted with a crotch strap, its use is recommended in the ORC special regulations, published annually in *Recommendations for Offshore Sailing.*

Such a device, while cumbersome, will help to ensure that the harness cannot be pulled off over the wearer's head.

Lanyard Attachment Fittings

Lanyard attachment fittings vary, from simple D-rings through which the lanyard is run to specially produced locking fittings that secure the harness to the wearer in the absence of the tether. D-rings have the disadvantage that, if the harness is adjusted tightly, they are uncomfortable and, because the rings do not lock together, it becomes more difficult to adjust the harness precisely. I much prefer the more specialized fittings that lock together, allowing the harness to be adjusted and worn ready for use.

Built-In Harnesses

A number of the more expensive foul-weather jackets have built in harnesses, which is extremely convenient. I have used this type of harness often. Once I am wearing the jacket it is simple to pull out the D-rings from the Velcro pockets and attach a lanyard. This type of harness uses the whole jacket to help secure it; adjustment then is not so critical, though with a loosely adjusted harness and a large jacket the whole lot could possibly pull off over your head while you're being towed behind a boat. There are many times when the use of a harness is indicated yet you won't want to wear a heavy foul-weather jacket. Because of this, a jacket with a built-in harness will only serve in addition to a regular harness.

Harnesses with Built-In Flotation

A number of products have become recently available that combine a safety harness with some automatic flotation should the wearer fall into the water. Though expensive, this combination offers double protection so long as the product does not compromise one feature for the other. To date, it seems that a few of these devices have harnesses that are not fully adjustable, do not fit correctly, and use D-rings for attaching the lanyard. I therefore have some doubts as to their appropriateness, because I believe a strong, well-adjusted harness is better than a less ideal one with built-in emergency flotation.

One additional factor to consider with a self-inflating harness is that it could inflate accidentally when you are on deck and deluged by some heavy seas.

Lanyards/Tether

To attach the harness to the boat you will need a strong tether. The material used for this should be at least as strong as that used for the harness or for the safety lines on deck. If rope is used, then nylon is a good choice as it has some elasticity to absorb part of the shock. A ⅜-inch rope (10 mm) has an approximate breaking strength of 4,400 pounds and should be the minimum size used. Flat webbing of the type used to make a harness, so long as it is sufficiently strong, is a better material.

A tether length of around six feet seems to work best, and most commercially available tethers are around this length. This will allow you relative freedom to walk along a side deck, yet it will be short enough to stop you from falling overboard to leeward if you are attached to the windward safety line. On occasions a shorter tether of three or four feet may be more appropriate so you can secure yourself fairly tightly, for instance when working at the mast.

Some tethers come with an attachment clip at one end and an eye splice at the other that is threaded through the harness clip. The line is then passed through the eye which means that if you have to unclip your harness you have to do so at the very end of the tether. There have been rare instances when, in order to survive, a person needed to unclip and could not reach the end of the line. A safety line should therefore have clips at both ends. Standard carbine hooks are often used for this purpose and are generally fine, though there is the very real possibility of the clip opening accidentally. This has happened to me more than once and is most likely to occur when the clip is attached to a padeye or U-bolt, such as is often used for a cockpit-harness attachment point. Safety clips to keep this from happening are preferable. The range of such clips include locking snap shackles, carbine hooks with a spring loaded or threaded barrel to lock the clip, and clips especially made for safety harnesses. I strongly favor the clip specifically manufactured for this purpose by Gibb. It is strong, safe, and easy to clip and unclip under load—even when wearing gloves.

Better than having a clip at both ends is to have three clips, one to attach to the harness and the other two for attaching to the boat. This system allows the user to transfer attachment points (for instance, from the starboard to the port safety line) while remaining clipped on at all times. The third clip is often positioned either halfway or two-thirds of the way along the lanyard, giving the option of a short or long lanyard. I have found a three-clip lanyard particularly useful when climbing mast steps at sea. Though I normally wait to attach my harness at the mast top if I am undertaking this task in port, at sea on a rolling boat when you already have a problem that necessitates a trip aloft, it is prudent to use the harness; and a treble clip lanyard allows the wearer to transfer clips from step to step while climbing, thus remaining clipped on at all times.

What to Look for in a Harness and Lanyard

In checking out your existing safety harness or in selecting a new one, make sure that:

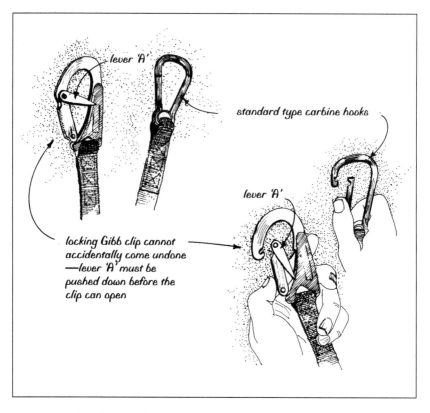

Figure 12. Locking safety carbine hooks such as the Gibb clip are best.

- The harness can be adjusted to fit outside your foul-weather gear when wearing several layers, and also to fit snugly over a thin shirt.
- Both shoulder straps and waist strap can be adjusted to ensure it fits correctly.
- The lanyard attachment point is comfortable and sufficiently strong.
- It is easy to put on, especially in the dark.
- It is not damaged.
- The lanyard has clips at both ends.
- The clips have a safety device to prevent accidental opening.
- The material used for the lanyard is in good condition and is adequately sized.

Harness Attachment Points

For a harness to be effective, there must be an adequate number of strong attachment points aboard the boat. These can be existing hardware such as cleats and rigging or specially installed harness eyes and safety lines.

Cockpit harness eyes

You are most at risk of falling overboard when you emerge from the main cabin. You are perhaps sleepy, not fully adjusted to the dark or to the boat's motion, and you are higher and in a more unstable position than at most other times. There will ideally be eye bolts in the cockpit that will allow you to put on the harness when below decks and then reach out the companionway to clip on the tether before emerging, thus ensuring you are attached to the boat. In practice, when I go below, I often leave my tether attached to these eyes, detaching from the harness end when below so that the tether is there, already attached when I next need to go up on deck.

A good location for harness eyes is low down, close to the companionway. If the cockpit is large, additional eyes may be needed close to the steering position, particularly if there are no other appropriate attachment points close at hand.

Harness eyes need to be strong enough to take a large shock loading, as could occur when a heavy crewmember is swept overboard. They must be of good quality, sufficiently large, and through-bolted with a substantial backing plate.

Safety lines

Safety lines (jacklines) running the length of the vessel are normally used to allow the crew to go forward on deck while remaining attached to the boat. Like a harness or tether, these lines need to be of sufficient strength, particularly since several crewmembers could be attached to a line at the same time.

For vessels undertaking only an occasional offshore passage, nylon lines run along either side of the boat from a bow cleat to a stern cleat will normally be adequate, though in preparing for cruising it is sensible to consider a more permanent arrangement. In this case, you may choose plastic-coated stainless steel wire, as is used for the safety lines that run through the stanchions; however, using such a wire on deck can be a hazard as it tends to roll under the foot as you walk forward. For this reason I have come to value flat webbing as an ideal material for a safety line. This can be obtained in bright colors and a one-inch wide line will have a breaking strain of 4,000 to 10,000 pounds. The stronger the better. Because they are flat they will lay easily on the side decks. Additionally, they will be unlike any other line used aboard the boat, and therefore there is a reduced risk of clipping onto a genoa sheet or boom preventer line at night instead of the safety line.

Lines should be run so that you can attach a tether while seated in the cockpit and then move forward to the bow without removing the tether. This is not always easy to arrange, when, for instance, you have genoa roller-furling lines running from the bow along the toerail then abruptly changing direction and crossing the side deck at the forward part of the cockpit. A similar difficulty can arise with center-cockpit boats where the genoa sheets are led aft to turning blocks before they cross the side decks to reach the winches at the aft end of the cockpit. The run of these lines must be carefully planned and on occasion only the use of a tether with a spare clip will ensure that the wearer remains attached while navigating such obstacles.

If cleats fore and aft are not located satisfactorily, stanchion bases, toerails, or other deck hardware may be considered as long as they are strong enough. Particularly when using flat webbing as a safety line, it will be important to ensure that the line will not chafe at the attachment point. To avoid this, it is a good idea to make or have made your safety lines to the exact length required aboard the boat, with locking carbine hooks at either end. The lines can then be attached quickly and easily before a passage, and removed at the end of it so they do not deteriorate in strong sunlight or risk general abrasion from the day-to-day use of the side deck.

Other harness attachment points

Besides cockpit harness eyes and safety lines, it is useful to consider what other strong points are available that may be used if necessary aboard the boat. In most cases, mast stays and shrouds will be more than strong enough: The mast itself may be used if the tether is passed around it and then clipped onto itself. Deck cleats may be used, particularly where it is possible to pass the line through the center of the cleat and clip it back on itself. When in the cockpit, the steering pedestal may be strong enough, but not all are, and I have seen what appears to be a strong, continuous, stainless-steel support bar for the pedestal but in fact are three separate pieces connected together somewhat superficially.

Personal Flotation Devices (PFDs)

Only once did I ask a crew to wear life jackets rather than a safety harness. Normally I would rather the crew remained attached to the boat rather than be afloat overboard. PFDs are bulky and uncomfortable to wear, making it often difficult to move around on deck or accomplish a particular task. However, I would not set out on a passage without sufficient good life vests aboard, and in the U.S. they are required by law.

While a safety harness will be used often, PFDs may rarely be seen in the cockpit. Nevertheless it is important that they be easily accessible and all crewmembers know where they are, for in an emergency it will be necessary to get them out quickly and easily. Cockpit lockers may be a good location for their storage so long as they do not remain buried below more frequently used equipment. A locker below decks reserved for their storage and marked accordingly may be a better location.

Unlike harnesses, the occasions when you will ask crew to wear life vests are rare and mainly limited to situations when there is a serious risk of having to abandon ship. The occasions when PFDs should be considered include:

- When a crewmember cannot swim.
- If there is a possibility of abandoning ship because of fire or sinking.
- In fog when the risk of collision is increased.
- When transferring from one boat to another.

Types of PFDs

There are many different types of devices that may be worn to provide additional flotation, ranging from a small emergency pack strapped to the waist to a large and bulky Mae West that makes it almost impossible to undertake any task while wearing it. Perhaps the easiest way to deal with these different types of life vest is to use the five categories specified in the U.S. Coast Guard regulations relating to personal flotation devices.

U.S. COAST GUARD REGULATIONS
RELATING TO PERSONAL FLOTATION DEVICES

Type	Definition	Observations	Comments
Type I	Offshore life jacket	It provides the most buoyancy. It is effective for all waters, especially open, rough, or remote waters where rescue may be delayed. It is designed to turn most unconscious wearers to a face-up position.	Though this is the highest USCG category, life vests with more flotation than required for a Type I vest are available. In big seas it is necessary that the crewmember's head be well out of the water.
Type II	Near-shore buoyant vest	It is intended for calm inland waters or where there is a good chance of quick rescue. This type will turn some unconscious wearers to a face-up position in the water.	Less than ideal for offshore cruising, especially for heavy crew.
Type III	Flotation aid	Good for calm inland waters.	In my opinion this is not appropriate for a cruising boat.
Type IV	Throwable device	Intended for calm inland water. Type IV devices include buoyant cushions, ring buoys, and horseshoe buoys.	Clearly these devices may have to be used in other than calm inland water. If you have just one, make sure it is a good one.
Type V	Special use device	It is intended for specific activities and may be carried instead of another PFD only if used according to the approval condition on the label.	Within this category there is some useful equipment for cruising sailors which could be carried in addition to Type I life vests.

To comply with the requirements of the USCG regulations, all recreational vessels in the U.S. (between 16 to 65 feet) are required to carry a Type I, II, III, or V PFD for each person aboard, plus one Type IV throwable device. Type V PFDs only count if worn.

Type I life vests provide a minimum of 22 pounds (9.07 kg) of permanent flotation and are designed to turn most unconscious wearers face-up in the water, and so this type is clearly the best for use in any offshore emergency. Type II devices offer 15½ pounds (7.03 kg) of flotation and are designed to turn some wearers face-up in the water. Type III devices also have 15½ pounds of flotation but will not turn the wearer face-up. Type IV must have at least 16½ pounds (7.48 kg) of buoyancy.

In the U.K. there are no legal requirements for recreational vessels to carry life vests though it would be reckless to consider a trip without them. If you plan to wear a life vest regularly, those offering little or no buoyancy until inflated (automatically or manually) offer a good compromise between restricted maneuverability and safety. But for those (rare) situations when you will want your crew to don life jackets, those complying to British Standards (BS) 3595 should be considered. These have built-in permanent buoyancy of around 20 pounds but can be further inflated to give a minimum of 35 pounds (15.9kg) of buoyancy.

How Best to Comply with U.S. Regulations

Prudent skippers will not only want to comply with the regulations; they will also want to ensure that the PFDs they carry are adequate for the intended use. Therefore it makes sense if preparing for a long cruise to have aboard sufficient Type I PFDs for all regular members of the crew. Type I life vests are the best of those categorized by the USCG though they still offer less buoyancy than recommended in many European countries. At least this amount of buoyancy, and preferably more, is required to lift a wearer's head sufficiently above the water to have any chance of breathing without swallowing a lot of water when in rough seas (a time when you are perhaps more likely to be overboard).

Type V devices only count if actually worn, and you won't want to wear them all the time. However, some Type V devices can be useful offshore, particularly because they offer some warmth to the wearer. They include life vests with a small amount of built-in flotation—allowing them to be relatively small, comfortable, and easy to operate in— and additional flotation that may be activated by an automatic inflation system, by mouth, or by both. As with all PFDs, they do not keep the person attached to the boat. When racing, a skipper or crewmember may spurn the restrictions imposed by a harness and choose to use a device of this type; most cruising skippers will prefer to ensure that they and their crew stay attached to the boat.

In addition to a PFD for each crewmember, a Type IV throwable device is required. Here the choice is between flotation cushions, ring buoys, or horseshoe buoys. You may choose to carry some flotation cushions aboard as they make good extra cockpit cushions. But these alone are not suited for serious offshore use as they require the person to hang onto them, which will be impossible when fatigue sets in as will happen within minutes in cold water. They offer little help in keeping the person's head above the water. Ring buoys are of limited value for similar reasons. That leaves the horseshoe buoys, which are really the best. These may be stowed ready for throwing either by themselves or with the addition of a man overboard pole or light. The Lifesling is a variant of this type and can appropriately be carried alone or in addition to another independent horseshoe buoy.

Other Flotation Devices

In addition to the PFDs traditionally covered by the Coast Guard regulations, there are a number of optional devices well worth considering. These include small packs that may be conveniently worn around the waist and which, on contact with the water, automatically inflate to provide some sort of flotation. Though I would be more than happy for any crewmember to use one of these, I do not believe they should be substituted for use of a harness when this is predicated, but they are well worth considering as an extra safety feature.

Inflatable jackets offer warmth and some protection from spray, but have little or no built-in flotation until inflated either automatically or manually. Coast Guard approved vests, belts, and suspenders are just coming on the market. The Coast Guard has approved the inflatables only for use by boaters over 16 years old. They are not recommended for non-swimmers.

To be effective, nearly all of these devices need to be serviced regularly, and the CO_2 cartridges inspected and replaced regularly.

Adjustment of Life Jackets

If a life vest is not adjusted correctly and does not have a crotch strap (many do not), there is a very real risk of the device slipping over the wearer's head. Though not always practical for bay or coastal sailing with a different crew each week, it becomes possible when cruising to allocate PFDs to each person. These can then be adjusted to fit, worn to ensure familiarity with all the straps and clips, and marked clearly with the appropriate name. Though this may seem overzealous, the reality is that with the many pressing things to be done before setting out, this may be the only occasion the crew can try these out before an emergency.

CHECKLIST

	YES	NO
Are there harnesses aboard for each crewmember?	❏	❏
Are they all adjustable at the waist and shoulder?	❏	❏
Are they comfortable?	❏	❏
Are they all undamaged and in good condition?	❏	❏
Have they been adjusted correctly?	❏	❏
If there are jackets with built-in harnesses, have these been adjusted?	❏	❏
Are there lanyards aboard for each crewmember?	❏	❏
Are these of an appropriate length?	❏	❏
Are they strong enough?	❏	❏
Do they have clips at each end?	❏	❏
Are the clips of the locking type?	❏	❏
Can the clips be released under load?	❏	❏
Are harness attachment points fitted in the cockpit?	❏	❏
Are they sufficiently strong?	❏	❏
Are they within easy reach of anyone below decks?	❏	❏
If necessary, are there additional attachment points at the steering position?	❏	❏

	YES	NO
Are safety lines fitted on deck?	❏	❏
Are the attachment points strong enough?	❏	❏
Do the lines allow you to travel the length of the deck without unclipping?	❏	❏
Have you identified other safe harness attachment points on deck?	❏	❏
Are there enough PFDs aboard for use offshore in rough seas?	❏	❏
Have they been inspected for damage?	❏	❏
Have they been adjusted and marked?	❏	❏
Do they comply with USCG regulations?	❏	❏
Is there a throwable device aboard?	❏	❏
If any of the life vests have automatic inflation:		
Have they been examined for damage?	❏	❏
Are spare inflation cartridges aboard?	❏	❏

CHAPTER TEN

Preparing for Heavy Weather

It was Wednesday and time for my departure. After pulling up my anchor I tied alongside a friend's boat temporarily so I could stow the anchor and rode securely before leaving. That done I said my farewells, cast off, and motored out of the tightly packed harbor of Lagos on the southern coast of Portugal. After a short run down the channel I was out in the Atlantic and, though the wind was light, the swells of the ocean soon became evident once I was past the limestone caves marking the headland that protected the port from the west.

I motored for five or six hours until, far enough from land, I picked up a light breeze. It was sufficiently strong for the Aries wind vane to commence steering. All day the winds remained below ten knots and the passage southwest looked like it was going to take a long time. Sometime during the late afternoon I cleared Cabo de São Vicente, the noble Cape St. Vincent in Browning's poem, to the north. I expected soon to feel the effects of the Portuguese trades as they swept south down the Atlantic coast of western Europe. But it was not to be, and I had a hard time that evening watching out for shipping hidden behind my deck-sweeping No. 1 genoa.

The next morning I noticed a dip in the barometer that I hoped would signal an increase in the wind. Later that morning it did a little, sufficiently for me to take down the No. 1 and replace it with the No. 2, which I set from a pendant at the tack, making it easier to see under the sail. Now at a steady four knots, I was beginning to settle into the passage. By the second evening I made myself a decent meal and opened one of the bottles of wine I had stocked up on while in Portugal. After supper, and with the sun setting, I was ready for my scheduled radio contact with friends back in England. Stretching the microphone cable, I could just reach the companionway, and I sat in the entrance to the cabin with headphones on and microphone in hand, and described the sunset as I headed on toward the Canary Islands some 700 miles distant.

I had not been on the radio long before the increasing wind caused me to end the contact and get ready to reef. With the No. 2 genoa set, I chose to first reduce the mainsail, putting three rolls around the boom using the through-mast boom furling system. By the time this was accomplished the wind had increased further and it was necessary to reduce the headsail area. By now it was dark as I went forward to take down the genoa. After I bagged it, I dragged it back to the cockpit and got out the working jib, which I took forward. This whole procedure had taken 40 minutes or so. By the time I found myself sitting again on the foredeck I realized I needed the storm jib rather than the working jib. Back to the cockpit and back again to the foredeck to raise the storm sail, then to the mast to further reduce the mainsail area.

I was exhausted when all this was done and I slumped into the cockpit. The wind and seas continued to build throughout the night as *Melos* rushed ahead on a broad reach, surfing down the seas as they passed beneath us. The sound of the rushing water was new to me; the surge as she was lifted up and propelled forward, and the lull as she was slowed in the trough before the next swell repeated the process, were new experiences. I was tired and apprehensive. But my course was downwind and I had plenty of sea room with the wind in the north. It was a restless night as I tried to get some sleep between trips to the cockpit to check for shipping.

As the sky began to lighten in the east and the seas turned gray, I was able to see how large the waves had become during the night. All day we continued to run downwind, heavily reefed and making speeds I didn't know *Melos* was capable of. In the troughs I could see nothing, while at the height of the crests I saw the gray panorama of the ocean, the white surf on the wave tops creating a formidable scene I had previously only been able to imagine. Sometime during the morning we passed a freighter heading north. It was closer than I would have liked.

By Sunday morning the winds were beginning to abate and I went forward to pole out the storm jib. A few hours later I returned to the foredeck to replace the storm sail with the working jib. It was then that I found my first flying fish on deck. I took time to carefully carry it back to the cockpit before continuing with the sail change, and later, with more sail set and the sun shining for the first time for a couple of days, I sat and examined the gossamer wings of the fish before returning the stiff body to the ocean. Only later when I saw more of them did I realize how pathetically small (two-inches long) the fish was that had excited me that morning. I think it was the relief that the storm had abated and I could relax a little.

It's not uncommon to have sailed for years yet never to have experienced a storm at sea, and there are many people who have cruised extensively but have never been caught out in heavy weather. In practice, bad weather is often no more than conditions that are more severe than you have previously experienced. I often hear other sailors describe as awful conditions that I am pretty certain were fairly moderate; yet I know that when I next experience a storm worse than I have previously known my anxiety will be high, for I will be in unknown territory, testing myself as much as my boat and her equipment.

If you are planning to cruise, the chances are that sooner or later you will find yourself in some rough conditions and you will want to ensure before you depart that you have the right equipment aboard to be able to cope with bad weather.

Reefing

To reef is to reduce the amount of sail being used, either by changing one sail for a smaller one or by reducing the working area of the sail already set. Your options vary depending on the rig of your vessel and the equipment.

Mainsail Reefing

Traditional reefing

Rarely seen except on older vessels, particularly those that are gaff rigged, traditionally reefed mainsails have rows of reef points sewn across the sail from luff to leech ending with large reinforced holes called cringles. Each point is reinforced with extra cloth and a line usually permanently fitted through the grommet. To reef, the main halyard is lowered until the next line of reef points and cringles can be conveniently tied around the boom. Once all reef points are secured, the halyard may be raised again until it is taut. This system should not be confused with the more modern jiffy reefing system that also has rows of reef points. When designed for traditional reefing, these points are strongly reinforced to take part of the load along the new foot.

Jiffy reefing

Jiffy reefing is by far the most common form of mainsail reefing and is a variation of the traditional reefing system described above. When a sail is fitted with jiffy reefing, there will still be reef points running from luff to leech, but the difference will be in the large cringles at either end. These cringles are large and well reinforced as they will become the new tack and clew for the reduced sail.

To reef, the halyard is lowered and, if necessary, sail slides removed until the large luff grommet may be attached to a permanently fitted hook at the boom gooseneck. That done, and the slack is taken out of the halyard to prevent the grommet from slipping off, a line running from the large grommet in the leech is hauled up tight until the grommet is close to the boom. After finally tensioning the halyard, the sail is reefed.

When a sail is made with jiffy reefing, the smaller grommets fitted between luff and leech are not reinforced very much as they are not designed to take any of the stress of the reefed sail. These points are merely there to allow the bag of sail created by the reef to be tidied up, to stop it from flogging around. When reefing during a short squall it is acceptable to merely allow the bag to billow out to leeward. However, if it is anticipated that the reef will remain in for some time, then the bag of sail may be rolled up and the reef points tied loosely. A common mistake is to tie these too tightly; when the clew is not positioned correctly, these points will take too much stress and rip out of the sail.

If the sail is fitted with slides along the foot, the reef points may be tied only around the sail and not around the boom. This is not possible on a sail fitted with a bolt rope at the foot unless slits have been made by the sailmaker. If you have jiffy reefing you probably will be familiar with this process of reefing. For cruising, though, you will need to pay particular attention to the exact arrangement of the lines, blocks, and hardware. When lowering the sail you may have to remove some of the sail slides. If you have to do this, make sure it can be done easily. The mast gate should be easy to open and close, and if it is necessary to remove a stopper, this should have a lanyard attached to it. Where it is not easy to remove the slides, as when the mainsail track is external to the mast, a line should be run through the few bottom slides so that it is no longer necessary to remove them.

Reefing hooks at the gooseneck for the cringle are often too weak for offshore sailing. A few years ago when I was helping a customer prepare his boat for offshore sailing, we had to replace the gooseneck fitting. An extremely competent rigger undertook the task and had the new one made. When I saw it, I realized it was not sturdy enough and he took it back to the machine shop to have it strengthened. The reinforced reefing hooks were certainly better, though I would have made them even stronger. My doubts were allayed by the rigger whose job it was to fit the equipment. His racing experience included the America's Cup and I did not feel I should question his authority a second time. But when the vessel returned after a double Atlantic crossing, both hooks were bent upwards until it was nearly impossible to keep the reefing cringle hooked on. One more good blow at sea and they would have been useless. If you are not sure that your hooks are strong enough, have them reinforced.

For a reefed mainsail to set correctly, the reef lines that pull the reef point down to the boom must be run so that the new clew of the reefed sail is pulled down close to the boom and back to the boom end, and both foot and leech are tensioned together. Some reefing systems fit the turning blocks for these lines on a short track that allows adjustment along the boom. If the blocks are permanently fitted it will be necessary to check their position. They may have been installed correctly for an earlier mainsail and now not be correctly positioned for a new sail, or they may have always been in the wrong place.

Reefing lines will normally be fitted with a bowline onto a boom

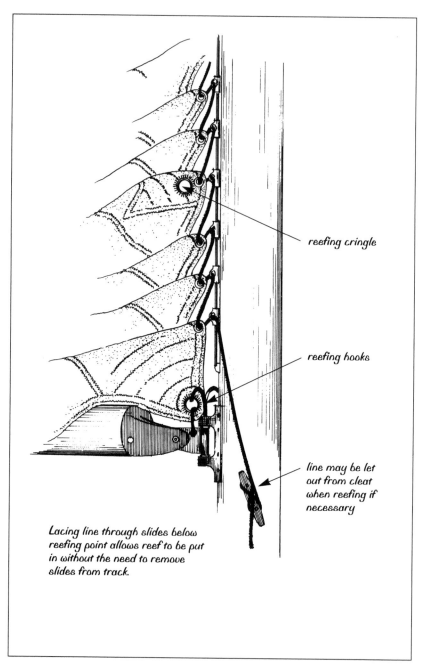

reefing cringle

reefing hooks

line may be let
out from cleat
when reefing if
necessary

Lacing line through slides below
reefing point allows reef to be put
in without the need to remove
slides from track.

Figure 13. A lacing line makes it unnecessary to remove sail slides when reefing.

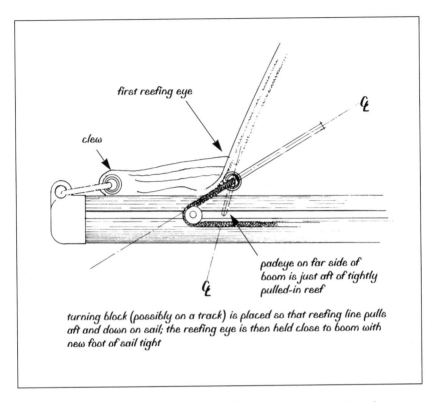

first reefing eye

clew

℄

padeye on far side of
boom is just aft of tightly
pulled-in reef

℄

*turning block (possibly on a track) is placed so that reefing line pulls
aft and down on sail; the reefing eye is then held close to boom with
new foot of sail tight*

Figure 14. *Turning blocks for jiffy reefing need to be positioned
correctly.*

padeye or around the boom itself, run up through the leech grommet
then back to a turning block before passing along the boom—either
inside or outside—toward the mast where they may be cleated.
Sometimes the lines run through jam cleats on the boom to a winch on
the boom, or more frequently to one on the aft edge of the mast, so that
they may be tensioned before cleating. If a winch is fitted, it is necessary
to make sure the lines run fairly to it so that riding turns do not occur
easily. Like all lines leading to a winch, they need to approach with a
slight angle to the winch base. If no winch is fitted and the lines merely
run to a cleat on the boom, it might be worthwhile to install a couple of
blocks that will increase the purchase power and allow sufficient tension
to be exerted on the clew. Though it may seem possible to get this tight
by using brute strength while dockside in a light breeze, it will be con-

siderably harder in a real blow when the boat will be rolling, the sail filling, and the boom swinging around.

Often a mainsail will be fitted with only two reef points and you will
have to decide whether to have a sailmaker fit a third set. This will clearly depend on a number of factors, such as the position of the second
reef, how deep it is, and whether you plan to carry a storm trysail or not.
Personally I always like to see three reefing points in a mainsail. Though
the third reef may rarely or ever be used, knowing it is there and that
you can further reduce sail if conditions worsen is good for your morale.
Also, if the sail rips around the second reef you will still be able to set
some sail, using the third reef points while repairing the sail.

When three reef points are fitted, it is usual to only fit reefing lines
through the first two leech grommets and lead these back to the cockpit.
The rationale is that once a second reef is put in, the line for the first
reef may be used for the third reef. Trying to thread a line through the
third reef cringle at a time when three reefs are necessary is not an easy
matter. Usually only two lines are run because there is space for only
two lines in the boom, or to save on hardware for a third reef that will
rarely be used. A good compromise is to run a line through the third
reef but leave it tied up at the boom end, ready to run through the
blocks if necessary.

To make reefing easier for all, it is a good idea for each reef to have
a different colored line to avoid confusion. This really helps in making
sure that the correct line is being tensioned if the lines are led aft to the
cockpit and a bimini obscures the sail.

Single-line reefing systems

Single-line reefing systems are a variant of jiffy reefing. One continuous line is used to pull in both luff and leech. The advantage of a single-
line reefing system is that, with lines led back to the cockpit, it is possible
to reef without leaving the cockpit to hook on the luff cringle, as is normally necessary with jiffy reefing. In practice it does not always work well,
as the friction caused by the number of blocks necessary is considerable. If
you are contemplating such a system you will probably need a sailmaker
to modify the mainsail so that blocks may be attached to the luff, and
unless you contemplate installing the hardware yourself, a rigger will be
used to fit the equipment. If you are using these professionals, ask them to

show you a system already installed on a boat and to arrange for you to talk with the owner about how it works. Often sailmakers and riggers have a background in racing, as opposed to cruising, and their actual experience using such a system may be very limited indeed.

A good system should eliminate the need to go forward to the mast except for a few occasions. A poor system or bad installation will be no easier to use than regular jiffy reefing, and in fact may require two crew to put in a reef, as one may be needed at the mast to help the line along while the other is needed in the cockpit to winch in the line. And in the end the sail may not be set all that well.

Roller-furling mainsails

Roller-furling mainsails are ideal for reducing sail area. While you need to compromise in order to have such a system in the first place, once fitted it allows you to infinitely reduce sail area from a full sail down to none. Because the sail is loose-footed, it is possible to reef or furl the sail from a far greater range of wind direction than with a normal mainsail. The only really difficult point of sail is when running, due to the possibility of the sail catching or ripping on the shrouds or spreaders, or if you put too much strain on the roller-furling gear while trying to reef with the sail still drawing. To alleviate this risk and lessen the strain, it will normally be sufficient to change course to a reach while changing the sail area. With no battens, the risk of the sail ripping when flogging or catching is greatly reduced.

The disadvantage of a roller-furling mainsail is the increased risk of the gear failing or the sail jamming so that it becomes impossible to reduce sail. If the jamming occurs with the sail fully out, it may be possible to take the sail completely off, though once this is done it will be difficult and dangerous in rough conditions to put it back up. If the failure or jam occurs with the sail partly furled, the options are considerably fewer and depend on the type of system being used.

There are four types of mainsail roller-furling systems available:

In-mast furling. The mast extrusion is specifically designed to accept a roller-furling gear. There is an advantage to having a system designed specifically for this purpose. The furling gear is normally fitted while the mast is off the boat so that the extrusion may be passed up inside the mast. Though most systems allow access to the mechanical furling gear near the mast base, access to the top bearings is often limited and it is usually not possible to remove the furling gear while the mast is on the boat. These limitations should be considered when planning for cruising.

With such a system, if the gear jams with the sail partly unfurled, it will not be possible to remove the sail or the reefing gear.

Aft-mast furling. This will retro-fit a mast designed for a conventional mainsail with a roller reefing system. A stay much like that used for headsail furling is mounted a few inches aft of the mast and the sail furls up around the stay. This system has similar advantages to headsail reefing gear and suffers from the same disadvantages. Should a jam occur it is easier to solve the problem with this system than with in-mast furling, though not in rough conditions.

In order to have the conveniences of roller furling/reefing you have to accept some of the disadvantages. For sail set this system is the worst. While all mainsail furling systems require the sail to be battenless, and thus also have a hollow leech, this system makes it difficult to keep the luff from sagging downwind and will suffer from poor sail shape when the sail is partially furled.

Retro-fitted in-mast furling. This system uses an aluminum extrusion fitted permanently to an existing mast that contains the roller-furling gear. In practice, the system behaves like an in-mast furling system, having similar advantages of sail set over the aft mast system while also having the disadvantages of access common to the in-mast system.

Boom furling. There are two types of boom reefing systems. The older system of boom roller furling is to wind the sail around the outside of the boom. As far as I know, it is no longer commercially available. It is this type of boom furling that I have aboard my boat. It has worked reasonably well but requires a claw fitting for the boom vang that sometimes gets caught when reefing, and the reefed sail has bag in the foot. I don't have plans to change it but I wouldn't choose this type of furling now. Modern boom roller reefing uses a hollow boom and operates in a way similar to in-mast roller furling. Boom roller furling keeps the gear at deck level with consequent increased accessibility. Should a jam occur, it is still possible to lower the sail and tie it temporarily outside the boom. An additional benefit over mast furling systems is that, in reducing sail from the top, the center of effort of the sail is kept low, which is desirable in heavy weather. Disadvantages of in-boom furling include the increased diameter of boom required—they are huge—and the difficulty of keeping sail shape as the sail area is reduced.

If your vessel has a roller-furling mainsail or you choose to fit one, make sure that the gear works easily. Any difficulty in furling or unfurling should be checked carefully as it may be the first sign of an impending jam. Because you will rarely adjust the main halyard tension or remove the sail, inspect the halyard for wear or chafe before setting out and before each major passage. Special shackles may be used to attach head and tack, and if this is the case, spares should be obtained for it is easy to lose these when removing or fitting a sail at sea.

Headsail Reefing

Headsails are reefed in two ways. The sail is either taken off and another, smaller one, set in its place, or the sail is partially furled using a headsail reefing system. Both headsail reefing systems have their pros and cons, and you must decide which system you prefer.

Hanked-on sails

This is the traditional method of reefing headsails. The boat will carry a number of sails from large genoas and drifters down to small working jibs and storm jibs. When the wind becomes too strong for one sail, it is taken down, bagged, and stowed, and the next smaller sail raised in its place. The system has simplicity and redundancy, for if a sail rips, the next size sail can be used while a repair is made. The sails are easily raised and lowered and the risk of jamming is minimal. However, an initial wardrobe of sails is expensive, and subsequent repairs are too. The two biggest disadvantages are the space needed for stowing the sails and the work involved in changing sails, which even in storm conditions requires someone to go onto the foredeck, take off a sail, and replace it with another.

Roller-reefing headsails

Ninety-five percent of boats have been equipped with roller-reefing gear in the last ten years. Roller-reefing gear allows a large headsail to be reduced from fully set to fully furled, and so any chosen amount of sail may be set.

Roller-reefing gear should not be confused with roller-furling gear. Some headstays may be fitted with a furling system that uses a drum at the base with a line led aft, and this type of gear may look like a roller-reefing system at first glance. This older type of gear does not have a fitted extrusion along the headstay, so the sail is furled around the wire stay. While this works fine to reduce sail completely, it is not possible to partially reduce sail using this system: It's all or nothing.

With roller reefing the furling line is led aft back to the cockpit. This is an additional safety factor. However, roller reefing presents some disadvantages. The gear is hard to get to should a problem occur and there may be times when a sail cannot be furled in, though this risk can be minimized if you use the more expensive and proven equipment. Buying budget roller-reefing gear will be more costly in the long run. A further inconvenience is that even if a sail is made especially to fit a roller-reefing gear, it will not set as well when partially furled as an equivalent separate sail. The problem usually stems from the bag or draft in the sail, which is put there deliberately by the sailmaker so the sail will draw correctly when fully unfurled. When only part of the sail is set, too much draft is left in the middle and, no matter how halyard tension and sheet fair leads are adjusted, the sail will not be able to be set ideally. The result is that in heavy weather, especially when trying to beat to windward, the performance of the sail is reduced and wear will increase due to the luffing bag in the sail. A separate storm jib is required.

In heavy weather, the biggest problem with roller-reefing gear is that it is difficult to set a storm jib. The choice is between using a small portion of the already set genoa or unfurling it all, pulling it off the head foil, and raising a storm jib. Neither is easy. A small portion of the genoa may work fine for running downwind, but the set will be so bad that it will work poorly when on a reach, and worse still if trying to beat, as may be necessary when trying to put distance between you and a lee shore. The alternative is to take down the genoa and raise a storm jib, but this requires first that the genoa be fully unfurled—at a time when you are contemplating the need for a storm sail—and then that a crewmember goes forward, pulls down the sail, and perhaps deals with some difficult shackles before the sail may be removed. And once down, you have a huge unattached sail on the foredeck just waiting to get caught by the next breaking wave. This certainly is more demanding than setting a storm jib when using hanked-on sails, and the risk of ripping the sail, losing it overboard, or losing the shackle pins is significant. And it does not include the difficulty of bagging a huge sail in these conditions. Because of these difficulties it is necessary to have some alternative method of setting a storm jib when using a roller-reefing headsail.

Storm Sails

Though bad storms are not common, the prudent sailor will be prepared, and make sure to have storm sails. No matter what the rig configuration of the vessel, it will normally be necessary to carry two storm sails: a storm jib and a storm trysail.

Storm Jibs

A storm jib is essentially no different from a regular jib other than being smaller. The ORC (Offshore Racing Council) special regulations give a maximum size for a storm jib no greater than five percent of the height of the foretriangle squared with a maximum luff length of 65 percent of the height of the foretriangle. In practice I have found that an appropriate size for a storm jib will be around 20 percent of a No. 1 genoa. Though similar to a regular jib, it may be cut a little flatter and will almost certainly be reinforced at the corners and have chafe protection there as well. The luff will usually have stainless wire to avoid stretching in the strong winds in which it will be used.

If using hanked-on headsails, raising the storm jib is no different than any other sail change. When cruising I prefer to take down the existing sail first, bag it, and stow it before returning to the foredeck with the storm sail. This will not help you win races but it does keep things simple.

If you have a roller-reefing headsail, special consideration has to be given to setting a storm jib because of the impracticality of removing the roller-furling sail at the time a storm jib is needed. Either an existing inner stay may be used or a removable stay installed for the storm jib.

Setting a storm jib on a cutter-rigged vessel

If a vessel is cutter-rigged, consider using the staysail stay for the storm jib, as this will keep the center of effort of the sail closer to the mast (thus aiding maneuverability and beating) while also keeping it away from the foredeck where it could be subject to the stress of big seas. Either the existing staysail itself is appropriate or you may choose to have a reef put in the staysail so that it can be used as a storm sail. Alternatively, the staysail can be removed and a storm jib raised on the stay.

On some boats, even the staysail may be fitted with roller-reefing gear, thus complicating the operation if the sail is too large to be a storm jib. You may decide that with the stay nearer the center of the boat and the sail smaller, it is practical to unfurl the staysail fully, remove it from the foil, and raise the storm jib. But if you decide this will not be easy, you will have to arrange for a temporary storm jib stay to be available, as is necessary aboard a non cutter-rigged boat.

Setting a storm sail on a vessel with headsail reefing gear and no staysail stay

Because of the need to have a storm sail and the difficulties discussed in using the existing headsail or headsail stay, the only realistic alternative is to provide a separate stay specifically for the storm jib. Usually this can be done in such a way that the stay can be removed and stowed out of the way when not required, and easily set and tensioned when needed. When fitting such a temporary stay you will need first to decide where to attach it on the mast, and secondly, how to secure it at deck level. This requires individual planning for your specific boat and you may need the advice of a rigger to assist at this stage.

Most regular inner forestays or staysail stays run parallel to the forestay and are then attached to a fitting on the mast somewhere between the spreaders and the mast head. Because this attachment point will be at an unsupported part of the mast, there is a need for running backstays. To avoid this, I usually try and fit the upper end of the temporary stay as near the top of the mast as possible. Often this can be done at a point just below where the upper shrouds attach, as the forestay will usually be fitted above the shrouds. Either a tang can be fitted to the mast at this point or a T-ball socket installed. If the latter is used, it is necessary to make a cover plate to ensure that the stay does not pop out of the socket when it is not being used, and hence slack.

At deck level it is necessary to find a strong enough point to attach the stay. I have often found the forward bulkhead to be a good location,

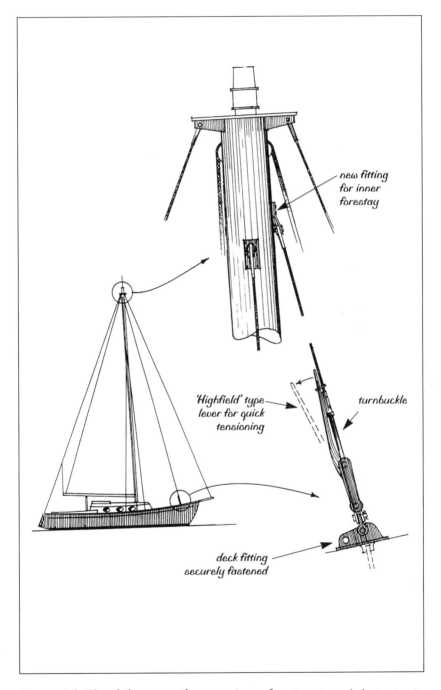

Figure 15. *The ability to easily set an inner forestay at sea is important.*

or somewhere close to where an anchor windlass is situated. If the bulkhead is bonded to the deck, a simple padeye may be sufficient at this position, but often it will be necessary to engineer a bracket below decks to transfer some of the load from the deck to the bulkhead.

Where the stay attaches to the deck it is necessary to fit some form of tensioning device so that, once fastened, the stay may be easily tightened before it is used. Though a turnbuckle could be used, it would not be that easy, quick, or convenient to attach and then tighten one. A large pelican hook or a highfield lever are preferable and provide a quick and easy method of attachment and tensioning.

Once the stay is fitted, you will need to arrange a means of raising the sail and attaching the tack. Normally a spare or spinnaker halyard will serve to raise the sail while a pendant and snap shackle attached to the deck padeye or tensioning lever will provide an easy attachment point for the tack.

Sheet leads for a storm jib

Once the sail is raised it becomes possible to consider the sheet leads. The existing genoa tracks should run sufficiently far forward to allow a satisfactory lead for the sheets. If they do not, you will have to consider using snatch blocks on the toerail, fitting padeyes at the appropriate position on deck, or having the sail recut so that you can use the existing genoa tracks. Of these three I much prefer having the sail recut if this can be accomplished satisfactorily. The aim in either recutting the sail or choosing a sheeting position is for the sail to set correctly when close-hauled. Because it is small, backwinding the mainsail will not be a problem and it therefore becomes possible to sheet the sail close to the centerline of the vessel with the sheets set inside the shrouds. Try and establish a sheeting position that will use existing hardware and will leave a fair run back to the cockpit. Once a sheeting position is decided upon, adjustment of the tack pendant—how far the tack of the sail is from the deck—will help in ensuring that foot and leech tensions are approximately equal.

If an existing staysail is being used, the sheets can lead to the cockpit normally. However, if a temporary stay has been installed for the storm jib, sheeting in the sail may require further attention. If there are existing winches available, such as spinnaker winches, these can often be used to sheet the storm jib satisfactorily. If none are available the genoa sheet winches will have to be used, which will necessitate removing the existing sheets and then cleating them securely. Though using the existing sheet winches will often work fine, I have found myself in circumstances where I would have liked to use both the storm jib and a portion of the rolled up genoa. In heavy squalls the genoa can be furled, leaving the storm jib, while in the lulls a little genoa can be let out to keep up boat speed. If this option is desired, then clearly the existing genoa winches cannot be used for both sails at once and some alternative sheeting arrangement will have to be found for the storm jib.

Storm Trysails

A storm trysail is a small, loose-footed sail that is raised aft of the main mast in place of a mainsail. Used less often than a storm jib, a storm trysail is a must when beating to windward, as may be necessary in storm conditions in order to avoid the dangers of a lee shore. A storm trysail will normally have an area around 80 percent of your mainsail fully reefed.

Because it is loose-footed, a trysail does not require the use of the boom, which should be lowered onto the boom gallows or to the deck and tied firmly. With the boom secured there is one less piece of heavy equipment swinging around during storm conditions, an additional benefit of using a trysail.

On vessels with a standard mainsail, the trysail can often use the same mast track as the mainsail as long as the sail slides can be easily fitted to the track. Where the mast has an externally fitted track, the only gate will probably be at the bottom, and thus fitting the trysail slides would necessitate opening the gate, removing the mainsail slides, fitting the trysail slides, and then closing the gate. This could be done, but it would be difficult and time consuming in storm conditions, and the bulk of the mainsail would be hanging loose from the boom. A simpler solution is to fit a second mast track for the storm sail to the side of the existing one.

If the track is internal, there may be more than one gate where slides may be introduced. If the head of the doused mainsail is below the upper gate it becomes possible to fit a trysail above the mainsail. In some cases it may be possible to install an additional gate when none is available. When a gate is not available and one cannot be fitted, again you must install a separate track.

Once a system is available for raising a trysail, you will need to think about a suitable tack attachment point and the sheet leads. Often the tack can be fitted with a swaged pendant and snap shackle that may be attached either at the boom gooseneck or at the mast base as is most convenient. Sheet leads are not so easy to deal with. If the vessel has an aluminum toerail, it may be possible to use snatch blocks there to provide a good sheet lead, but these tend to be too far outboard. It will often be necessary to coordinate sail cut with the vessel so that the clew may be led to a convenient position on deck where a block can be attached or a padeye fitted for this purpose. Needless to say, this procedure should be carried out well before a planned departure. As for the headsail, the sheeting position should be arranged for the close-hauled position as this will be the point of sail most often desired when using a storm trysail.

Preparing on Deck

While you will prepare for heavy weather shortly before it arrives, you must plan for it before departure. If you normally carry a lot of equipment tied on deck, plan for stowage below decks or in a cockpit locker if at all possible. If some items have to be left on deck, you can't use too many lines. Even small items secured to the lifelines can have sufficient resistance to a big sea to cause the stanchions to bend or the lifelines to break. In fact, a big sea can cause stanchions to bend even when nothing is attached to them. Once the decks are cleared storm boards may be fitted, companionway boards secured, and dorades removed.

Storm Boards

Large ports or windows aboard a boat are susceptible to damage in storm conditions. Should one break it would, at a minimum, result in a lot of water below decks. Consequently, if the vessel has large windows, ports, or hatches, it is prudent to have boards that can either be fitted for protection against damage, or fitted to seal a hole. Windows facing forward are particularly vulnerable, as are large hatches that can be "sucked" off in big seas.

Storm boards are normally fitted to the outside of the vessel and are through-bolted. They are not easy to attach. If they are to be through-bolted to the deck or cabin top, holes are required for the bolts—and these then become another source of potential leaks. Though somewhat unsightly, one solution is to glass-in the bolts from the inside of the boat and fit dome nuts on the outside to protect the exposed studs while the boards are not being used.

Boards may be marine plywood, a minimum of one-half inch thick, and more where the area is large. When made of wood, storm boards should be painted or epoxied to seal the edges. Though more work, fiberglass boards could be made that would certainly be sufficiently strong and durable.

Companionway Hatches and Boards

One of the recommendations made after the 1979 Fastnet race, when many boats capsized, was the need for companionway wash boards to be secured in position and attached to the ship. In a number of cases these boards floated free during a knockdown, letting large quantities of water below. Particularly vulnerable are wash boards that fit in a tapering companionway, as they need be raised only a few inches in order to be free. Boards can either have individual barrel bolts that allow them to be secured in place or be attached via a lanyard that can be adjusted through a cleat.

Hatch covers are often free to slide open and can only be locked from the outside. In order to stop a huge sea from forcing it open, the hatch should be fitted with a means of locking that can be used at sea by crew either in the cockpit or below decks.

Dorade Boxes

While large vent cowls on dorade boxes are essential to channel sufficient air below decks, they are extremely vulnerable to damage should a sea break on deck, and those forward of the mast can be ripped off long before you are in storm conditions. It is therefore essential that these cowls can be removed easily and that cover plates are available to replace them.

Securing Items Below Decks

When heavy weather is anticipated it will be prudent to stow any loose items around the cabin and to make sure that items in the galley, such as knives, are particularly well-secured, as are navigation items such as dividers. Small items can gain a surprising velocity when the vessel comes to a sudden stop in a heavy sea.

Storm Tactics

Though how to deal with a particular storm will depend on the individual circumstances, preparation for all techniques should be made before departure and the necessary equipment obtained.

Heaving-to

The surprising stability of the boat that results when hove-to is impressive and this is a storm technique that can often be used, particularly when beating, to make it possible to prepare a meal, eat, get some sleep, or undertake repairs. Every vessel will handle differently when hove-to and so it is essential to practice the technique in order to learn how to set the sails and helm aboard your boat.

With the jib or genoa set aback, either the windward sheet or the sail itself will be pressed hard against the mast or windward shrouds, with a consequent risk of serious chafe if this position is held for long. Better the sheets chafe than the sail, so often it will be necessary to reduce sail before heaving-to. So long as the clew is forward of the lower shrouds when beating, it will not catch when hove-to. Protecting the sheets is not so easy, though installation of chafe protection on all shrouds will be very useful. If it is anticipated that the vessel will remain hove-to for some time, chafe protection should be fitted at the rub points.

When hove-to, the wheel or tiller should be locked in place and a simple and effective system should be available. Most wheels have a lock on the pedestal, but some do not and you should consider installing one. A tiller can often be secured with a line if cleats are readily available.

Running Downwind

Running before a storm will often be the chosen technique as it is so much easier on the crew. In using this technique it is essential to adjust the speed of the boat to the conditions, so that it is going neither too fast nor too slow. Too fast and the boat will be out of control with the risk of broaching and damage; too slow and the following seas may poop the vessel. While you will use initially storm sails, mainly the storm jib, when conditions further deteriorate, even with no sail up if the vessel is traveling too fast, you must be able to slow the boat down. This can be done by trailing a long line behind the boat, usually in a bight from one stern cleat to the other. If this is not sufficient, additional drag will be required. If you have a drogue, you will need to use it, if not, you could use a car tire fed along the trailing line. A drogue, like a sea anchor, is designed to be towed behind a vessel and not set from the bow. A series drogue consists of many small drogues placed along a line so that the more the line is let out, the more the drag increases. Though I have never used a series drogue, this appears to offer the ideal solution as the line may be adjusted to give the required amount of drag, and thus the vessel's speed is adjusted appropriately.

Using Sea Anchors

A traditional method for weathering storms, sea anchors have been around for many years, and much has been written about their ineffectiveness. A sea anchor is designed to be set from the bow. The principle is that as the boat drifts downwind the line will become taut due to the drag of the anchor, acting like a parachute in the water, and the bow will be kept pointing up into the wind and seas. If this were to actually happen sea anchors could be effective, but it does not. The vessel will yaw from one side to the other, and while generally keeping the bow into the wind, much of the time it will be more sideways onto the seas; when this happens there is a serious risk of damage to the boat.

Though I have been on a number of vessels that carried a sea anchor, I have never used one and so I have no firsthand experience. However, my experience of how boats behave during a hurricane when using conventional anchors showed me how even in relatively flat waters the boats will yaw considerably, weaving almost continually. All vessels appear to behave in this manner, though to varying degrees, and I believe this behavior is partially responsible for the chafe that occurs when using nylon rodes in these conditions.

Additional difficulties occur due to the extreme stress put on the line, causing deck fittings to fail and bar-taut lines to chafe and break easily. Once set, a sea anchor will be difficult or impossible to recover unless a tripping line has been set. Pulling on the tripping line causes the anchor to collapse so that it may then be hauled aboard. One problem with tripping lines is their tendency to become tangled with the rode, so care needs to be taken in how the line is rigged. Some manufacturers use a short line from the sea anchor to a float from which the tripping line runs back to the boat, thus keeping it away from the rode; and in one instance that I am familiar with this worked entirely satisfactorily.

There are circumstances when you may choose to use a sea anchor and for this reason alone it is sensible to have one aboard. If the boat is drifting down onto a lee shore and it has become impossible to either sail or motor to windward, all that is left is to reduce the amount of leeway being made in the hope the storm will abate before the vessel reaches the shore. Here a sea anchor could be used, as it will certainly help in this way, though at the same time it may be increasing the risk of damage from a breaking sea. In other circumstances, perhaps when conditions are less severe, a sea anchor allows a crew to rest or to repair a damaged rudder.

Tropical Storms

By far the best method of dealing with tropical storms is to avoid them. Known more precisely as tropical revolving storms, they are also referred to as hurricanes, cyclones, and typhoons, depending on where they occur in the world.

The simplest technique of avoiding these storms is not to sail in areas where they can occur at a time of year when they are most likely. Many cruising folk follow this advice. But it is not always practical. For instance, the sailing season along the East Coast of the U.S. coincides to some extent with the hurricane season, and if you are planning to cruise to Japan there is a permanent risk of hurricanes as they can occur at any time of the year. Even if you choose not to sail in tropical storm areas during the tropical storm season, it is prudent to have some plan for coping if caught by an out-of-season storm.

Assuming your vessel is well-found and well-equipped, what will be needed most is accurate information and a knowledge of how such storms behave. Given the right equipment aboard the boat, the information you need to make your decisions should be available; what use you make of it depends on the knowledge and experience of the skipper. I recall being in St. Maarten on the approach of Hurricane Hugo in 1989. Tied up at the marina at the time was a 60-foot megayacht run by a captain and owned by a Venezuelan businessman who was not aboard. Choosing not to anchor in the lagoon, the only real option for all small sailboats such as mine, the captain decided to head for a marina in Puerto Rico, where the yacht arrived safely only to sink later at the dock as the storm swept the island. The captain could have made other choices. At the time of the storm's approach it was traveling in a west-north-westerly direction at about ten knots. Knowing that storms in this area rarely go south of their current latitude, that the vessel he was captain of could outrun the storm, and that he could easily reach a safe port before the storm arrived, he could have gone south. Instead he chose a port he was familiar with but which was in the direction the storm was heading.

Before you depart, make sure you thoroughly understand these storms, have adequate information about safe ports and hurricane holes, and monitor the weather regularly when at sea. As Adlard Coles says in his authoritative book, *Heavy Weather Sailing*, when referring to the action of skippers during the 1979 Fastnet race, "It was encouraging to read that a considerable proportion [of skippers] had read *Heavy Weather Sailing* and a few even referred to the book during the course of the storm although, like seasick pills, the contents should be taken before the arrival of rough weather." (Appendix 7, p. 327) It's all part of preparing yourself as well as the boat.

CHECKLIST

	YES	NO
If you have mainsail jiffy reefing:		
Are the gooseneck hooks strong enough?	❑	❑
If sail slides have to be removed to reef, can this be done easily?	❑	❑
Are all reefing lines run?	❑	❑
Do the lines have different colors?	❑	❑
Are the cockpit jammers labeled?	❑	❑
Is the winch in the correct position to avoid riding turns?	❑	❑
Can the reefing lines be tightened satisfactorily?	❑	❑
Does the sail set correctly when the reefing line is tight?	❑	❑
If you have mainsail roller reefing:		
Does the system work easily and show no signs of jamming?	❑	❑
Are you familiar with how it works?	❑	❑
Can you get to the important parts of the mechanism?	❑	❑
If it uses special shackles to attach the sail, do you have spares?	❑	❑
Do you have a storm jib?	❑	❑
Can you raise it easily?	❑	❑
Is the tack easily attached?	❑	❑
Are the sheet leads satisfactory?	❑	❑
Is there a means of winching in the sheets?	❑	❑
Do you have a storm trysail?	❑	❑
Can you raise it without removing the mainsail?	❑	❑
Can you attach the tack easily?	❑	❑
Does the sheet lead satisfactorily?	❑	❑
Can you winch in the sheet?	❑	❑
If your vessel has large ports or hatches, do you have storm boards for them?	❑	❑
Can the storm boards be easily and securely installed?	❑	❑
Do you have places to stow items that are normally on deck?	❑	❑

	YES	NO
Can you secure the main companionway hatch from:		
The cockpit?	❏	❏
Below decks?	❏	❏
Are you able to lock the companionway boards in place?	❏	❏
If you have dorade boxes, do you have cover plates for them?	❏	❏
Have you arranged stowage below decks for dangerous items?	❏	❏
Do you know how to get the vessel to heave-to properly?	❏	❏
When hove-to can you:		
Lock the wheel or tiller in position?	❏	❏
Ensure the jib or jib sheets won't chafe?	❏	❏
Do you have:		
A line suitable to trail as a warp to slow the boat?	❏	❏
Strong enough cleats or other attachment points?	❏	❏
A drogue or other equipment to further slow down the vessel?	❏	❏
A sea anchor?	❏	❏
Have you studied and practiced various storm tactics?	❏	❏

CHAPTER ELEVEN

Man Overboard

I first met John in Tenerife where we were both anchored at Los Cristianos waiting to leave for our Atlantic crossing. I was alone aboard my Rival 32; he was with his wife, two children, and cat aboard their Freedom 40. I left before them, not expecting to see them again. But we did meet again six months later in St. Maarten. It was over a beer that John told me their story.

Several days out from the Canary Islands their Freedom 40 was under full sail, wing-and-wing with preventers on both booms. They had been going well all day, hardly needing to touch the sails and beginning to really enjoy their passage. After it got dark around 6:00 P.M. they began their formal watch system, he and the younger child remaining on deck while the other two family members got some sleep. After some time they heard the sound of a flying fish land on deck and a second later the cat, who had been asleep below, arrived to investigate. Just as the cat reached the fish a sudden wave caught the boat and the cat and fish together fell overboard.

Hearing the screams of "cat overboard" the rest of the crew came on deck. After what seemed like an age they started the engine, released the two preventers, and began turning the boat into the wind to head back along their reciprocal course in search of the cat. It was a hopeless task to try to locate a cat in the ocean. They had no idea how far to return or even if they were on an exact reciprocal course. It was dark and their searchlight, which in port illuminated the whole boat, seemed a pathetically inadequate pencil beam when searching the ocean. Then to the astonished delight of all the crew, they saw him, the cat's eyes reflecting in the beam. But getting close enough was hard and it took several attempts before they had him alongside. The fishing landing net was used to get him back aboard. Wet, frightened, and bedraggled, the cat was back, at least one of his nine lives used up.

I gather the cat didn't really take to the cruising lifestyle after that, for no sooner had they made their landfall in the Caribbean and tied up to a dock for fuel than the cat escaped ashore, never to return. Perhaps it realized the perils of the sea.

Even in fairly protected waters loss of life occurs all too frequently. It seems that at least once a year someone is lost in the local bay, despite all the support available. Offshore, even when making a short coastal passage, it is likely that help will be a long time in coming and if a person is in the water the chances of rescue are not good. For these reasons safety harnesses are essential. But *what if . . . What if* a crewmember falls overboard? It can happen so easily even in calm conditions. What equipment is really needed to get the person back aboard and what expertise do you need to achieve this?

Providing Flotation

One of the first tasks when someone goes overboard is to provide some additional flotation even if a life jacket is worn. In any kind of seas it is extremely difficult to keep your head sufficiently above water to breathe easily and often a substantial amount of water is swallowed. (Think how this happens in a swimming pool when there are a lot of people around.)

Throwable Buoys

The best kind of device is the horseshoe buoy, which you can easily put on, forcing it under your arms and thus raising yourself out of the water. Ring buoys are almost impossible to wear and require that you hold onto them, a task that will quickly become impossible in cold water. For similar reasons, flotation cushions are not that useful.

In one minute a boat traveling at five knots will be 170 yards away from the person in the water. It takes some seconds to react to an emergency and so the immediate release of the horseshoe buoy or other device is critical if it is to be of any use. But herein lies a real difficulty, because if the buoy is too easy to remove, a passing sea or a strong gust may launch it inadvertently. Horseshoe buoys in the conventional wire holders are not secure and many owners resort to tying them down. A better method is to secure them with a quick release pin attached to a lanyard that can be reached readily. A flat braid or a distinctive colored line used for the lanyard will be quickly recognized in an emergency.

Lifeslings

This new device is often the only one carried, which is fine as long as you realize that it must be deployed quickly and easily. If it takes too long or the line tangles, its use is severely restricted until you can get the boat back to the crewmember in the water. It is a good idea to carry a separate, easily deployable horseshoe buoy in addition to a Lifesling.

Man Overboard Modules

These are units carried at the transom in a rigid container that may be deployed by pulling on the release handle. The units contain an inflatable horseshoe buoy, an inflatable man overboard pole, and a drogue. Though it may seem that such a comprehensive unit is desirable there are some drawbacks to the system. Because the unit inflates using a CO_2 cartridge there is a need for regular servicing and inspection to ensure that it will deploy when needed. Because it is carried at the transom where it will occasionally be deluged by salt water there is a real risk of corrosion.

Another problem with these units is that they are extremely light, which means that in any wind the unit will blow away, sometimes before the drogue can set. The inflated pole will not stand upright in a strong wind and will not be as visible as may be expected.

Despite these drawbacks man overboard modules, which provide flotation and mark location, are useful, but in addition to other equipment rather than as a replacement.

Marking the Position

Once you have thrown flotation, the next priority will be to mark the position where the person is. A person's head is so small that seeing it from even a short distance away is difficult and in any size swells it will be visible only occasionally. Unless the position is marked it will be difficult or impossible to find again. Marking the position may be done visually, by use of man overboard poles or lights or electronic navigation equipment.

By Sight

So long as a person overboard remains in sight there is a good chance of recovery. Once lost the chances diminish dramatically. When someone is overboard it is an emergency situation, adrenaline levels will be high and the boat will be altering course dramatically. At sea with no points of reference it is impossible to keep one's bearings unless the victim in the water is kept in sight. Given sufficient crew this should be possible, but in practice it becomes difficult. Often, when being taught man overboard recovery, the crew loses sight of the cushion or life vest used for practice. With all that is going on aboard, rescue is extremely difficult and so any device that helps to mark the location is desirable.

Man Overboard Poles

These poles can be jettisoned after the immediate flotation and will flag the position. With the top of the pole between six and ten feet above water, finding it will be considerably easier than finding the victim. It is my opinion that man overboard poles are an essential piece of safety equipment and should be chosen with care and mounted in a manner that allows easy deployment. A simple and convenient method is to use short lengths of plastic water pipe attached to the backstay. The weighted base is contained in the bottom piece and the flag stowed in the upper tube. To release, the pole is lifted up and then pulled down.

Some man overboard poles are equipped with a small parachute sea anchor to stop the pole from blowing downwind and away from the body in the water. This is only useful if the sea anchor does not delay deployment.

The man overboard pole is sometimes attached via a line to the throwable horseshoe buoy so that the two remain together in the water. The principle is sound but in practice the difficulty in launching both at the same time increases the delay and reduces the distance they can be thrown. I believe the two should operate independently, each piece of equipment ready to be deployed quickly and easily.

A flag will not be visible at night and some man overboard poles are equipped with a light activated upon immersion of the pole.

Lights

For a night-time rescue to stand a realistic chance of success it is necessary to mark the position with a light. Lights can be fitted to the man overboard pole, as mentioned above, tied to the horseshoe buoy, or independently deployed. An alternative is for each crewmember to wear a personal strobe light. Each system has its advantages and disadvantages and some compromise has to be made. For ease of use I prefer to keep a horseshoe buoy unattached and so tying a strobe light to the man overboard pole may be sensible.

The light must be reliable, bright, and easily deployable. If a good man-overboard strobe light is carried it will have to be fitted so that it can be easily released—intentionally and not accidentally—and a secure device with a quick release pin is recommended. As with a horseshoe buoy, a brightly colored lanyard can be attached to the release pin.

Personal strobe lights that attach to a life vest or safety harness can be useful in identifying the victim in the water once nearby; their low wattage, together with the fact that they are at water level, makes them next to useless for identifying the location from any distance. They are really useful as an extra piece of equipment, not a primary device.

Personal Radio Beacons

The recent development of personal radio beacons is a significant advance should anyone fall overboard. These personal locator beacons are currently available in Europe, though to date they have not received FCC licensing for their use in the U.S.

Each crewmember wears a small transmitter about the size of a pack of cigarettes. Should someone fall overboard, the transmitter is activated manually or automatically and the receiver aboard the vessel will sound a loud alarm. A visual homing receiver can then direct the vessel back to the person in the water.

These devices would seem particularly useful for cruising couples. With its loud alarm, the receiver could wake the sleeping crewmember and provide sufficient information for a successful rescue.

Using Electronic Navigation Equipment

With the wide availability of GPS navigation systems it has become possible to establish electronically the location where someone goes overboard so that, no matter how far the vessel travels, it is possible to return to the position. This is of tremendous advantage in locating a person overboard. If the GPS unit is located in the navigation area, it will be impossible to activate the man overboard feature until more important tasks, such as throwing flotation, have been accomplished. With a crew of two, and one of them in the water, it is questionable whether it is more important to go below to activate the MOB (man overboard) button than to keep the person in sight and return to the position as soon as possible. Therefore such a feature must be available in the cockpit to be really useful.

Some GPS units have a large red button marked MOB, but many are not so easy to use. There are some units that omit this feature altogether. Keep this in mind when choosing a GPS receiver.

Recovery

Once the victim has been located, getting him aboard is the next most difficult task. First you must connect with the person in the water and then the victim must be brought aboard.

Some years ago, Rob James, a famous round-the-world sailor, lost his life just a short distance from the shore on the south coast of England because of the difficulty of getting him aboard. As skipper aboard a racing multihull with a fairly inexperienced crew, he was reaching back and forth outside the entrance to Salcombe Harbour in Devon, waiting for the tide to rise sufficiently so they could enter. He slipped and fell into the cold water and the crew did manage to find him. However with his strength quickly failing in the cold water, and no easy way to get him aboard, the crew could not save him. This could easily happen to you, too.

Making the Connection

There are varying methods of returning to a person in the water, depending on the circumstances when the emergency happens. For many years the *reach-tack-reach* tactic was favored because of its applicability on all points of sail. More recently the *quick-stop maneuver* has been advocated because it ensures that the boat and the crewmember in the water stay closer to each other, but this method is not easy to use at all times, on all points of sail.

The boat's engine will generally be used in such an emergency, creating two problems. If the engine is used when close to the victim in the water there is a risk of serious injury and so extreme prudence has to be exercised as there is little room for error. Another difficulty that arises all too frequently is that in the rush to drop the sail and start the engine, a sheet gets knocked overboard and subsequently fouls the prop, thus making it impossible to use the engine or reset the sail.

It is clearly an emergency when someone falls overboard; as a result there will be considerable tension and anxiety among the crew. Being able to fall back on a well-rehearsed plan helps considerably and practice is essential.

When approaching a person in the water a decision has to be made whether to stay upwind or downwind. If the vessel stays upwind it can be allowed to drift slowly down, with the engine off or in neutral, to the victim who is kept protected from the seas by the lee of the vessel. Conversely, staying downwind ensures that there is no risk of injury as the vessel drifts, rising and falling in the swells. Only the conditions at the time will allow judgment to be made as to what approach to take. In my opinion this is a matter of experience, seamanship, and boat handling skills, all of which can only be learned through actual practice on the water.

Using a Lifesling

Many boats carry a Lifesling when setting off cruising. The equipment is affordable and it allows easy connection without the need to bring the vessel very close to the person. Once deployed, the vessel circles the person in the water, using the engine, until the line with its horseshoe buoy is brought close enough to grab. Once this has been accomplished all power is stopped and the crewmember in the water puts the horseshoe buoy under both arms. The line can then be pulled in to bring the person close to the vessel, and hoisted on deck with a halyard.

Though this is a great piece of equipment, it does require some agility by the person in the water and anyone injured or close to drowning might be unable to use it.

The Lifesling must be in good condition. The line from the buoy to the boat is polypropylene so that it will float. But polypropylene line degrades quickly in sunlight and so the portion of the line emerging from the bag and going to a cleat or other strong point is covered in nylon braid for protection. Make sure that no polypropylene line is exposed permanently, as this will produce a weak link in the line. Ensure also that the line is stowed in the bag in the correct manner, with the bitter end at the bottom, so that it will deploy easily from the top.

Recovering the Person Aboard

If the victim in the water is conscious and still has energy, a boarding ladder will be sufficient. The ladder may be permanently attached to the boat or a removable one can be put over the side, though in both cases the steps should go down well below the surface. A ladder that is fine for getting down into a dinghy may be almost impossible to use by someone in the water, particularly a person drained of strength. Check to make sure that your ladder is easy to use and long enough.

If a Lifesling is being used, the sling may be hoisted aboard with the person so long as the necessary equipment is on hand. Ideally you should have a block and tackle especially for this purpose which can be attached to the main halyard. If you don't, the ship's boom and mainsheet tackle could be used. This is not the best solution, however, since you already have one major problem aboard and a wildly swinging boom could easily create another. If you have a Lifesling and anticipate using it to bring someone aboard, then practice at least once to find out what works and what doesn't. Like many things it's not as easy as it looks.

If the crewmember in the water is injured, unconscious, or very weak, it will be necessary to have some alternative means such as an inflatable dinghy. With the dinghy partially deflated in the water, the victim may be floated aboard the dinghy, which can then be re-inflated. An alternative involves using the mainsail. If the sail is detached at the luff but remains attached at the foot, it can be lowered into the water. With the halyard attached it will form a cot into which a person can be floated

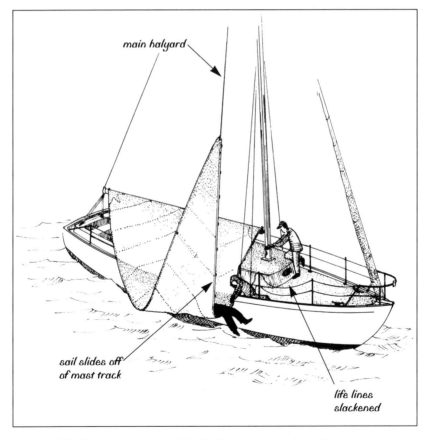

Figure 16. *Using the mainsail to bring a victim aboard.*

before winching-in on the halyard. If this method is to be used easily, some way of releasing the lifelines amidships is required. An alternative to using the mainsail is to use a storm jib, attaching tack and clew at deck level, and using the head with a halyard, as with the mainsail.

CHECKLIST

	YES	NO
Do you have a throwable buoy other than a Lifesling?	❏	❏
Is it easily deployable?	❏	❏
Is it secure in rough conditions?	❏	❏
If you have a lifesling:		
Is the line attached securely?	❏	❏
Is the nylon protective covering in place?	❏	❏
Is the line stowed correctly for easy deployment?	❏	❏
If you have a man overboard module:		
Has it been checked recently?	❏	❏
Do you have spare cartridges aboard?	❏	❏
Do you have a man overboard pole?	❏	❏
Is it easily deployable?	❏	❏
If a light is fitted, does it work?	❏	❏
Do you have a deployable light for use at night?	❏	❏
Does it work?	❏	❏
Is it easy to deploy?	❏	❏
Do you have spare batteries?	❏	❏
If your GPS has a man overboard (MOB) facility:		
Is it accessible?	❏	❏
Do you know how to use it?	❏	❏
Do the crew know how to use it?	❏	❏
Have you practiced man overboard recovery procedures?	❏	❏
If you have a Lifesling:		
Have you practiced using it?	❏	❏
Can you bring the person aboard?	❏	❏
Do you have a boarding ladder?	❏	❏
Can it be used if you are in the water?	❏	❏
Do you have a means of bringing an injured or unconscious person aboard?	❏	❏

CHAPTER TWELVE

Taking on Water

I had covered nearly five hundred miles of my passage from Lisbon towards Tenerife in the Canary Islands. It had been a quick passage assisted by a three day gale. The winds dropped to nearly nothing and with 80 miles to go I started the engine. It would still be another 16 hours before I arrived but at least it would only mean one night with little sleep.

Sometime after dark I went below and found water swilling around the floor boards. For a moment I was ready to panic but, after switching on the large electric bilge pump, I calmed down and was able to focus on the likely cause. I needed to check the stern gland first, and that meant clearing the quarter berth of a considerable amount of gear. In what must have been less than a minute I had done this and was crawling head first along the berth towards the stern. Once I removed the engine access panel, I could see that the gland was the source of the leak, as water was freely entering around the stern tube.

With the water level reduced to a few inches in the bilge I realized that my bilge pump was more than adequate for the task provided the leak did not worsen. I stopped the engine and went back down the quarter berth with some caulking cotton and a couple of small screwdrivers with which to force it in around the leak. I recalled that while departing from Lisbon I had caught my anchor tripping line around the prop. I realized it must have wrenched the stern gland sufficiently so that once the prop shaft began turning it started to leak badly.

With the caulking cotton in place I started the engine again and found I was able to run it with the leak somewhat reduced. From then until my arrival in Darsena Pesquera, Tenerife, I ran the bilge pump every ten minutes, timing it until it sucked air. Every so often when the bilge pump indicated that more water was entering, I had to go and restuff caulking around the stern tube. Even after I had arrived in Tenerife and tied up alongside another boat, I had to pack it again before I could risk going to sleep for a few hours.

Fortunately the leak was not too bad and I had been able to contain the inflow and even run the engine. But even a small leak, small enough that it could be packed with caulking cotton, lets in a surprising amount of water. If the stern tube had really come free I would have had a real emergency to contend with. As it was, I remained apprehensive until my arrival.

Taking on water is a major emergency. A small leak can quickly worsen, while a major leak could result in the vessel sinking within minutes. Knowing what to do and having the means to contain the inflow of water is an essential part of preparation for cruising.

Pumps

When planning for cruising you must decide which pumps will be necessary for a number of different situations. You will need a pump to remove small quantities of water from the bilge that may accumulate from the normal drip of the stern gland, from refrigerator condensation, from a leaking port, or from your foul-weather gear. Other pumps will be needed for removing water if you have a major leak, for instance in case a through-hull fitting breaks or the hull is damaged, or for removing water that has entered the companionway during a knockdown or worse.

Manual Bilge Pumps

Regardless of all other systems aboard your boat, manual bilge pumps are a good backup for removing water but their capacity is limited. While adequate to cope with relatively small leaks, even the one I had to deal with would have meant considerable work and the pumping would have been very tiring.

One of the recommendations resulting from the experiences during the 1979 Fastnet race and repeated in the ORC Special Regulations is that all vessels should have two manual bilge pumps, one accessible from the cockpit and another from below decks. But even a large manual bilge pump operated by an energetic crewmember will only be able to pump at a rate of about 40 gallons per minute, and most manual bilge pumps will pump at only half this rate.

Manual bilge pumps will only be used in an emergency, either to assist other pumps or when you have no power available.

Cockpit mounting

Cockpit bilge pumps should not be located where the handle needs to be inserted inside a locker. The pump needs to be operable from within the cockpit, with all lockers dogged. The operator should be able to sit comfortably and pull and push the operating handle. Pumps that are difficult to operate are next to useless.

Below decks mounting

A bilge pump operable from below is more efficient because the operator can remain warm and dry while pumping. In extreme conditions the crew can pump the boat without a trip topsides.

For the pump to reach its optimum pumping capacity it should be easy to use, and not mounted in galley or head lockers. If at all possible the pump should be mounted on the cabin sole, or just below, where it can be operated from either side.

Suction and discharge hoses

The suction end of a bilge pump hose should have a fitted strainer to filter out large debris that could clog the pump. The hose itself must be secured so that it cannot float up out of the bilge, yet you may need to get to the strainer in a hurry if it becomes blocked, as may well occur after a knockdown when all sorts of things may end up in the bilge. One solution is to fit the strainer with a weight or use a bronze strainer to keep it at the bottom of the bilge.

The discharge hose from a manual pump should be sufficiently large, as short as possible, free of elbows or other joints. It should discharge well above the waterline so that even when the boat is heeled there is no chance of it siphoning back to fill the boat with water.

Electric Bilge Pumps

The most effective bilge pumps found on recreational boats are submersible electric pumps. There is also an electrically operated diaphragm pump, which needs to be mounted out of the water as high as possible.

The largest electric pumps have a greater output than the largest manual bilge pump. Their great advantage is that while the pump is operating you and your crew can either help with manual pumping or work to reduce the inflow.

Ideally a cruising sailboat will have at least one high-capacity electric bilge pump, though in an emergency the more the better. If possible fit pumps forward and aft and have each independently wired with separate discharges.

On a vessel with a generator or other source of 110-volt power, a commercial sump pump can be fitted in addition to the regular 12-volt pumps. These pumps usually have greater output than the low voltage ones, and in a real emergency may give you sufficient time to attempt a repair or to at least salvage as much as possible before abandoning ship.

Mounting

Submersible bilge pumps need to be fixed in position. On one boat that I sailed, the electric pump slid around so much that it caught on the high side of the bilge while the water level increased on the low side. But even if a pump is secured, it may be necessary to remove it in order to clear the strainer from debris. In deep bilges this can be accomplished if a mounting bracket for the pump is secured just below the cabin sole. If the bilge is shallow the pump can be mounted on an easily removable base.

Non-submersible pumps need to be mounted as high as possible so that in the event of severe flooding they remain above water for as long as possible.

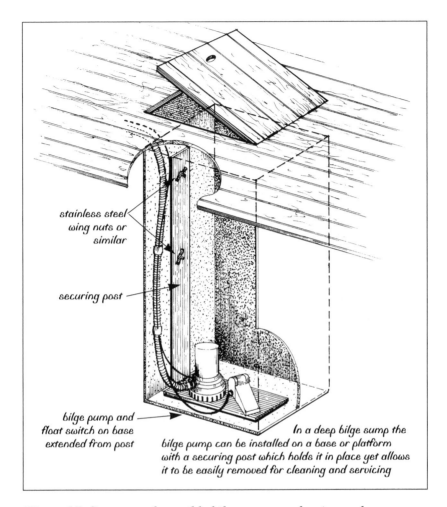

stainless steel
wing nuts or
similar

securing post

bilge pump and
float switch on base
extended from post

In a deep bilge sump the
bilge pump can be installed on a base or platform
with a securing post which holds it in place yet allows
it to be easily removed for cleaning and servicing

Figure 17. *Secure a submersible bilge pump so that it may be removed easily.*

Electrical connections

If your electric bilge pump is to be used in an emergency you would rather have the pump motor burn out from constant running than have the connecting wires melt or a breaker trip all the time. Consider using oversize electrical cables together with a high-rated breaker. All connections need to be sealed using heat shrink tubing or something equally effective. If you have sealed batteries you may want to consider connecting one of the bilge pumps via a switch and fuse directly to the battery. If the battery terminals are subsequently insulated using waterproof tape and/or a liquid seal, the pump should continue to run even if the battery becomes submerged.

If you choose to fit a submersible 110-volt pump, special care must be taken with these connections, both to avoid the possibility of electrocution and to guarantee sufficient electrical insulation, thus preventing electrolysis. A large Hatteras sports fishing boat nearly sank because of such a fault; the pump had shorted to the casing and power was being introduced into the bilge at a level insufficient to trip the breaker but large enough to corrode two through-hull fittings in a couple of days. When the problem was noticed because of a cycling bilge pump, the through-hull fittings were found attached to the hull only by the sealant used to bed them in.

Mechanically Driven Pumps

Except for incredibly large engines, much larger than seen on most recreational vessels, the raw water pump has a minuscule output of around a few hundred gallons per hour compared to a few thousand for an electrical submersible pump. Even a specially mounted engine-driven pump is likely to have only a moderate output and installation costs are considerable.

It makes sense to use your vessel's engine to provide electrical power via the alternator to the electrical pumps rather than use a mechanically driven pump.

Use of Other Pumps in an Emergency

If you are fighting a losing battle with the water you will want to use everything you have to pump it out. Other pumps aboard could perhaps be used in an extreme emergency.

Buckets
It's often said that the most effective pump in an emergency is a frightened person with a bucket. Simple and effective, buckets can remove a large amount of water from below about as quickly and easily as anything. But you need to have several good quality buckets aboard.

Head pumps

In some installations it may be possible to use a manual head or holding tank pump as a supplementary bilge pump. If this is possible, consider fitting a Y-valve to the pump input with a hose leading to the bilge.

Macerator pumps

If your holding tank system uses a macerator pump for overboard discharge at sea you may be able to use this in an emergency. Consider installing a Y-valve with a hose to the bilge.

Air conditioning sea-water pumps

Air conditioning sea-water circulating pumps usually run on a 110-volt supply. At sea you will need a generator. If this is possible consider using the pump in an emergency. Close the intake seacock, cut the hose, and turn on the pump.

Fresh water pumps

Your fresh-water pressure pump also could be used in an emergency. It is probably not a good idea to install a Y-valve because of the possibility of contaminating your fresh water system, but in an emergency you could cut the supply line from the tank and let the water run into the galley and head sinks, hoping it drains overboard.

Hull Repair

If the cause of flooding is a hole in the boat, as opposed to sea water entering during a knockdown or roll-over, you will want to find the cause and attempt damage control. Water most often enters as a result of:

A *hole in the hull*: If you heard a bang and felt the boat hit something, the bow of the boat below the waterline could have been damaged.

A *lost prop shaft*: If the engine was running and you lost forward motion at the same time you could have lost the prop shaft.

A *fracture of the through-hull*: If neither of the above, suspect a through-hull fitting below the waterline.

Of these, the most serious is a hole resulting from a collision, though a broken through-hull fitting can just as easily result in the vessel sinking if you can't find the source before the water becomes too deep.

Repairing a Hole in the Hull

So far I have never done this, other than in a boat yard, and I hope I never have to because chances are I will have little time to accomplish anything before abandoning ship. My plan would be as follows:
• Isolate the damaged area.
• Attempt to heel the boat, using the sails to get the damaged area above the water.
• Use cushions and pillows from the inside of the hull to reduce the inflow.
• Attempt to brace a board of some kind against the broken area of the hull.
• Repair with plywood and screws.

You need to be able to access the forward area of the hull if it is damaged. Fitted fuel or water tanks may hinder this, as will extensive built-in furniture. If possible try and arrange a method of quick access to this vulnerable section of the vessel. Some boats have a collision bulkhead forward in anticipation of this problem.

Having suitable materials at hand is also important. Thin plywood, a hand-drill, and screws may enable you to make a repair within a reasonable period of time if you have pumps or crew or both keeping the water level down while you work. While underwater setting epoxy is a useful material to have aboard, I cannot imagine having enough to make a major repair, though it could be used for minor holes.

Fixing Holes Caused by a Lost Shaft or Broken Through-Hull/Seacock

The traditional remedy for a small circular hole in the boat, such as from a corroded through-hull or a ripped out depth transducer, is a soft wood plug. These plugs are readily available at marine stores and it is often recommended that a suitably sized plug be fitted to each through-hull. I have two reasons for not following this advice, preferring to keep my selection together in a place that I will remember. First, you need to understand how they work: When a dry plug is inserted in a hole the soft wood absorbs water and swells, thus locking the plug in the hole. If a plug is wired to a through-hull, it will probably be soaked through when you get to it, either from bilge water or from a fitting that has been leaking before it finally fails. If the plug is already sodden it will not seal the hole as well. My second reason is that it is just not possible to know what size the hole will be because a through-hull has a number of diameters at which it may fail. As through-hull fittings often contain zinc as part of their alloy, if electrolysis occurs the zinc will erode away leaving the fitting extremely brittle and liable to crack or part easily. The whole fitting could corrode and come away from the hull or a dezinctified seacock could crack anywhere. I keep my soft wood plugs in a locker where they all remain dry until needed.

If a stern tube has come loose, water will be entering around the shaft, yet there will be no empty hole to plug. Stuff cloth down the stern tube and around the shaft, though this will inevitably mean the engine can no longer be used for propulsion.

CHECKLIST

	YES	NO
Do you have a manual bilge pump?	❏	❏
Does it work?	❏	❏
Is it easy to use?	❏	❏
Have you considered having two manual bilge pumps: one operable from the cockpit and one operable below?	❏	❏
Is the suction end of the pump fitted with a strainer?	❏	❏
Can you get at this easily to unblock it if necessary?	❏	❏
Do you have one or more electric bilge pumps?	❏	❏
Are they mounted securely?	❏	❏
Are the electrical connections watertight?	❏	❏
Are the wires, fuses, or breakers sufficiently large?	❏	❏
If you have 110-volt bilge pumps: Are the electrical connections watertight?	❏	❏

	YES	NO
Have you considered the possibility of failure, resulting in serious electrolysis?	❏	❏
Do you have other backup pumps that could be used in an emergency?	❏	❏
Do you know how you would do this?	❏	❏
Have you considered installing Y-valves for this purpose?	❏	❏
Do you have materials aboard to repair a hole in the hull?	❏	❏
Do you have soft wood plugs to seal a broken through-hull, seacock, or hose?	❏	❏
Do you have materials to seal a broken stern tube or stern gland?	❏	❏

CHAPTER THIRTEEN

Abandoning Ship

After cruising in the Caribbean, Alison and I sailed back to Florida and then on to Texas. She had a job to start and I planned to work inland for a while before we went cruising again. But our relationship did not last. I returned to live on the boat and set up my own marine-related business while she continued working while dreaming of more sailing. I think that was why she took a job as crew aboard a boat being delivered up the East Coast.

Her only real sailing experience had been when we were cruising. This was an opportunity to learn how to prepare for an ocean voyage and how to cope at sea. The passage was to take place in August, at the height of the hurricane season, and the vessel left with Alison as crew when a tropical depression was somewhere out in the Atlantic. The depression became a storm and then a hurricane. Alison as well as the skipper and the other crewmember found themselves fighting for their lives as the vessel foundered in the huge seas and began filling with water. They had a liferaft, which was launched, but no prepacked emergency bag. Hurriedly they threw together everything they could think of into a sail bag that was passed down into the raft. But the conditions were terrible and the heavy bag was dropped and lost almost immediately.

Alison and the two others did make it into the raft and survived, but only after ten days at sea with little or no provisions or equipment. When they were found, almost by chance, they were drifting east across the North Atlantic and had resorted to drinking sea water. They could not have survived much longer.

A liferaft is a spare boat that you can take with you. The conditions aboard are almost certainly going to be uncomfortable and unpleasant but there are hundreds of people alive today thanks to a liferaft. Passagemaking will always have its risks and having a liferaft does not guarantee safety. But it does give you a backup to the main vessel, and as such it should be part of the equipment a prudent sailor will insist upon having.

A liferaft alone is not enough. It is doubtful that many who have survived long passages in a raft could have done so without additional equipment.

Liferafts

Choosing a Liferaft

Liferafts are made for many different purposes. Commercial airliners carry them, so do commercial vessels, and the armed forces have special needs. But none of these are really suited to the small boat cruising sailor. Friends of mine thought they had a deal when they purchased an ex-airline raft at an auction. They had it inspected and it was O.K., so they took it with them on a cruise. On their return they tried launching it but nothing happened: it would not inflate. But even if it had done so, it would have been unsuitable. Designed to take 20 passengers, it was a large flat raft. With only two people in it, there would have been little stability and moderate winds or seas would have easily capsized it. If not, the lack of a canopy would have resulted in hypothermia or sunstroke or both within a relatively short period of time.

Liferafts designed for recreational vessels are available:
• In sizes for four, six, eight, or ten people.
• For coastal or offshore use.
• In a valise (soft bag) or in a rigid (fiberglass) container.
• With or without an inflatable floor.
• With varying quantities of equipment stored inside.

The decision about which type of liferaft to purchase is clearly important, for your choices could affect your chances of survival. But as with everything in preparing for a cruise, some risks will have to be taken.

Size
In determining what size raft to choose, bear in mind that a four person raft will barely fit four people. A common suggestion is to pick a raft one size larger than the number of crew you will have. But don't get one that is too big because a large part of the stability of a raft is derived from the weight of its occupants. A liferaft with too few persons will more easily capsize in rough conditions.

Coastal or offshore
Though rafts vary in design, most offer two basic choices. A coastal raft will generally have only a single support tube, no inflatable arch for the canopy, and will come with little or no additional equipment. Offshore liferafts normally have two independently inflated buoyancy rings, an automatically inflated canopy arch, and a bag of additional equipment.

Valise or rigid container
All liferafts are available in a soft bag that can be stowed relatively easily or in a rigid fiberglass container. The bag takes up the smallest space but has to be stowed somewhere, making it more difficult and time consuming to launch in an emergency. A rigid container will be larger, heavier, and in most cases it needs to be permanently mounted on deck. While mounting it will often entail a further expense, the raft will be much easier to get to and launch. Having a sealed rigid container, the raft itself is pretty well protected and is unlikely to be damaged prior to use.

Inflatable floors
Offshore rafts come with or without an inflatable double floor. Some rafts will have a removable inflatable floor. This provides insulation from the cold water, thus making the raft more comfortable and protecting against hypothermia. An additional benefit commented on by many liferaft survivors is how uncomfortable a single floor raft becomes, particularly when fish or sharks nudge the underside.

Additional equipment

If you ever have to take to the raft, having additional equipment will increase your chances of survival and early rescue. But whether this additional equipment should be in the raft or in a separate grab bag is a matter of decision. Most sailors like to include a range of basic equipment in the raft and then supplement this with additional items in a grab bag. You do not need to accept the manufacturer's standard equipment package; make sure you take a look at the items individually and then make your choice about what to include.

Liferaft Inspection

If your liferaft is not new it needs to be inspected. Though this is not a compulsory procedure for non-commercial vessels, it is necessary. You could do it yourself, and some cruisers do, but unless you know what you are doing it is far better to pay a recognized service center to do this for you. Don't just drop off the raft and pick it up later. Stay and check it out, or arrange to call back before it is packed so that you can see just what you've got.

In an inspection the raft will be inflated using an air line, rather than the CO_2 cylinder in the raft, in order not to stress the raft with unnecessarily high pressures. In most cases this will mean that your cylinder will only need weighing rather than recharging. When the raft is inflated it is visually inspected and the equipment checked. Expired items are replaced and the equipment bag repacked. The raft itself will be left inflated for a set period, usually 24 hours, to ensure that it maintains its pressure. This is checked, making due allowance for changes in temperature and atmospheric pressure when necessary. The raft is then repacked and sealed ready for use.

Equipment Included in the Liferaft

When the raft is inflated you will have an opportunity to examine it and become familiar with it so that if you need to use it you know what to expect. But it is also an opportunity to add additional equipment, so long as it fits, or replace items that you don't consider appropriate. Perhaps you wish to change the type of seasickness tablets included, add extra water, or improve the medical kit. One item worth improving is the fishing kit. Some are more appropriate for Walden Pond than the North Atlantic.

Consider including a hand operated water-maker. This small and relatively inexpensive item could be a lifesaver and should be added to the equipment bag of the raft if it is not part of the grab bag.

Other possible items are extra lengths of line, additional batteries that could perhaps repower a dead handheld VHF radio, knives, provisions, or space blankets.

Mounting or Stowage

Rigid container liferafts

Special compartments designed for a liferaft are provided on some vessels at the stern of the boat—on vessels with sugar scoop transoms—or occasionally in the cockpit or cockpit sole. If you plan on using these you will need to ensure that the locker is secure enough so that the raft will not fall out yet is easy to access. On one boat that I saw the liferaft locker in the cockpit sole required a special key to lock the lid, which meant either leaving it unlocked and risking loss during a capsize or accepting the risk of a lost key.

Most boats will not have a locker for the raft and it will need to be mounted on deck. Unless the position for a raft has already been determined, and you are happy with this, choose a location accessible in an emergency and from where the raft can be easily launched. While an area forward of the mast may seem ideal, a better location would be just forward or aft of the cockpit where it can be reached quickly.

The mounts for the raft and the securing straps need to be strong yet easy to release. Make sure that you can do this quickly. You want the raft to stay aboard during a roll-over yet be released intentionally within seconds. One point worth noting concerns the stainless steel bands often used to secure the two halves of a canister. One person I know was told to remove these before setting off. This should not be done. The bands are designed to hold the two halves together and thus maintain a seal, yet they have weak points that will break when the raft is fired. Check with the service center if you are in any doubt.

Make sure before you depart that the launch line has been attached to a strong point on the vessel so that in an emergency the inflated raft does not blow away without you.

Valise rafts

A valise raft should not be permanently mounted on deck but should be easily available. If you do not have an extra cockpit locker for the raft, try and make a shelf near the top of a locker especially for it. If this is not possible then stowage under a seat at the transom or in some other place where the bag will not get trampled on is a good idea. As with any liferaft, make sure that the launch line is secured to the boat and, if it is stowed on deck, that the raft is secure enough to resist a breaking sea or roll-over, yet can be quickly released.

When in port, a valise raft that is normally on deck should be taken below where it will not suffer further from dirt, water, or sunlight deterioration.

Launching

I have never had to launch a liferaft but I still remind my crew of this rule: *You should step up into the raft.* In other words, your vessel should be about to go under when you use the raft. The most written about yachting tragedy, the 1979 Fastnet race, showed that on any number of boats the crews were too quick to launch their liferafts. Lives were subsequently lost from the rafts yet the mother ship was later found abandoned but still floating. Another temptation is to launch the raft but keep it tied close by, ready to use. This also would not be sensible because during conditions in which you are contemplating using the raft, it is likely to become airborne, capsize, sever the painter, and disappear. I have seen heavy dinghies tied close to the stern of a boat at anchor become airborne and flip in strong winds; a liferaft will certainly take off without crew weight in it.

Have a plan before you launch the raft. Do things in the following order:

- Launch the raft to leeward;
- Pull the line to fire the inflation cylinder;
- Pull the raft close and get most crew inside;
- Pass aboard as much equipment as you have time for;
- Get in yourself;
- Cut the painter as close to the vessel as possible. You may need the line later.

Grab Bags

A grab bag or emergency bag contains additional equipment that cannot be included with the liferaft or items that you would rather not include, such as flares that you may like to have available for use from the main vessel as well as from a raft.

For a grab bag to be effective:

- It must be easy to get to in an emergency.
- It must be light enough to carry.
- The bag or the contents should be waterproof.
- It should be buoyant.

Contents

In preparing a list of items to include in a grab bag, start with what you will need most urgently. My first hope will be to be rescued quickly but if this does not happen I will need to avoid hypothermia if I am to survive for long. After that I will need water, and only after that will I need food.

ITEMS TO SUMMON ASSISTANCE

Handheld VHF radio	Waterproof or in a waterproof bag. Offshore a handheld is not much use, should be put in the grab bag.
EPIRB	A small EPIRB to use after the main ship's EPIRB has died or as a backup.
Flares	You could include flares with a recent expiration date rather than disposing of them before you leave.
Mirror	For signaling.

ITEMS TO AVOID HYPOTHERMIA

Aluminum foil blankets	
An inflatable air bed	
Extra life vest	Provides some warmth but also extra buoyancy for the bag.
Clothes	Especially a warm quick-drying jacket and long johns.

ITEMS TO AVOID DEHYDRATION

Seasickness medication.	Maybe a different type than that included in the raft.
Handheld water maker	If it is not included in the raft. I prefer to keep this item in the grab bag in case I want to use it without launching the raft.
Extra water	A plastic container partially filled with water will provide extra water, some buoyancy for the bag, and be a container or bailer for the raft.

ITEMS TO AVOID STARVATION

Food	High-energy food.
Fishing gear	Include a cutting board and knives if possible.

OTHER ITEMS

Extra medical supplies	These could include band-aids, antibiotic cream, pills to control diarrhea, analgesics, and sunscreen.
Raft repair equipment	Additional glue and patches, clamps, needle, and thread.
Writing paper	To record your journal for future publication! It will help morale.
Flashlights	
Games	

Abandon-ship Duties

In preparing for a passage I usually do a watch roster and include with it a list of responsibilities in an emergency. Depending on the number of crew this can either be formal or informal, but having a list will be helpful when the adrenaline is running high. The following items appear on my list and are allocated according to knowledge and abilities:

- Transmit Mayday distress signal.
- Launch liferaft.

- Set off 406 MHz EPIRB and attach painter to raft.
- Grab bag.
- Extra flares.
- Water.
- Medical kit.
- Food.

CHECKLIST

	YES	NO
Do you have a liferaft?	❏	❏
Is it a sensible size?	❏	❏
Is it the correct type for your intended cruising?	❏	❏
Has it been inspected recently?	❏	❏
Do you know what additional equipment it contains?	❏	❏
If it has a rigid container, is it mounted securely?	❏	❏
If it is a valise raft, is it secure yet easily accessible?	❏	❏
Is the painter already secured to a strong point?	❏	❏
Is it easy to launch?	❏	❏
Do you have a grab bag? Is it:		
Easy to get to in an emergency?	❏	❏
Light enough to pick up easily?	❏	❏
Buoyant?	❏	❏
Are the contents waterproof?	❏	❏
Do you have a list of abandon-ship duties for the crew?	❏	❏

CHAPTER FOURTEEN

Ground Tackle

In 1989 I was working for a yacht charter company on the Dutch island of St. Maarten in the eastern Caribbean. It was a fairly prolific year for hurricanes, and twice before the onset of Hurricane Hugo all the local boats had been moved to the lagoon and anchored for what in the end turned out to be an anticlimax of light winds and hazy skies. This time, as the depression became a storm and started tracking westward it became obvious that it could be for real.

I took a friend's boat down to the lagoon first and anchored it. I returned to anchor the Cal 46, the charter boat I was skippering, making sure there was plenty of chafe protection at the bow to protect the nylon rode. And then, the day before the hurricane was due to arrive, I took my boat down and anchored her. I had on board four anchors and decided to set three of them like spokes of a wheel, in the directions of the anticipated winds, with a heavy weight and a rising chain from the center hub to the bow.

I spent a tense night aboard my boat waiting for the arrival of the storm. The winds began to build around 9:00 A.M. the next morning. From then on winds over 100 knots blew for 24 hours. Every hour it seemed another boat around me lost its anchor and disappeared. A boat close by lost a stay and shortly afterwards its mast. On the radio there were screams and shouts as one boat after another drifted downwind dragging its anchor and tripping others. By nightfall it was chaos, with

215

huge seas building in a fetch of only a few hundred yards and in water only seven or eight feet deep. I ventured out of the cabin a couple of times with full foul-weather gear and safety harness on. Crawling forward toward the bow I could not face the sting of the rain and after checking the anchor chain I was glad to return below.

By the time of first light, the winds were noticeably reduced and after a few more hours they were down to a mere breeze. It was over; my anchors had held but many others had not. Now it was time to see how the other boats had fared.

Anchors

For many sailors setting out on an extended cruise, anchoring is a skill that is yet to be learned. With floating docks and hundreds of marinas around the coast, most passages in home waters end in another harbor where you will be docking. For the uninitiated, there is almost a mystique about anchoring, and to compensate for the lack of knowledge in this area there is a tendency to choose unnecessarily large anchors.

How Anchors Work

Anchors work by burying themselves in the seabed. But their design must also allow for them to be easily recovered. When pulled horizontally along the sea bottom they will bury themselves and thus hold securely, but when pulled vertically they will release their hold. Understanding this will enable you to see why an anchor can unintentionally pull out from the bottom and drag. If the pull from the anchor rode is not nearly horizontal to the seabed the efficiency of the anchor will be substantially reduced.

Tripping lines

Even when pulled from directly above, an anchor can be difficult to raise if it has hooked onto an obstruction in the seabed. This could be an old anchor chain from a big ship, a rock, or even the anchor line of a neighboring vessel. To assist recovery in these situations, nearly all anchors are fitted with an eye at their crown where a tripping line can be attached. Pulling on this line will almost certainly bring an anchor aboard.

Attach a tripping line to the crown of the anchor as a safety device if you suspect the bottom to be full of obstacles. Once the anchor is set, the line can be loosely led back to the boat. Using a tripping line can be risky. When pulled, it is designed to trip your anchor and if this happens accidentally you could find yourself unexpectedly drifting. This can occur if the tripping line becomes tangled with the main anchor rode as a vessel turns with the tide or current. To reduce this risk, tripping lines are often buoyed with a float, such as a small fender, and allowed to rise almost directly to the surface from the anchor. Now the risk of the line tangling with the main rode is reduced yet it is replaced by another risk, as friends of mine found out when using a tripping line with a float. They returned to their vessel to find a small fishing boat tied off to the tripping line, the owner thinking it was a permanent mooring buoy.

Types of Anchors

For recreational vessels there are essentially four types of anchors available. First you need to decide which types to carry aboard your boat.

Traditional anchors

The traditional yachtsman's or fisherman's anchor is the type often pictured with a folding stock and two arrow-like flukes. Its efficiency in most ground conditions is largely dependent upon its weight, and so for this type of anchor the bigger the better. It is for this reason that most vessels do not carry such an anchor, since an anchor of around 100 pounds could easily be needed to hold a 40-foot sailboat . Even this would have been a relatively small anchor for Joshua Slocum aboard his vessel *Spray*. He reports in *Sailing Alone Around the World*, "I had three anchors, weighing forty pounds, one hundred pounds and one hundred and eighty pounds respectively."

Fluke type anchors

Anchors such as the Danforth and the Fortress have large flat flukes. They are designed to fall flat on the sea bottom and no matter which side they fall on, one of the spade-like flukes will begin to bury itself when a strain is taken on the anchor rode. These anchors are incredibly efficient once buried and even a small anchor can hold a

large boat. The weight of the anchor is only important in ensuring
that it is large enough so it won't bend under load and that it will
begin to sink into the bottom. What is important is the specific design;
some anchors are less efficient at burying themselves and as a consequence are hard to set.

Plow anchors

The most common plow anchor is the aptly named CQR (Secure)
made by Simpson Lawrence in Scotland. Most other plow anchors are
to some extent a copy of their patented design. Like a farmer's plow, the
shape and weight cause the single heavy fluke to bury itself as the
anchor is pulled from ahead. Because of its design and weight, the plow
anchor works in most bottom conditions and is the anchor of choice for
many. If you choose a plow, make sure that it really does work. Simpson
Lawrence make two claims for their CQR that are worth bearing in
mind. They claim that the precise design is important for its holding
power, and that a few degrees difference in the design can make a substantial difference. And because their anchor is forged, it will not break
as some of the cast imitations would. Since an anchor may be all that's
between you and a shipwreck, if you choose a plow as your main
anchor you will want to pick the CQR with its proven record.

Bruce anchors

The Bruce anchor is a particular patent anchor that is among the
anchors of choice for cruising sailors. Designed initially to hold floating
oil rigs in the stormy conditions of the North Sea, the Bruce anchor has
no moving parts yet will bury and hold extremely well in many bottom
conditions. Its only real drawback is its physical size, which makes it
more difficult to stow securely.

Other designs

With continued development, new patented designs are always
appearing on the market and each type of anchor will no doubt have its
advantages and disadvantages. However it would probably not be prudent
seamanship to choose a relatively new and unproven design as your main
anchor, though it may be a good choice for a second or third anchor.

How Many Anchors

On most occasions one anchor, set properly, will be all that is needed and many cruising people find that their other anchors often remain unused. However, it will sometimes be necessary to use two anchors and occasionally three.

Two anchors from the bow will be needed if using a Bahamian mooring, while bow and stern anchors may be needed in a river to keep your vessel parallel to the shore. In some anchorages the prevailing wind may come off the land but a swell entering the harbor may necessitate a second anchor to keep the vessel's bow into the swell. On other occasions a second anchor may be needed to anchor the vessel while the first is retrieved from the bottom or the rode removed from the prop.

Occasionally you may want to set three anchors, or set two and keep one aboard should you need to cut and run. And having a third anchor aboard does mean that if you lose one, you still have sufficient anchors to secure the vessel.

What Size Anchors

In most cases it is not so much the size of an anchor that determines its holding power as the method by which it is set and the type and amount of anchor rode used. As Joshua Slocum found out, even his huge anchors did not always hold his relatively small boat, though it is reasonable to assume that many of the current designs could have done so with a weight in pounds no greater than the length of the boat in feet. While his 180-pound anchor did not hold the *Spray* in the Straits of Magellan, I have seen a small spade anchor of around 20 pounds hold a huge and heavy ferro-cement ketch in conditions when a large ship broke its chain and went aground. The experience during Hurricane Hugo was similar, with one 100-foot vessel dragging a huge anchor across the bottom while others held with small well-set anchors.

Most manufacturers produce tables of recommended sizes for the use of their anchors and you should refer to these. Most cruising boats will be heavily laden and put a considerable strain on their anchors in a blow, particularly as they yaw from side to side, snapping at the rode with a considerable shock loading. If a manufacturer's table puts your vessel close to the maximum size for a particular anchor, it may be a prudent choice to go to the next size up. But larger than this will be unnecessary. Money spent on a larger anchor than recommended could provide more security if spent on larger anchor rode. Besides, a heavier anchor will be harder to haul up, by hand or by windlass. It will mean a heavier weight carried on the bow or more work for you moving it to and from there, and it will be harder to secure for passage.

If you decide to carry three anchors, at least two should be sufficient to hold the boat in all conditions. The third may be smaller.

Anchor Rodes

As important as the anchors you choose are the rodes used to secure them to the vessel. Essentially there are two types: all chain or rope and chain. Both have advantages.

All Chain Rode

Having an all chain rode has a number of practical advantages for the cruising yachtsman. It is strong, will not chafe, will stow itself, and it enables you to anchor on a shorter scope than with nylon line.

Because the rode is all steel, its resistance to abrasion is an extremely important benefit. Often in unknown anchorages, a rock, coral head, or other obstruction on the bottom can cause a nylon line to part. Once, when anchored by bow and stern, another vessel swung over my stern line at night and in a few hours nearly sawed through the line with its keel. I had to subsequently cut the line at this point. When you are cruising you will be often be anchored close to the shore, and I always feel safer with an all chain anchor rode for my main anchor.

The other significant advantage of chain is its ability to self-stow, making raising and lowering the anchor a semi-automatic process. Given a good design and layout for the windlass, hawse pipe, and anchor locker, the chain can be winched-in over the bow, fall down into the anchor locker below the windlass and stow itself—something rope cannot do.

Offsetting these advantages, chain is heavy, will eventually corrode, and does not stretch. This last point is important, for in strong gusts the anchor rode has to absorb sudden increases in strain. An all chain rode will do this to some extent because of the weight of the chain, which under normal conditions forms a curve from bow to anchor called a catenary curve. In the gusts this curve is stretched but in severe weather it may become bar-taut, transferring large loads to the bow of your vessel.

Rope and Chain Rodes

Most vessels in the U.S. are equipped with this type of anchor rode. A short length of chain is attached to the anchor to provide extra weight, while to some extent protecting against chafe where the rode is closest to the seabed. But the majority of the rode is nylon line, which has the dual advantages of being lightweight and elastic so that it will stretch under load and absorb the strains imposed during strong gusts. So long as sufficient line is used when anchoring, nylon rode works extremely well.

What Length of Rode

The length of rode you will need when cruising depends initially on whether it is all chain or rope and chain. Because of its weight, an all chain rode will provide a near horizontal pull along the sea bed if a length of about three times the depth of water is used. Nylon line requires a length of chain at the anchor and a length about six times the depth to achieve the same. In rough conditions or where the holding is poor a greater length will be needed—say five times the depth for chain, ten times the depth for nylon—and in really severe conditions you will want to use all that you have.

In most anchorages you will probably be able to anchor in around ten to twenty feet, occasionally more. The most that I have encountered in an anchorage often used by small vessels is around 40 feet. Thus a minimum length of chain would be around 200 feet or 400 feet of nylon line. Given that most anchorages are considerably shallower than 40 feet, this will provide quite a margin for those times when it will be needed.

Rode Thickness

When choosing an anchor rode you will want to be sure that it will not part under load. In extremely severe conditions, chain links can stretch until they break, and nylon line can part, though to my knowledge neither caused any boat to lose its anchor during Hurricane Hugo. Most often chain rodes will part where corroded or when the rode is too short and snubbing taut occurs. While nylon is extremely strong, a line under tension is much more easily abraded and under extreme conditions a small amount of chafe will cause the line to part. So long as consideration is given to these points, the anchor rode sizing provided should be more than adequate. Compared to other tables, these sizes are conservative as I have made allowance for the fact that most cruising vessels will be heavier than average and that the anchors will not be used merely as lunch hooks.

		Chain		_Strand Nylon Rode_	
L.O.A. ft (M approx)	Typical Load lbs (Kg approx)	Size inches (mm closest)	Working load lbs (Kg approx)	Size inches (mm closest)	Average breaking strain lbs (Kg approx)
<25 (<7.5)	1000 (450)	¼ (6)	1250 (550)	⅜ (10)	4400 (2000)
25–30 (7.5–9)	1500 (700)	⁵⁄₁₆ (8)	1900 (900)	⅜ (10)	4400 (2000)
30–35 (9–10.5)	2000 (900)	⁵⁄₁₆ (8)	1900 (900)	⁷⁄₁₆ (12)	5900 (2700)
35–40(10.5–12)	2500 (1100)	⅜ (10)	2650 (1200)	½ (14)	7500 (3400)
40–50 (12–15)	3500 (1600)	½ (13)	4500 (2000)	⅝ (16)	12200 (5500)
50–60 (15–18)	4000 (1800)	½ (13)	4500 (2000)	¾ (20)	16700 (7600)

Table 2. Suggested Sizes for Chain and Rode Aboard a Cruising Sailboat

Connecting and Stowing Anchor Rodes

The anchor rode for the main anchor will need to be available for almost immediate use at all times.

If all chain is used it should be stowed near the bow, though given its weight it should be as low as possible. One end should be permanently attached to the anchor with a shackle and the shackle pin seized to ensure it does not come undone. Rather than choosing a shackle that is too small—a weak link in the chain!—use one a little larger than the chain size if possible. The bitter end of the rode must be attached to the vessel so that in an emergency it is not lost overboard with the anchor. But to secure this below decks is a mistake for in other emergencies you may need to cut your anchors and run. If an all chain rode is used, a short length of nylon line should be attached to the bitter end and this secured below. The line should be sufficiently long that it will reach up to deck level so that it can be cut easily if necessary.

Nylon anchor rode should be connected to the anchor via a length of chain. In order for the join between rope and chain to pass easily through a hawse pipe hole, or to pass around a windlass gypsy, they should be connected using a rope to chain splice though this is rarely done. The alternative, a thimble and eye splice, often means the join has to be coaxed out of the hawse pipe hole by a deft twist, making the procedure difficult in an emergency. When stowing nylon anchor rode it should be done in such a way that it can be paid out easily later. Neatly coiled lines may look good but will result in kinks as the line is fed out. If you really want to stow it neatly, faking it in a figure-of-eight will put twists in the line in opposite directions at each turn so that they cancel out as the line is paid out. The alternative is to stow nylon line in a heap, letting it fall naturally. Most times this is fine but there is a risk of loops tangling to form a knot when the line is used. If this happens below decks it could mean a quick trip below at a crucial time. Since nylon is not too heavy it can be stowed in a foredeck anchor well where it will be easily accessible.

Windlasses

Pulling anchor and rode up from the bottom is rarely easy. Most times they are heavy, the anchor is well buried, and occasionally there is a strong breeze. Most cruising sailors will consider an anchor windlass an essential piece of equipment. It is important to have one that works easily and efficiently .

Windlass Types

Windlasses can be manual or powered and have either a horizontal or vertical action. Manual windlasses are simple, reliable, and powerful, but they are often very tiring to use when only a few inches of rode are recovered at each stroke. Powered windlasses are convenient and usually perform well, yet even large ones will struggle against a strong wind.

Installation

If fitting a windlass, choose one sufficiently large. Make sure that powered windlasses can be operated manually in an emergency. Generally the horizontal action windlasses are easier to use and if using all chain rode it is easier to self-feed down into the chain locker. But an advantage of the vertical action windlass is its compact size, with usually only the drum and gypsy above deck and the power section below.

If using all chain anchor rode, try to arrange for the chain gypsy to line up with the bow roller so that a straight pull is obtained. Make sure that the windlass gypsy matches the type and size of the chain.

When using nylon rode, the lead to the drum is all important if you are to avoid riding turns. It should come from a few degrees below its base, to the side on horizontal action windlasses. Consider what you will do when you reach the chain part of the rode. Often a chain gypsy is on the opposite side of a horizontal action windlass, making it almost impossible to use when the nylon rode is already on the drum. Vertical action types are a little easier but it is still not simple. Once the chain section of the rode has been reached a line can be attached to the chain, taken aft through a block and back to the windlass so that the chain is pulled up on deck and aft until the anchor is at the bow. This complication is one disadvantage of using a nylon rode.

If the windlass is electric, it must be well installed. Because a windlass uses a lot of power, large cables are needed to connect it to the ship's batteries and where this run is long, even larger cables are needed. Having a separate windlass battery mounted forward works extremely well. The large cables can be kept short and only lightweight wires need to be run from the engine room to charge the battery. As with all electrical connections aboard a boat, they need to be protected from salt water and corrosion. With windlass connections this is particularly important because of their location at the bow, where there will inevitably be much water at sea. Heat shrink tubing works well.

CHECKLIST

	YES	NO
Do you have a main anchor of sufficient size for the vessel?	❑	❑
Is the anchor chain:		
Of sufficient length?	❑	❑
Of a large enough size?	❑	❑
Marked along its length?	❑	❑
Attached and seized to the anchor?	❑	❑
If a line is used in addition to chain, is it:		
Of sufficient length?	❑	❑
Of a large enough size?	❑	❑
Marked along its length?	❑	❑
Is the bitter end secured to the vessel?	❑	❑
Do you have a second anchor of a similar size?	❑	❑
Is the anchor chain:		
Of sufficient length?	❑	❑
Of a large enough size?	❑	❑
Marked along its length?	❑	❑
If a line is used in addition to chain, is it:		
Of sufficient length?	❑	❑
Of a large enough size?	❑	❑
Marked along its length?	❑	❑
Do you have a third anchor?	❑	❑
If a windlass is fitted:		
Is it of sufficient size?	❑	❑
Does the anchor chain fit the gypsy?	❑	❑
If using nylon line, is it positioned to avoid riding turns?	❑	❑
Is the windlass wired with a separate battery or with cables of sufficient size?	❑	❑
Are the electrical connections waterproofed?	❑	❑

CHAPTER FIFTEEN

Running Aground

After a night crossing from the Bahamas, I arrived somewhat south of my intended destination off the U.S. mainland, as I had conservatively allowed too much for the northward flow of the Gulf Stream. After a short passage north along the Florida coast, we turned and entered the Palm Beach inlet around 10:00 A.M. Once inside we knew that we had to report to Customs immediately. Seeing a marina and fuel dock nearby we turned toward it so that I could go ashore and make my call to Customs' hot line. I saw several moored sailboats fairly close. As it turned out they were not that close. Between us and them was a mud bank that we found unexpectedly. Of course it was on our Intracoastal Waterway chart and, if I had been paying attention, we would not have run aground. Fortunately the bottom was soft mud and we were soon able to free the boat and take the less direct path to the marina.

Since then I have been aground a number of times in the Intracoastal Waterway or in the shallow backwaters of the Texas coast, but always when nudging-in under power and at a relatively slow speed.

Where I learned to sail in England, many small boats went aground twice a day with the ebbing tide. On a sandy or muddy bottom they would either sit upright on their twin keels or gently fall over on their side until the rising waters would float them again. But in other areas where jagged rocks were close beneath the surface, going aground was a frightening prospect. The boat would almost certainly be damaged severely as it fell onto the rocks with each passing wave, and it was a lucky owner who was able to rescue his boat from a falling tide.

While in some areas going aground is a matter-of-fact occurrence, in many places it could be the end of your boat. Anyone who has spent time in the Caribbean is aware of boats that end up on a reef where they are pounded by the surf and cut by the coral until they are holed. There vessels rarely float off intact.

With good seamanship, accurate navigation, and satisfactory ground tackle, you can avoid serious groundings on a reef or beach, but getting stuck in the mud or caught on a sand bar on an ebbing tide are possibilities you must prepare for.

Equipment

Anchors

To pull the vessel off you will need to use your own anchors. A lightweight anchor with good holding power, such as the Fortress, will come into its own. This together with a nylon rode will be much easier and quicker to deploy than a main anchor and an all chain rode.

If you are not sure about the bottom conditions, consider a tripping line for the anchor, especially if you have to set it in shallow water to get the right pull on your vessel. An anchor that has just been used to pull your boat into deeper water will be well buried and almost impossible to get up manually from the dinghy.

Winches and Windlasses

Your main sheet winches and windlasses can be utilized when it comes to pulling your boat off. But often the problem is to get a fair lead to the drum and avoid riding turns. It is helpful to have aboard a couple of sizable snatch blocks that can be quickly attached to a cleat, stanchion base, or toerail.

Dinghy

Unless you are planning to swim out with an anchor, you will need to use your dinghy. Having it ready to go makes the whole process quicker and simpler. A dinghy on davits is ideal as you can launch it easily. An inflatable stowed below or at the bottom of a locker will take you half an hour to get ready, during which time the tide could have fallen significantly.

Getting Off

Once aground, it is desirable to get off again as soon as possible in order to minimize any damage. If the wind is blowing you further aground and the tide is rising, you must set an anchor immediately to stop your vessel from being blown further aground. If the tide is falling, unless you can get off quickly you could be there for a number of hours.

In preparing your vessel for the possibility of a grounding you will need to consider the following:

Using the Engine

Probably your first attempts to get off will be by using the engine. Try putting it in reverse and rocking the boat using crew weight, keeping someone at the helm or tying off the wheel or tiller securely so that it doesn't slam hard over as you start coming off. Adjust the trim of the boat by moving weight forward or aft, or heel the boat with crew out on the boom. While doing all of this, watch your engine temperature and monitor the water from your exhaust. When aground your engine intake can easily become blocked with sand, weed, or mud.

Kedging Off

If you have gone aground when going forward, your best bet is to get off the way you went on because you know that there is sufficient depth on that reciprocal course. Setting a kedge anchor astern will be necessary. Plan how you will run the anchor line. Are the stern fair leads adequate? If you plan to use the primary sheet winches, how will you make sure that you have a fair lead to them that will avoid riding turns on the winch? Is it possible to make use of the windlass using snatch blocks?

Heeling the Vessel

If you plan to heel the vessel using a halyard, how will you do this? Genoa and mainsheet halyards will chafe badly and possibly jump off the masthead sheave and jamb if pulled athwartships. If you want to be able to heel the boat you will either need to use a spinnaker halyard, which should be fitted with a swivel block, or you will need some means of attaching a block at the masthead.

Given a wind direction that will push you back into deeper water, the sails may be used to heel the boat and pull her off. If possible try to do this with just the genoa, as once off and sailing it can be freed easily to give you time to get things under control. While you may need all the sail you can get and thus have to raise the main, once off it may be hard to round up into the wind and get it down before you are blown across a channel and end up aground again, but this time on the leeward side.

Accepting a Tow

I have sometimes been able to help other vessels by pulling them off and this has been paid back to me by others when I have been aground. Thoughts of salvage may enter your mind, yet most times other boaters will be glad to help, though it's wise to use your own lines if at all possible, and to agree on the price in advance—perhaps a couple of beers. If a commercial tow appears you will definitely want to determine the price first.

When preparing for a tow, you will need lines of sufficient length and diameter for your vessel. A good guide will be the recommended size for a nylon anchor rode. But using the anchor rode itself, with its attached chain, will often not be easy. Instead have available a separate line of several boat lengths that can be used for towing.

In preparing for cruising, you should expect that at some time you will go aground and be pulled off, or you will help some other vessel in this way. Having planned ahead how you will connect the lines to your vessel in these circumstances will help ensure that you can act quickly and sensibly.

Make sure that the cleats you are intending to use are sufficiently strong and well mounted. Many cleats that for years have secured your vessel to a floating dock in a marina will not be strong enough. If your mast is keel stepped, consider taking a line around it and leading the lines through fair leads or chocks at bow or stern. However, trying this with a deck stepped mast could result in losing your rig.

If you plan to use bow or stern fair leads or chocks, make sure these are sufficiently strong. Whereas the cleats themselves may be through-bolted with backing plates, fair leads may only be attached with wood screws. Unless you are certain that they will hold up when the pull puts them under sideways stress, plan to use something else. It may be better to run the lines through blocks rather than the fair leads.

When preparing a towing line, I always like to attach the line via a bridle. This spreads the heavy loads rather than putting all the strain on one cleat, while allowing the tow to be slipped easily should this become necessary. But this can only be done if you have cleated the lines using the bitter end rather than the standing part, or have tied a line with a knot that can be undone under tension; a bowline tied around the mast could not be undone whereas a round turn and two hitches could.

Offering a Tow to Others

There will probably be situations when you want to offer help to another vessel aground. While this is a pretty decent thing to do, be aware of the risks you may be taking. You could end up aground yourself, damage could occur to your vessel, a crewmember be injured, or you could end up causing damage to the other boat.

Try and stay in deep water yourself, if necessary putting out an anchor. If possible stay to windward and float a line down to the other vessel using a fender or PFD as a float. Try to establish communication via VHF radio so that you can stay in contact as you begin to maneuver. Plan things carefully and always be ready to release the tow. And watch that the tow line does not get caught around your own propeller.

If towing another vessel, use a bridle to keep the tow line aft of

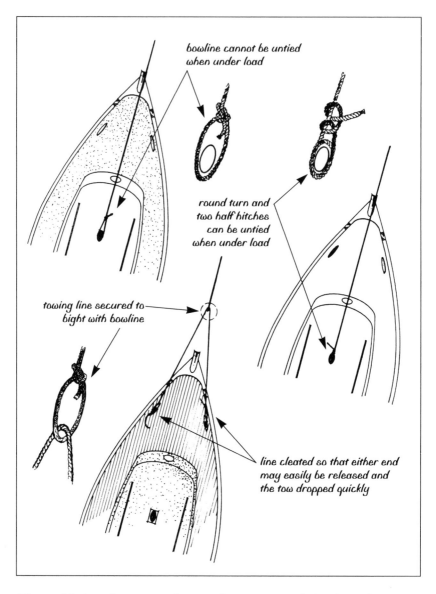

Figure 18. *Attach a towing line so that it can easily be slipped.*

antennas, self-steering gear, stern ladders, or other equipment at the stern. If the two ends of the bridle are led to secure points on your boat forward of the rudder post you will gain steerage when pulling.

CHECKLIST

	YES	NO
Do you have a suitable kedge anchor?	❏	❏
Does it have its own anchor rode?	❏	❏
Do you know how to rig a tripping line?	❏	❏
Do you have a couple of large snatch blocks to help ensure a fair lead when using sheet winches or windlass to pull the boat off?	❏	❏
Can you use your dinghy in a hurry?	❏	❏
Are the bow and stern fair leads strong enough to be used when kedging off?	❏	❏
Do you have a halyard that can be used to heel the vessel?	❏	❏
Do you know what to do when offered a commercial tow?	❏	❏
Will this result in a salvage claim against you?	❏	❏
How will you attach the towing line to your vessel?	❏	❏
If you offer to tow another vessel how will you rig the lines to avoid damage to gear at the stern?	❏	❏

CHAPTER SIXTEEN

Seasickness and Medical Emergencies

As I crossed the Atlantic alone, it was a sobering experience to listen to the reports of the seriously ill crewmember in the Indian Ocean. The skipper had already died from severe food poisoning after eating a bad can of meat. He died also, and the vessel was eventually found mid-ocean and towed to land by a cruising couple.

On my second crossing of the Atlantic I was with a girlfriend. I had been trailing a line for just a short time when I got a bite and hauled in a good sized dorado but I lost him as we tried to gaff him at the stern. Within 15 minutes I had another bite and was impressed with my new, triple-hooked diving spoon that was producing such great results. This time I managed to get the fish alongside and gaffed, so we brought him into the cockpit. I gave him the regulation few hits on the head with a winch handle, a method I had refined after a lesson from Venezuelan fishermen. Next I had to remove the hook and get the line out of the way, as I was not using a reel and the cockpit sole, where the line lay, was to be the gutting table. Somewhat apprehensively I grasped the hook and attempted to pull it out but as I did so the fish, still alive, gave a spasm that resulted in one of the other hooks embedding itself in my finger. It was a good catch for the fish, with the barb well-in, and I found myself now attached to the flapping fish with a finger going numb. I imagined all sorts of potential complications occurring before I could make landfall in a couple of weeks.

But first things first. We both stepped on the fish hard to stop it moving. Then my girlfriend went to get my toolbox and with a pair of side cutters I was able to detach myself from the fish, though the hook was still in my finger. After making sure that the fish was dead, and returning the line overboard, I went below to extract the hook. It wasn't easy or pleasant. I wish I had known then that I could have used an ice cube as an anesthetic. Fortunately there were no complications. I washed the wound as best as I could, applied antibiotic ointment and a band-aid, and then cleaned and cooked the fish.

This simple mistake could easily have resulted in complications that would have been hard to remedy 1500 miles from land.

Coping with Seasickness

While not usually an emergency, seasickness is by far the most common (and annoying) medical problem at sea. Much has been written about seasickness but, despite considerable medical research, the malady remains almost as severe as it must have been hundreds of years ago. If you are planning to go offshore you really need to know how you will cope. If only to lay this problem to rest, you need to spend some time offshore.

In my experience, no remedy is perfect, but these days sailors use Scopolamine patches, which have to be obtained on prescription from a doctor, or non-prescription pills such as Dramamine and Bonine. The patches and pills are not without some negative side effects; if you are not sure whether you will be sick or not, I think it best to set off without taking any medication. This way, you will find out.

On nearly every passage I suffer from some early signs of seasickness including listlessness, yawning, and a tense stomach, but I have learned how to cope so that they are not a problem. Before setting off I usually arrange for sandwiches to be prepared and snack food to be easily available. When I start feeling tension in my stomach I eat right away, usually snacking on fruit or cookies or the sandwiches. Usually my symptoms diminish almost immediately. During the first 24 hours I try not to spend unnecessary time below unless I am lying down. That does not preclude me from any necessary chartwork or making a hot drink in the galley, but I don't go below to read, prepare gourmet meals, or unblock the head unless it is really essential.

Symptoms

Symptoms associated with seasickness affect most people in a similar way. It usually begins with a feeling of tiredness and lethargy—not plotting a position on the chart when necessary, or failing to adjust the sails to a change in course or wind direction. I always experience a tense stomach, burping, and wind. Those on lookout may miss obvious things such as crab pots, floating debris, and even big freighters. Carelessness is almost always a good early indication. If not busy, those affected may become quiet, still, and cold; they may begin lying down in the cockpit. Soon after these symptoms occur they may begin turning white or green and start vomiting.

Look out for the following signs in yourself and other crewmembers:
• Yawning
• Feeling cold/goose bumps
• Being listless
• Burping
• Staying quiet/not talking
• Lying down
• Lacking concentration
• Making simple mistakes and showing carelessness
• Turning white/green
• Visiting the head
• Hanging over the side

Aggravating Factors

Just as I have learned how to deal with the early signs of seasickness and avoid its serious effects, so can you. But it cannot be done during just one short offshore passage. You will need to experiment and if necessary try out different seasickness remedies to find out which suits you best. First, try and reduce those factors that commonly exacerbate the malady.

Anxiety

When I was a charter skipper in the Caribbean, I soon learned that if I could reassure my passengers of my competence early on I would have less seasickness to deal with during the trip. Many were sailing for the first time and were tense at setting out offshore. They were afraid of falling overboard, getting sick, or of the boat heeling. Merely telling them of my experience as we motored out the harbor, and explaining how the boat would heel or the seas increase as we rounded the headland showed them I knew what I was doing and they could relax. With more relaxed passengers I had less seasickness to cope with, and the passage became easier.

Going below

For those who seem immune to the onset of seasickness, going below will often provoke a queasiness and a quick return topsides. Unless you are sure you will not be affected, stay in the cockpit during the first couple of days, unless you lie down immediately when you go below. Seasickness is connected with the balance mechanism in your inner ear and by lying down you avoid the need to use this. If you are seriously affected when going below, get your foul-weather gear off while still in the cockpit, so long as it's safe to do so, and make sure you lie down as soon as practical.

Diesel fumes

If you have ever gone out on a day fishing charter you will probably have experienced diesel or exhaust fumes for at least part of the trip. The smell is nauseating by itself and only serves to exacerbate any tendency to seasickness.

The motion of the boat

Sometimes you will feel fine until the motion of the boat changes and then a lurching or rolling motion just becomes too much. If this is the case and the navigation allows for it, you can choose your point of sail to minimize this, at least for the first day at sea.

Boredom

I recall feeling a little queasy and listless during one of my first English Channel crossings until I had to put a reef in the mainsail. It took some effort to start moving, but then I completely forgot about my seasickness until after it was all done and I was once again back in the cockpit. Being occupied helps; being bored increases the likelihood of seasickness.

Alleviating seasickness

If you have minimized the aggravating factors and still find yourself becoming sick even after several coastal or offshore passages, you may want to try medication—but before you do so try the following ideas.

Eat something. Though it is always difficult for me to persuade crew who are feeling a little sick to eat, this works every time for me and for those few I have been able to persuade. I have found fresh and dried fruit, cookies, and sandwiches really help, and I always try to ensure they are readily available.

Keep busy. If I have something to do it really helps. It's not often these days that I go offshore as crew rather than skipper, but when I do I often experience more of a problem with sickness and I'm sure it's because I have less responsibility and less to do. If you are skipper and you notice the early signs of sickness, try and give the crewmembers something constructive to do. Putting them on the helm nearly always helps.

Medical Preparations

If cruising was without danger it would not be so appealing. While we must try to minimize all the risks, medical risks must be reduced as much as possible by careful training and preparation. It makes sense for at least one of the crew to have taken a recent first-aid and CPR (Cardiopulmonary Resuscitation) course and ideally, if there will be just two of you, both should do this. Consider a more advanced class, a wilderness survival course, or a private lesson with a nurse or doctor. But even if you are a medic yourself, you are still taking risks when you set off on a passage. To be able to cope with the most common medical occurrences, you must have aboard sufficient equipment and medications as well as a communications system that will permit you to get professional advice.

The medical problems you are likely to deal with are to a large extent related to your preparations in other areas:
- A well-fitted vessel with strong safe equipment is less likely to incur breakages in which a crewmember may be injured.
- An experienced skipper and crew are less likely to make mistakes, such as accidental jibes, that could result in injury.
- A fit, healthy person who has undergone a comprehensive health check before leaving is less likely to become ill or suffer, for instance, a heart attack.

What Medical Emergencies to Prepare for

Though you imagine the worst type of emergencies, the most likely ones to occur are those that result from your specific activities: Bee stings or snake bites are unlikely but coral cuts are; contagious infection is unlikely but ciguatera poisoning from fish is a possibility. Burns or scalds in the galley are common. In the following discussion I have tried to cover the most likely problems that occur while cruising, with suggestions on what you can bring, or what knowledge you need to deal with them. I have consulted with a number of medics, all experienced boaters, but in the end the decision to include or omit an item has been mine. I have not made specific recommendations for medications or treatment as I am not medically qualified and, in all cases, the skipper should make these decisions based on the particular circumstances of the crew and the intended voyage.

Marine related problems

By setting out to go cruising, you are decreasing the risk of some medical problems while increasing others. Marine-related medical problems are not only among the most common situations with which you will have to deal, they are likely to be underplayed by medics with little or no cruising experience, so don't expect your local family doctor to be of much help.

You will probably spend a large amount of your time in warm sunny climes where you may have to deal with sunburn, sunstroke, and the increased risk of melanomas. Prevention should be your first thought. But you will still need to know how to recognize the onset of these problems and how to deal with them if they occur.

An all-pervading element of your cruising will be water and this brings with it a number of potential problems. You need to anticipate the possibility of hypothermia and drowning in order to prevent these in the first place and respond appropriately if you have to cope with them.

In tropical areas you need to exercise caution when swimming around coral to avoid coral cuts. You also need to know how to treat the cuts.

Household type injuries

If you plan to use your boat as your home, you will suffer the same type of injuries you would in a house. Most of these injuries are likely to occur below decks. You may get cuts as you are knocked around the cabin in a big sea or flying galley utensils that have not been stowed correctly may hurt you. Burns occur as you attempt to work on the engine or scalds result from a pot containing hot soup flying off the stove. Be prepared to deal with at least minor eye injuries.

Sailing injuries

Some injuries are more likely on a sailboat where the boom swings around, lines are under tremendous tensions, and powerful equipment is being used. Besides knocks and bruises, which are all but inevitable, you should be prepared to deal with sprains and fractures if you will be making long passages. You need the basic knowledge of what to do in these circumstances, together with medication for treatment—such as some pretty strong analgesics and possibly antibiotics.

Infections

While infections can result from coral cuts or compound fractures, they may also result from contaminated food—aboard or eaten immediately before you leave. If you anticipate any passages of more than a few days you will need to have aboard medications to treat such problems, even if you do not feel competent to diagnose and prescribe for these situations. While you can get medical advice via radio, the only medications available to you will be the ones that you take with you.

Allergic reactions

Severe allergic (anaphylactic) reactions to bites, stings, drugs, or other substances can be fatal yet there is a simple treatment for an emergency reaction. Though it is perhaps unlikely to occur, it does make sense to have aboard the necessary medication.

Dental problems

With a good check-up and any necessary treatment before you leave, the chances of dental problems occurring can be greatly minimized. However, with a little knowledge from your dentist and some pretty common prescription drugs, you will be able to control most problems at least until you reach land. A dentist can provide a temporary filling material which is easy to use in an emergency.

Major injuries or illnesses

If you are aware of a specific illness, risk or injury, you may obtain specialist advice and equipment before departure. But it is just not possible to take along everything you might need. This is one reason why many people who talk of setting off never do. But if you are serious about cruising you will plan and prepare well, while recognizing that some things could happen that cannot be planned or provided for, such as a collision with submerged objects at sea or a serious accident or illness.

Where to Get Medical Assistance

In an emergency you may need to get advice on how to treat an injury or illness. The radio communications equipment you have will be of major importance. You can use a VHF radio to call any vessels in the vicinity and see if they either have a doctor aboard or longer-range transmission equipment. If you have a ham or SSB radio aboard you will be able to obtain medical advice relatively easily.

A call to any ham radio operator or ham net will probably result in all the help you need, while a call on a marine SSB frequency to an

AT&T operator will get you the same. Or, failing either of these, you can make a Pan-Pan broadcast on the radio distress frequencies.

Make sure that more than one crewmember knows how to transmit so there will be a backup if the radio operator is the one to need assistance. Having written instructions posted close to the radio will help in an emergency. Include information on how to transmit a distress message, as well as how to reach the main SSB frequencies and ham radio nets.

CHECKLIST

	YES	NO
Do you get seasick?	❏	❏
If you do, do you know what:		
Makes it worse?	❏	❏
Helps you reduce the problem?	❏	❏
Medication works best for you?	❏	❏
Can you recognize the first signs of seasickness in others?	❏	❏
Have you or at least one of the crew:		
Any medical training?	❏	❏
Passed a recent first-aid course?	❏	❏
Taken a CPR class?	❏	❏
Consulted with a doctor regarding medications?	❏	❏
Consulted with a dentist regarding medications?	❏	❏
Have you considered how you will deal with the following:		
Sunburn, sunstroke, and risk of melanomas?	❏	❏
Hypothermia and drowning?	❏	❏
Coral cuts?	❏	❏
Serious lacerations?	❏	❏
Burns and scalds?	❏	❏
Sprains and fractures?	❏	❏
Infections?	❏	❏
Allergic reactions?	❏	❏
Dental problems?	❏	❏

	YES	NO
Do you or your crew have any special medical conditions that will require specific medications or treatment?	❏	❏
Do you have the means to summon medical assistance if necessary?	❏	❏

CHAPTER SEVENTEEN

Fire Safety

I was working in a boatyard at the time. We had a full service yard and the possibility of fire was always present. Paints, resins, thinners, glues, and other chemicals were used daily. There were the power cords to the boats and the cigarettes smoked by the yard help. Fortunately we never had a fire. But across a fairly narrow canal was a power boat dealer and a couple of small marine businesses, together with a number of boat slips. One morning just before lunch one of our crew saw the fire, black smoke pouring from the engine room of a 30-foot power boat tied up at one of the slips. We all went to look. By the time I arrived flames were engulfing the stern of the boat and the few people around were trying to push the boat out of the slip, away from the other boats. Then the fire truck arrived and shortly after the local fire boat. They were very effective and put out the fire before the boat could burn down to the waterline and sink. But it was not worth repairing.

I've not seen any other fires on boats but I have seen the results. When help is at hand the fire is often extinguished, though not before the vessel is damaged almost beyond repair.

Then there are the other fires aboard where there is no immediate help. You never see the boats again for they burn to the waterline and sink. You don't want this to happen to your boat.

Fire Prevention

A fire at sea would be a disaster that could have been prevented. This really is one aspect of preparation where you make your own luck. Do it wrong and you may not live to regret it.

Engine Room

The engine room is the one area where a fire can easily start and get out of control. You have electrical cables carrying substantial currents, fuel lines, and high temperatures: all the volatile ingredients to start a fire. So what can be done to minimize the risk of an engine room fire?

Electrical connections

All electrical connections are a potential source of fire; the thicker wires that carry stronger currents are the ones to pay most attention to. These include the heavy duty cables from the battery to the starter motor solenoid, the ground cable connected to the engine, and the output wire from the alternator. If any of these wires have poor, loose connections they will not function well and are likely to become hot when in use. Ensure that the cables are routed away from the hottest parts of the engine, such as the exhaust manifold and exhaust, where the covering may melt, and that they are secured so they cannot become caught in any of the moving parts, such as the belts.

Fuel lines

The fuel lines of the engine are likely to be rigid tubing, though the supply line from the tank via the primary filter will almost always be flexible. Check that all connections are sound and not leaking, that the supply hose is in good condition, and that there is plenty of flexibility to allow for engine vibration. Routing the supply hose on the side of the engine away from the exhaust and exhaust manifold is a sensible precaution so that if a leak develops there is no danger of fuel spilling onto these hot surfaces.

Engine exhaust

The engine exhaust is the most likely cause of an engine room fire as it can become extremely hot. While most exhausts have the engine cooling water injected into them just a short distance from the manifold, thus cooling the exhaust, some have relatively long fixed exhausts that are often wrapped in an attempt to insulate them from any surrounding combustible materials. There is a risk of fire if the uncooled exhaust passes close to anything that can burn or passes through a bulkhead. In most cases it should be possible to redesign the exhaust system to remove this potential risk.

If your engine ever runs without the cooling effects of the raw (sea) water, it will overheat. But be aware that by the time the fresh-water cooling system has become hot enough for the temperature alarm to sound, the uncooled exhaust could have become extremely hot and anything touching it may be a fire risk.

The Galley

The galley is a potential source of fire or explosion. Galley fires can result from poor design, inexperienced sea cooks, or both, while explosions can occur if care is not taken in the use of compressed gas. The following elements should be considered:

Design

Galley fires can result when the surrounding furniture gets too close to the burners. This can easily happen when the vessel is heeled and the stove gimballed. Allow sufficient room at the sides of the stove and, before you use it at sea, move the stove by hand and check to see if any surfaces come close to the burners. Any such surface can perhaps be protected with a thin stainless steel sheet. Overhead clearance above the burners should be a sufficient distance to ensure that these surfaces do not ignite.

Galley use

At sea when the vessel is pitching, it is difficult to do much in the galley. However, there are those hardy sailors, apparently immune to seasickness, who can eat fried eggs in the roughest weather. Using the galley to fry food is a potential source of fire. Hot fat will easily ignite and a flaming pan is a very definite danger. In rough conditions stick to boiling or reheating liquids.

Risk of explosion

When you use compressed gas as fuel, be extremely careful to avoid a build up of gas in the bilge and a resultant explosion. All fittings should be sealed and checked periodically for leaks. Flexible hoses that connect the stove to the supply are a potential source of leaks as the hose can easily chafe or become trapped between sharp corners while the stove gimbals. It should be inspected regularly. Look for rupture in the flexible hose where it connects to the brass fittings that create a hard spot.

In addition to good design and regular maintenance, the use of gas solenoid valves and a gas sensing alarm help ensure that leaks do not result in a catastrophe.

Smoking

Being a non-smoker, I recall being amused at the quantities of cigarettes that ocean sailors would take with them to avoid running out while at sea. Lately, sailors who smoke are less common, but for those who do, limiting smoking to above decks is a sensible precaution. Not only does this considerably reduce the risk of a fire below, it also keeps the cabin cleaner and more pleasant for the non-smokers. I always have a rule that smoking is only allowed on deck.

The Bosun's Locker

The cruising sailor will take all manner of paints, resins, and glues for repair and maintenance along the way. To do so safely make sure that they are fixed in place and that any spills will be contained. Having a portion of the cockpit locker set aside for these items is a good idea if they can be well secured in position.

Gasoline

It is often necessary to carry gasoline for outboard engines and portable generators. This defeats to some extent one of the biggest advantages of having a diesel engine in the boat. If you carry a can of gasoline, and most cruisers do, store it in a locker where it cannot leak into the engine compartment, even if the can breaks. The locker where it is kept should be separate from the rest of the vessel and ventilated. For safety and aesthetic reasons I prefer not to store gasoline containers on deck. In some ways this is safer than keeping them below or in a cockpit locker beside the engine, but a container on deck can become extremely hot from the sun with the result of a potential build up of fumes or pressure. Gasoline is about the most dangerous substance aboard your boat; make sure you stow it safely.

Fire Fighting

If a fire does occur on your boat, you will have relatively little time to bring it under control before you have to begin abandoning ship. Having the right equipment, conveniently placed and in good condition, will help considerably.

Fire extinguishers are required by the U.S. Coast Guard if one or more of the following conditions exist:

Inboard engines; closed compartments and compartments under seats where portable fuel may be stored; double bottoms not sealed to the hull or that are not completely filled with flotation materials; closed living spaces; closed stowage compartments in which combustible or flammable materials are stored; and permanently installed fuel tanks. Fire extinguishers with a UL approval and approved for marine use are required. They do not necessarily have to be Coast Guard approved.

In the U.S., the Coast Guard has determined the minimum requirements for fire extinguishers aboard virtually all recreational vessels as follows:

Vessel Length	No Fixed System	With Approved Fixed System
Less than 26 feet	1 B-I	0
26 to less than 40 feet	2 B-I or 1 B-II	1 B-I
40 to 65 feet	3 B-I or 1 B-II	2 B-I or 1 B-II

Table 3. *Number and Size of Extinguishers Required by the United States Coast Guard.*

Types of Fire Extinguishers

The Coast Guard requires that vessels use Type B fire extinguishers. These are designed to extinguish flammable liquids such as gasoline, oil, and grease fires. Class A fire extinguishers are primarily designed to put out normal combustible materials such as wood, paper, or cloth; while Class C fire extinguishers are designed for electrical fires. Because of the Coast Guard requirements, and because Class B extinguishers will work on most fires encountered aboard a boat, it makes sense to use this type.

Sizes

The number following the type letter on an extinguisher relates to its size. Type I is considerably smaller than Type II as shown in Table 4:

Classes	Foam (Gals)	Dry CO_2 (Lbs)	Chemical (Lbs)	Halon (Lbs)
B-I	1.25	4	2	2.5
B-II	2.5	15	10	10

Table 4. Sizes and Contents of Different Types of Extinguishers (USCG).

In determining which sizes to use, take account of where you will mount the extinguishers. You will want at least one extinguisher:
- at each exit from the boat
- in each cabin
- at each potential fire hazard (galley, engine room, electrical panel)

In the U.K. there are no legal requirements to carry fire extinguishers though to omit them would be reckless. Fire extinguishers should comply with BS 5423 though the U.K. and U.S. classifications and requirements are similar and many marine fire extinguishers comply with both U.S. Coast Guard and British Standards requirements where each type is designated by a letter as discussed above. For marine use you should consider having sufficient Class B extinguishers which are suitable for engine or galley fires though the Royal Yachting Association (RYA) recommend you also carry a Class A extinguisher which will effectively extinguish burning embers and prevent a fire from re-lighting.

Automatic engine-room extinguishers

Automatic engine-room fire extinguishers normally contain a halon gas no longer manufactured, though this type of extinguisher is still available. The extinguisher is mounted in the engine room and will release the fire damping gas when a preset temperature is reached. A running engine or bilge blower will exhaust the gas from the engine room quickly. They need to be turned off if the extinguisher is to work effectively.

Fire blankets

Fire blankets are great to have aboard for use in galley fires or other small localized situations. They are normally made of glass cloth and work by covering the fire and excluding oxygen. They are safe, easy to use, and reusable. I believe that every vessel should have one mounted prominently in the galley.

Checking Fire Extinguishers

Just because the fire extinguishers were new when you installed them, or no mention was made about them when you had the vessel surveyed, does not mean that they are still O.K. When I replaced two fire extinguishers that were beyond their expiration date, I decided to try them out. One worked, the other did not. Just as easily, both could have been fine or both could have failed.

Make sure that you check fire extinguishers regularly. If they are fitted with a gauge, check to make sure they do not need recharging. Look for signs of corrosion or leakage. See if all extinguishers of the same type are of the same weight. Or better still, replace them routinely every couple of years.

CHECKLIST

	YES	NO
In the engine room have you:		
Checked all electrical connections?	❑	❑
Secured all loose cables?	❑	❑
Checked all fuel lines, especially the flexible ones?	❑	❑
Checked the uncooled section of the exhaust?	❑	❑
In the galley have you:		
Ensured sufficient room at the sides of the stove?	❑	❑
Checked to ensure that all surfaces remain at a sufficient distance from the burners when the stove is gimballed?	❑	❑
If you use propane as your galley fuel:		
Have you checked all connections for leaks?	❑	❑
Checked flexible hoses for chafe?	❑	❑
Installed a gas sensing alarm?	❑	❑
Have you stowed all paints and chemicals securely?	❑	❑
If you have gasoline aboard the vessel:		
Is it stowed where it cannot leak into the engine room?	❑	❑
Are the containers in good condition?	❑	❑
Will you accept the inherent risks of gasoline?	❑	❑
Do you have aboard the vessel:		
Sufficient fire extinguishers to comply with Coast Guard requirements?	❑	❑
Sufficient fire extinguishers of the appropriate type?	❑	❑
A fire extinguisher at each exit?	❑	❑
In each cabin?	❑	❑
In the galley?	❑	❑
In the engine room?	❑	❑
A fire blanket for the galley?	❑	❑
Are all the fire extinguishers charged, inspected, and in good condition?	❑	❑

CHAPTER EIGHTEEN

Spares and Repairs

On the way back from the bi-annual race to Vera Cruz, Mexico, the women were on watch when the compass light failed. I would have expected them to call me but they did not. Instead they wrapped a small flashlight with a red head scarf and attached it to the compass binnacle using headbands. It worked well but the batteries failed pretty quickly and the next day we had to fix the light. First we unscrewed the compass using one of the large screwdrivers we had aboard to make sure that it was not a bad connection. No, the bulb had failed when we checked it with the test meter. We went in search of a spare compass light bulb but could not find one though there seemed to be bulbs for about everything else. We carried on sailing while I wandered around looking for inspiration. Then I found it: the bottle of Pussers rum! It was not the rum I was looking at but the tropical fish flashlight that was hung around the neck of the bottle. It had a red LED (light emitting diode) that ran from a small watch battery inside. We took the flashlight apart and removed the LED, which just fitted in place of the compass light bulb. All we needed to do was tape a couple of D-cells to the steering pedestal frame and wire it up. Presto. We had an almost perfect compass light that lasted for the remainder of our five-day voyage!

Of course we should have had a spare compass light bulb aboard the boat as its failure is one of the most frustrating problems that has happened to me—on several occasions. But you cannot have a spare for everything, even if you could anticipate all that can go wrong.

When you prepare your spares' list, don't forget the rum. In other words, take along some things that may be useful in improvising a repair underway.

Part of good preparation is the anticipation of problems and in this chapter I want to list some useful items that you should consider taking with you. Without spares you could find yourself at the end of an escalating spiral of failures that could be disastrous. For want of a pump impeller for your engine you may not be able to run it. Without an engine your batteries do not get charged. Without batteries you can end up without navigation lights, electronics, and communications. You could end up wrecked. And all for the want of an impeller.

Spares

Having a Backup System

For some items aboard it is possible to have spares as well as a backup system. For instance, on a sailboat you will probably have both sails and an engine to provide propulsion with repair items for each. But the engine does more than provide propulsion; it also charges the batteries via the alternator. And because your batteries are essential to safe navigation (navigation lights and equipment) you probably need a backup charging system.

Backup equipment

Consider what backup system you will use if the following items fail:

Item	Possible Backup
Electronic navigation systems	Second GPS, sextant, and tables
Battery charging systems	Solar panels, wind generator, towing generator
Automatic bilge pumps	Spare electric pump and switch, manual pump
Steering	Emergency tiller, wind vane, autopilot

Item	Possible Backup
Cooking	Gimballed stove, portable kerosene stove, propane torch
Water tanks	Spare container of water
Fuel tanks	Spare container of fuel

What Spares

Just to be sure that you have the right spare for your bilge pump, you could take a whole spare pump. But what about the engine, or the galley stove, or the mast? Figuring out what spares to take means playing *what if . . .* What if the bilge pump fails, the stove won't light, or the engine stops running? In selecting spares to take with you when cruising, your goal is to have aboard sufficient items to repair or jury-rig *at sea* all essential items aboard. You will probably want to take items to fix the hull or rigging should they fail; you probably don't need to consider spares for the stereo or the cockpit awning since neither are essential to your safety at sea.

Tools

Having a spare pump impeller is of little use if you do not have the tools aboard to remove the old one. You need to take some tools with you when you set off cruising, but which ones do you really need? Power tools are of little use without a 110-volt supply; metric wrenches are no use on your Westerbeke diesel, though they are on your Yanmar; small screwdrivers may be needed to fit a new breaker in the electrical panel but it may take a very large one to remove the compass binnacle bolts.

Fitting Spares before You Leave

The best method of finding out what tools to take with you is to fit spare parts before you leave. This achieves four useful purposes:
- You are sure that you have the right tools to undertake the job at sea.
- You are sure that the spare part is the correct one and is really complete.

• You learn how to replace the item, which will make it easier next time.
• Your boat gets the benefit of a new part.

This suggestion of fitting spares before you leave works especially well for the mechanical systems aboard your boat such as engine, generator, and pumps. Many spares look alike and it is all too easy to buy a replacement engine filter only to find that it is too large to fit the space available, even though it has the right thread. Pump spares kits vary as the models change over the years; when you actually get around to fitting the parts, you could find out that the kit you have is for an earlier or later model.

Saving the Old Parts

Once you have removed a part to replace it with a new one, label the old one, and keep it as a spare. You know that it will fit if you need to use it, while it also serves as the best thing to take with you to a marine store to get an additional spare.

List of Spares

Item	Spares/repair	Notes
Hull and deck	Fiberglass cloth and mat Resin Underwater setting epoxy Wood, screws, and bolts	If your vessel is not fiberglass then repair items as appropriate
Standing Rigging	Wire of the correct size and type to replace the longest stay or shroud Toggle, turnbuckle, Sta-Lok or Norseman terminals, cable clamps, T-ball, or other specialized fittings used for the standing rigging	If wire sizes vary, as they often do, make sure you have spares for each size. All must be for the correct wire size

Item	Spares/repair	Notes
Running Rigging	Spare halyards run for all sails Sheets and miscellaneous lines Roller-reefing furling lines Wind vane steering lines Cleats, blocks, and shackles	
Sails	Needles, thread, sail palm, awl, piston hanks, sail slides (if used) Sail cloth (differing weights), adhesive sailcloth, sewn cringles, reinforcing tape, leather for chafe protection, sewing machine, and sail battens (if used)	
Engine and/or generator	Water pump impellers with gasket and spare cover plate screws Primary and secondary fuel filters Oil and oil filters Thermostat Drive belts Control cables Gasket paper and gasket sealant Replacement hoses, assorted hoses, and hose clips Alternator, starter motor Fuel lift pump, injector pump, and injectors, with spare copper/aluminum washers	Pump impeller cover plate, screws, and injector sealing washers are specific items easily lost in the bilge
Transmission and stern gear	Hoses for oil cooler (if fitted) Oil Shift cable Packing material for stern gland Cutlass bearing Shaft zincs, propeller nut, and woodruff key Propeller	While it may not be possible to fit some of these items at sea, you may be able to do so in an anchorage before docking

Item	Spares/repair	Notes
Steering systems	Stainless steel wire for cables, cable clamps, quadrant eye bolt Hydraulic oil Emergency tiller Wind vane spares, spares/repair kit, breakaway couplings, lines, vanes Items to jury-rig a rudder	If an electronic auto pilot is considered an essential piece of equipment, you will need spares and/or a replacement for this
Navigation equipment	Spare compass Backup position finding system Bulbs for: side, masthead, anchor, tricolor, compass, cabin, engine, safety lights Pencils, erasers, plotting instruments Knot log impeller	
Electrical	Wire, fuses, circuit breakers Test meter Plugs, sockets, connectors	You'll need some knowledge of the electrical systems aboard
Communi-cations	Backup VHF radio such as a handheld Spare VHF antenna Dipole antenna for SSB/ham radio	The dipole antenna for the SSB/ham radio can be plugged directly into the radio and used if the tuner unit or the permanent antenna fails
Heads and plumbing	Repair kits for all pumps	
Man overboard	Extra PFDs Bulbs for MOB lights and MOB pole	
Safety harnesses	Spare harness and lanyard	
Ground tackle	Spare anchor and rode Shackles and thimbles	
Medical	Medical kit	With appropriate items for the intended cruise

Making Repairs

Fitting spares and making repairs is easy for some sailors but not for most. The best method of learning is by watching others and then doing it yourself. See how a pump impeller is removed and then actually do it on your boat. Try removing the backstay and rigging a jury one. Will this mean a trip up the mast while it has a missing stay or not?

Much of making do, fixing things aboard ship, and jury-rigging a repair until you can get to port comes down to seamanship. It just takes experience. Before you leave, make sure that you have prepared yourself as well as you have your vessel.

Also make sure that your on-board reference library covers all of the essential topics you might need to look up.

CHAPTER NINETEEN

Before You Set Off

What happens the first few days after departure will set the mood for the remainder of the trip, perhaps for the whole cruise. If you start in a relaxed manner, confident in your abilities and in the vessel, and if the weather is fine, you and your crew will enjoy yourselves from the start. But if you are tense and anxious, if you have problems with the boat, and if the weather turns bad when you are too far away to put into port, it will not be fun and you will have created a hurdle that will have to be overcome when you next set off.

If you have followed the suggestions in this book, even half followed them, then you are ahead by a few nautical miles. But there are still a couple of things to consider before you finally set off cruising. Pay attention and you will have done all you can to ensure that you, too, enjoy cruising. And eventually, on your return, you will be able to enthuse others with your adventures.

Weather

You may have prepared for heavy weather. Perhaps you have already experienced some in preparing yourself, but you don't want to experience it at the beginning of your cruise.

261

Planning

Plan your departure for the right time of year so that you will most likely have good weather during your first weeks or months. Sailing around the Caribbean during hurricane season is fine if you monitor the weather and know where the hurricane holes are, but making an open water passage to get there at this time may not be such a good idea. Planning to set off south from the Northeast is O.K. but you don't want to get caught out in the Gulf Stream when a norther hits.

Check the Weather before You Leave

You have planned to leave during a certain month, perhaps even on a given date, but don't tie yourself to this. Monitor the weather for several weeks beforehand to get a feel for the weather patterns. Check the weather carefully:
  • Several days before your departure
  • The day before
  • The day of departure

Anticipate a Delay

It's fine if you plan to leave on a certain date, but anticipate a delay. Be prepared to postpone departure until the weather looks fine. This is clear evidence of good seamanship.

Crew Briefings

Even if it is just you and your partner who are setting off, it pays to review procedures prior to departure. And if you have crew who will be sailing with you for the first time, a crew briefing is almost essential.

What to Cover

Besides any idiosyncrasies of the vessel that you can think of, such as how to operate the electric aft head or whatever, plan to cover the following topics with your partner and crew:

- When to use safety harnesses and where to attach the lanyards.
- Where the PFDs are stowed and the conditions under which you may need them.
- Man overboard procedures, including use of electronics to record the position, plans to get back to the person, and methods of recovery.
- The watch system you will be using and where it will be posted.
- The navigation plan and when you expect the crew to make log book entries or plot a position on the chart.
- Where the first-aid kit is, what is included in it, and what is not.
- Where the food is stowed, where the snacks are, and who is responsible for meal preparations.
- The duties each crewmember will have in an emergency.
- What the plan is for the trip.
- Who you have filed a float plan with and the information it contains.
- Questions from the crew.

A Shake-down Sail

After you have done everything you can think of, all essential projects aboard have been finished, and you have completed your plan for gaining sufficient experience, it is time for a short shake-down sail before your final departure.

Plan a day cruise to a convenient destination. Plan to anchor for the night. Perhaps undertake a night sail the next evening. A plan that I have seen used by a number of sailors is to set off for a day or so in the opposite direction of your planned cruise. You can then spend a couple of days living aboard before you return to your home berth for final tasks and provisioning. This way, you will not mind turning around to head back as you will, in a way, be starting your cruise.

But why undertake a shake-down sail anyway? The only convincing answer is that you will know why after you have done it. Despite your most meticulous planning, there are always things that have been overlooked, things that you did not anticipate such as:

- The sheet leads are wrong for the new genoa.
- The engine battery doesn't charge, though the house batteries do.

- Air gets into the fuel lines only when the engine is running under a heavy load.
- Lockers that you thought would be fine come open each time you tack.
- The sink in the head fills and overflows on starboard tack.
- You need another handhold in the main cabin.
- The radar only works on one range.

and the list can go on . . .

Don't use this list. Don't bother checking for these things because they are only a small sample of the hundreds of things that you could find out during a shake-down sail. Undertake this short cruise, try out all your sails and equipment, and then you will know why it was necessary. And when you have done this, and fixed everything that needs fixing, you will finally be ready to go. You can set off for the happy, carefree cruising that has been your dream for all these years.

Bibliography

Callahan, Steve. *Adrift*. Ballantine Books, New York, NY, 1986.

Casey, Don, and Hackler, Lew. *Sensible Cruising: The Thoreau Approach.* Seascape Enterprises, Colonial Heights, VA, 1986.

Coles, K. Adlard. *Heavy Weather Sailing*, 3rd revised edition. Adlard Coles Nautical, London and International Marine, Camden, ME, 1992.

Nicolson, Ian. The Log of the Maken. In *The Ian Nicolson Omnibus.* Sheridan House, Dobbs Ferry, NY, 1986.

Offshore Racing Council, Recommendations for Offshore Sailing. Available from the United States Sailing Association, 1-800-US-SAIL-1

Rousmaniere, John. *The Annapolis Book of Seamanship.* Revised edition. Simon & Schuster, New York, NY, 1989.

Rousmaniere, John. *"Fastnet, Force 10."* W.W. Norton, New York, NY, 1979.

Slocum, Joshua. *Sailing Alone Around the World.* Edited by W. M. Teller. Sheridan House, Dobbs Ferry, NY, 1995.

Index